THE LIFE OF JOHN KNOX

IOANNES CNOXVS

*Reduced from Theodore de Beza's "Images of
Illustrious Men," 1580.*

See pp. 270-71.

The Life of JOHN KNOX

———

BY

REV. THOMAS M'CRIE, D.D.

Author of "Life of Andrew Melville,"
&c.

———

FREE PRESBYTERIAN PUBLICATIONS
133 WOODLANDS ROAD
GLASGOW G.3

1976

FOREWORD

—:—

It is a good historian whose work merits study a century and a half after its first publication. It is an absolutely outstanding one whose work merits republication after that length of time. Thomas McCrie was one of the best historians that Scotland has produced. He had unrivalled diligence in sifting the records, the raw materials of history, when this was much harder to do than it is now. He had the literary gifts to bring his findings to life. Most important of all, he chose, in writing of John Knox and Andrew Melville, a theme that was worthy of his talents. Here were two giants of Scottish history. Here were two Evangelical Christians with whose cause he could wholeheartedly identify himself. The founders of the Free Church in 1843 had read McCrie. They knew the weighty claims of the church by law established: but inspired partly by McCrie, they strove to put the claims of the Gospel first. The same inspiration can be found in his works today.

What would McCrie wish to see in an introduction to the reissue of his life of Knox? As a historian, he would no doubt wish to see more recent work acknowledged. As an Evangelical Christian, he would surely wish to see Knox's lasting significance reaffirmed.

Several detailed biographies of Knox have been
written, from Peter Hume Brown's in 1895 to Eustace
Percy's in 1937 and Jasper Ridley's in 1968. Other biog-
raphers have used Knox as a peg for their own ideas;
Edwin Muir's biography (1929) may be mentioned as the
work of a sensitive poet who nevertheless chose to
write the kind of insensitive and ill-informed attack on
Calvinism that is rather common in modern Scotland.

The quatercentenary of the Scottish Reformation
produced much important work, surveyed by Maurice
Lee in the *Scottish Historical Review* (volume 44, pp.
135-147), and the quatercentenary of Knox's death
occasioned *John Knox: A Quatercentenary Reappraisal*,
essays edited by Duncan Shaw (1975). Books like
Gordon Donaldson's *The Scottish Reformation* (1960)
and *Essays on the Scottish Reformation*, edited by
David McRoberts (1962), have brought out the econ-
omic social and cultural implications of the Reformation.
This does not conflict with the view of the Reformation
as a basically spiritual event, but rather enriches our
understanding of it. And Knox, who put the Gospel
first, stands out the more clearly from the ranks of those
in all parties who did not. But Knox did have worthy
colleagues, and greater understanding of them does not
diminish the stature of Knox: Duncan Shaw has
written, for instance, of John Willock in the book of
essays, *Reformation and Revolution* (1967), which he also
edited.

Certain books have particularly helped to ensure that Knox will be remembered as McCrie would have wished. In 1949 William Croft Dickinson produced a splendid two-volume edition of Knox's *History of the Reformation in Scotland:* Knox's own forthright words were again made freely available. James K. Cameron has re-edited *The First Book of Discipline* (1972), which revealed the vision of a Christian commonwealth held by Knox and his friends. John MacLeod dealt briefly with Knox in his *Scottish Theology* (1943, reprinted 1974), and James S. McEwen said a great deal that was fresh in *The Faith of John Knox* (1961): these books remind us how Knox's strenuous public career was sustained by his earnest private communion with God, and McEwen suggests that Knox was a theologian of originality. Finally, Pierre Janton's *John Knox (ca.* 1513-1572): *l'homme et l'oeuvre* (Paris, 1967) and his *Concept et sentiment de l'Eglise chez John Knox* (Paris, 1972) remind us that Knox remains of interest not merely to his fellow-Scots.

If we were to change our view of Knox, it would scarcely be on the basis of new facts discovered since McCrie's day. Knox seems to have been born in 1514 and not in 1505. And he probably did study at St. Andrews University under John Major, as McCrie believed, though this was hard to explain until his later date of birth was established and he could be assumed to have gone to university at about fifteen years of age, as was then customary.

Old facts can of course be used to sustain new interpretations.   Thus Eustace Percy, while recognising
Knox as 'a leader who deserved better things of his
countrymen', concluded that 'he found himself the slave
of the sword he had invoked', so that his life could be
seen as tragic.   McCrie would perhaps have countered
these arguments as follows.   Had Knox been a notably
meek man, the work of reformation would have been
left to others.   Knox could scarcely be held responsible
for many of the things that happened in a Scotland
where the rulers were determined to keep churchmen in
check.   And it is hard to be confident, in our own
century as in the sixteenth, that faith can always be
defended by gentleness alone.   Indeed, Percy was aware
that Knox lived in 'desperate times', and like a fair
historian he leaves room for his readers to reach con-
clusions different from his own.

Historians are human, and their disagreements are not
of the first importance.   Knox too was human, as McCrie
pointed out: and Knox's writings reveal, deliberately
and otherwise, enough of himself, of human feelings,
human foible, human frailty, for the reader to feel
affection for him as well as awe.   But McCrie's strength
as a biographer was not just his love of Knox, but of
Knox's cause.   Knox himself would scarcely have
troubled about Eustace Percy's view of his character.
Knox did not seek to write an autobiography—though
his writings may furnish one incidentally—but a history

of God's Reformation in Scotland. His life and his writings were at root the proclamation of 'the light of Christ Jesus'. New interpretations which ignore this will miss the mark: new interpretations which allow this will not dishonour his memory. McCrie saw Knox's career as a proof of 'the superintendence of a wise and merciful providence'. No change in historical fashion need tempt us to revise this view.

JOHN M. SIMPSON, M.A.,
Department of Scottish History,
University of Edinburgh.
January, 1976.

PREFACE

—:—

THE Reformation from Popery marks an epoch unquestionably the most important in the history of modern Europe. The effects of the change which it produced, in religion, in manners, in politics, and in literature,
continue to be felt at the present day. Nothing, surely,
can be more interesting than an investigation of the
history of that period, and of those men who were the
instruments, under Providence, of accomplishing a
revolution which has proved so beneficial to mankind.

Though many able writers have employed their talents
in tracing the causes and consequences of the Reformation, and though the leading facts respecting its progress
in Scotland have been repeatedly stated, it occurred to me
that the subject was by no means exhausted. I was
confirmed in this opinion by a more minute examination
of the ecclesiastical history of this country, which I
began for my own satisfaction several years ago. While I
was pleased at finding that there existed such ample
materials for illustrating the history of the Scottish
Reformation, I could not but regret that no one had

undertaken to digest and exhibit the information on this subject which lay hid in manuscripts, and in books which are now little known or consulted. Not presuming, however, that I had the ability or the leisure requisite for executing a task of such difficulty and extent, I formed the design of drawing up memorials of our national Reformer, in which his personal history might be combined with illustrations of the progress of that great undertaking, in the advancement of which he acted so conspicuous a part.

A work of this kind seemed to be wanting. The name of KNOX, indeed, often occurs in the general histories of the period, and some of our historians have drawn, with their usual ability, the leading traits of a character with which they could not fail to be struck; but it was foreign to their object to detail the events of his life, and it was not to be expected that they would bestow that minute and critical attention on his history which is necessary to form a complete and accurate idea of his character. Memoirs of his life have been prefixed to editions of some of his works, and inserted in biographical collections and periodical publications; but in many instances their authors were destitute of proper information, and in others they were precluded, by the limits to which they were confined, from entering into those minute statements, which are so useful for illustrating individual character, and render biography both pleasing and instructive. Nor can it escape observation, that a number of writers have been guilty of great injustice to the memory of our Reformer, and, from prejudice, from ignorance, or from inattention, have exhibited a distorted caricature, instead of a genuine portrait.

I was encouraged to prosecute my design, in consequence of my possessing a manuscript volume of Knox's Letters, which throw considerable light upon his character and history. The advantages which I have derived from this volume will appear in the course of the work.

The other MSS. which I have chiefly made use of are Calderwood's large History of the Church of Scotland, Row's History, and Wodrow's Collections. Calderwood's History, besides much valuable information respecting the early period of the Reformation, contains a collection of letters written by Knox between 1559 and 1572, which, together with those in my possession, extend over twenty years of the most active period of his life. I have carefully consulted this history as far as it relates to the period of which I write.

Row, in composing the early part of his *Historie of the Kirk*, had the assistance of Memoirs written by David Ferguson, his father-in-law, who was admitted minister of Dunfermline at the establishment of the Reformation. Copies of this History seem to have been taken before the author had put the finishing hand to it, which may account for the additional matter to be found in some of them. I have occasionally quoted the copy which belongs to the Divinity Library in Edinburgh, but more frequently one transcribed in 1726, which is more full than any other copy that I have had access to see.

The industrious Wodrow had amassed a valuable collection of MSS. relating to the ecclesiastical history of Scotland, the greater part of which is now deposited in our public libraries. In the library of the university of Glasgow there are a number of volumes in folio, containing collections which he had made for illustrating the lives of the Scottish Reformers and Divines of the sixteenth century. These have supplied me with some interesting facts.

For the transactions of the General Assembly I have consulted the Register, commonly called the *Book of the Universal Kirk*. There are several copies of this MS. in the country. That which is followed in this work, and which is the oldest that I have examined, belongs to the Advocates Library.

I have endeavoured to avail myself of the printed histories of the period, and of books published in the age of the Reformation, which often incidentally mention facts which are not recorded by historians. In the Advocates Library, which contains an invaluable treasure of information respecting Scottish affairs, I had the opportunity of examining the original editions of most of the Reformer's works. The rarest of all his tracts is the narrative of his Disputation with the Abbot of Crossraguel, which scarcely any writer since Knox's time seems to have seen. After I had given up all hopes of procuring a sight of this curious tract, I was accidentally informed that a copy of it was in the library of Alexander Boswell, Esq. of Auchinleck who very politely communicated it to me.

In pointing out the sources which I have consulted, I wish not to be understood as intimating that the reader may expect, in the following work, much information which is absolutely new. Those who engage in researches of this kind must lay their account with finding the result of their discoveries reduced within a small compass, and should be prepared to expect that many of their readers will only glance with a cursory eye what they produced with great, perhaps with unnecessary labour. The principal facts respecting the Reformation and the Reformer are already known. I flatter myself, however, that I have been able to place some of them in a new and more just light, and to bring forward others which have not hitherto been generally known.

No apology, I trust, will be deemed necessary for the freedom with which I have expressed my sentiments on the public questions which naturally occurred in the course of the narrative. Some of these are at variance with opinions which are popular in the present age; but it does not follow from this that they are false, or that they should have been suppressed. I have not become the indiscriminate panegyrist of the Reformer, but neither have I been deterred, by the apprehension of incurring this charge, from vindicating him wherever I considered his conduct to be justifiable, or from apologising for him against uncandid and exaggerated censures. The attacks which have been made on his character from so many quarters, and the attempts to wound the Reformation through him, must be my excuse for having so often adopted the language of apology.

CONTENTS

—:—

PERIOD I.

PERIOD II.

PERIOD III.

PERIOD IV.

PERIOD V.

PERIOD IV.

PERIOD VII.

PERIOD VIII.

THE LIFE OF JOHN KNOX.

———◆———

PERIOD I.

FROM HIS BIRTH, ANNO 1505, TO HIS EMBRACING OF THE REFORMED RELIGION, ANNO 1542.

JOHN KNOX was born in the year 1505. The place of his nativity has been disputed. That he was born at Gifford, a village in East Lothian, has been the most prevailing opinion; but the tradition of the country fixes his birth at Haddington, the principal town of the county. The house in which he is said to have been born is still shewn by the inhabitants, in one of the suburbs of the town, called the Gifford-gate. This house, with some adjoining acres of land, continued to be possessed by the family until about fifty years ago, when it was purchased from them by the Earl of Wemyss.

The name of his mother was Sinclair. His father was descended from an ancient and respectable family, who possessed the lands of Knock, Ranferly, and Craigends, in the shire of Renfrew. The descendants of this family have been accustomed to claim him as a cadet, and to enumerate among the honours of their

PERIOD
I.
1505–1542
A.D.

house, that it gave birth to the Scottish Reformer, a bishop of Raphoe, and of the Isles. At what particular period his ancestors removed from their original seat and settled in Lothian, I have not been able exactly to ascertain.

Obscurity of parentage can reflect no dishonour upon him who has raised himself to distinction by his virtues and talents. But the assertion of some writers, that our Reformer's parents were in poor circumstances, is contradicted by facts. They were able to give their son a liberal education, which, in that age, was far from being common. In his youth he was put to the grammar-school of Haddington; and, after acquiring the principles of the Latin language there, was sent, by his father, to the university of St. Andrew's, at that time the most celebrated seminary in the kingdom. This was about the year 1524; at which time George Buchanan commenced his studies, under the same masters, and in the same college of St. Salvador.

Educa-
tion.

The state of learning in Scotland at this period, and the progress which it made in the subsequent part of the century, have not been examined with the attention which they deserve, and which has been bestowed on contemporaneous subjects of inferior importance. There were unquestionably learned Scotsmen in the early part of the sixteenth century; but the most of them owed their chief acquirements to the advantage of a foreign education. Those improvements, which the revival of literature had introduced into the schools of Italy and France, were long in reaching the universities of Scotland, originally formed upon their model, and, when they did arrive, were regarded with a suspicious eye. The principal branches cultivated in our universities were the Aristotelian philosophy, scholastic theology, with canon and civil law. The schools erected in the principal towns of the kingdom afforded the means of instruction in the Latin tongue, the knowledge of which, in some degree, was requisite for enabling the clergy to perform

Backward
state of
learning
in Scot-
land.

the religious service. But the Greek language, long after it had been enthusiastically studied on the continent, and after it had become a fixed branch of education in the neighbouring kingdom, continued to be almost unknown in Scotland. Individuals acquired the knowledge of it abroad; but the first attempts to teach it in this country were of a private nature, and exposed their patrons to the suspicion of heresy. The town of Montrose is distinguished by being the first place, as far as I have been able to discover, in which Greek was taught in Scotland; and John Erskine of Dun is entitled to the honour of being regarded as the first of his countrymen who patronized the study of that polite and useful language. As early as the year 1534, that enlightened and public-spirited baron, on returning from his travels, brought with him a Frenchman, skilled in the Greek tongue, whom he settled in Montrose; and upon his removal, he liberally encouraged others to come from France and succeed to his place. From this private seminary many Greek scholars proceeded, and the knowledge of the language was gradually diffused through the kingdom. After this statement, I need scarcely add, that the oriental tongues were at this time utterly unknown in this country. It was not until the establishment of the Reformation, that Hebrew began to be studied; and John Row was the first who taught it, having opened a class for this purpose in the year 1560, immediately upon his settlement as minister in Perth. From that time, the knowledge of Greek and the Eastern languages advanced among our countrymen with a rapid pace.

Knox acquired the Greek language before he reached middle age; but we find him acknowledging, as late as the year 1550, that he was ignorant of Hebrew, a defect in his education which he exceedingly lamented, and which he afterwards got supplied during his exile on the continent.

John Mair, better known by his Latin name, Major.

PERIOD
I.
1505–1542
A.D.

John
Major,
born at
Hadding-
ton 1478
A.D.

was professor of philosophy and theology at St. Andrews, when Knox attended the university. The minds
of young men, and their future train of thinking, often
receive an important direction from the master under
whom they were first trained to study, especially if his
reputation be high. Major was at that time deemed
an oracle in the sciences which he taught; and as he was
the preceptor of Knox and the celebrated scholar Buchanan, it may be proper to advert to some of his
opinions. He had received the greater part of his education in France, and acted for some time as professor in
the university of Paris. In that situation, he had acquired a habit of thinking and expressing himself on
certain subjects, more liberally than was adopted in his
native country and other parts of Europe. He had imbibed the sentiments concerning ecclesiastical polity,
maintained by John Gerson, Peter D'Ailly, and others
who defended the decrees of the Council of Constance,
and liberties of the Gallican church, against those who
asserted the incontrollable authority of the sovereign
pontiff. He taught that a general council was superior
to the Pope, might judge, rebuke, restrain, and even
depose him from his dignity; denied the temporal supremacy of the Bishop of Rome, and his right to inaugu-
rate or dethrone princes; maintained that ecclesiastical
censures and even papal excommunications had no force,
if pronounced on invalid or irrelevant grounds; he held
that tithes were merely of human appointment, not divine
right; censured the avarice, ambition, and secular pomp
of the court of Rome and the episcopal order; was no
warm friend of the regular clergy; and advised the
reduction of monasteries and holidays.

His opinions respecting civil government were ana-
lagous to those which he held as to ecclesiastical policy.
He taught that the authority of kings and princes was
originally derived from the people; that the former are
not superior to the latter collectively considered; that if
rulers become tyrannical, or employ their power for the

destruction of their subjects, they may lawfully be con-
trolled by them, and, proving incorrigible, may be
deposed by the community as the superior power; and
that tyrants may be judicially proceeded against, even
to capital punishment.

The affinity between these, and the political principles
afterwards avowed by Knox, and defended by the clas-
sic pen of Buchanan, is too striking to require illustration. Though Major was not the first Scottish writer
who had expressed some of these sentiments, it is highly probable, that the oral instructions and writings of
their teacher first suggested to them those principles
which were confirmed by subsequent reading and reflection; and consequently contributed to bring about
those great changes which were afterwards effected by
means of them. Nor would his ecclesiastical opinions
fail to have their share of influence upon the train of
their thoughts.

But though, in these respects, the opinions of Major
were more free and rational than those generally entertained at that time, it must be confessed, that the portion
of instruction which his scholars could derive from him
was extremely small, if we allow his publications to be
a fair specimen of his academical prelections. Many
of the questions which he discusses are utterly useless
and trifling; the rest are rendered disgusting by the most
servile adherence to all the minutiæ of the scholastic
mode of reasoning. The reader of his works must be
content with painfully picking a grain of truth from
the rubbish of many pages; nor will the drudgery be
compensated by those discoveries of inventive genius
and acute discrimination, for which the writings of Aqui-
nas, and some others of that subtle school, may still
deserve to be consulted. Major is entitled to praise,
for exposing to his countrymen several of the more
glaring errors and abuses of his time; but his mind was
deeply tinctured with superstition, and he defended
some of the absurdest tenets of popery by the most

ridiculous and puerile arguments. His talents were moderate; with the writings of the ancients he appears to have been acquainted only through the medium of the collectors of the middle ages; nor does he ever hazard an opinion, or pursue a speculation beyond what he found marked out by some approved doctor of the church. Add to this, that his style is, to an uncommon degree, harsh and forbidding; " *exile, aridum, conscissum, ac minutum.*"

Knox and Buchanan soon became disgusted with such studies, and began to seek entertainment more gratifying to their ardent and inquisitive minds. Having set out in search of knowledge, they released themselves from the trammels, and overleaped the boundaries, prescribed to them by their timid conductor. Each following the native bent of his genius and inclination, they separated in the prosecution of their studies; Buchanan, indulging in a more excursive range, explored the extensive fields of literature, and wandered in the flowery mead of poesy; while Knox, passing through the avenues of secular learning, devoted himself to the study of divine truth, and the labours of the sacred ministry. Both, however, kept uniformly in view the advancement of true religion and liberty, with the love of which they were equally smitten; and as they suffered a long and painful exile, and were exposed to many dangers during their lives, for adherence to this kindred cause, so their memories have not been divided, in the profuse but honourable obloquy with which they have been aspersed by its enemies; or in the deserved grateful recollection of its genuine friends.

Knox and Buchanan compared.

But we must not suppose, that Knox was able at once to divest himself of the prejudices of his education and of the times. Barren and repulsive as the scholastic studies appear to our minds, there was something in the intricate and subtle sophistry then in vogue, calculated to fascinate the youthful and ingenious mind. It had a shew of wisdom; it exercised although it did not feed the understanding; it even gave play to the imagination, while it exceedingly flattered the pride of the adept. Nor was it easy for the person who had suffered himself to be drawn in, to break through or extricate himself from the mazy labyrinth. Accordingly, Knox continued for some time captivated with these studies, and prosecuted them with great success. After he was created master of arts, he taught philosophy, most probably as an assistant, or private lecturer in the university. His class became celebrated; and he was considered as equalling, if not excelling, his master, in the subtleties of the dialectic art. About the same time, he was advanced to clerical orders, and ordained a priest, before he reached the age fixed by the canons of the church; although he had no other interest, except what was procured by his own merit, or the recommendations of his teachers. This must have taken place previous to the year 1530, at which time he was twenty-five years of age.

PERIOD I. 1505–1542 A.D.

Knox ordained a priest.

It was not long, however, till his studies received a new direction, which led to a complete revolution in his religious sentiments, and had an important influence on the whole of his future life. Not satisfied with the excerpts from ancient authors, which he found in the writings of the scholastic divines and canonists, he resolved to have recourse to the original works. In them he found a method of investigating and communicating truth to which he had hitherto been a stranger; the simplicity of which recommended itself to his mind, in spite of the prejudices of education, and the pride of superior attainments in his own favourite art. Among the fathers of the Christian church, Jerom and Augustine attracted his particular attention. By the writings of the former, he was led to the scriptures as the only pure fountain of divine truth, and instructed in the utility of studying them in the original languages. In the works of the latter, he found religious sentiments very opposite to those taught in the Romish church, who, while she retained his name as a saint in her calendar, had banished his doctrine, as heretical, from her pulpits. From this time, he renounced the study of scholastic theology; and, although not yet completely emancipated from superstition, his mind was fitted for improving the means which Providence had prepared, for leading him to a fuller and more comprehensive view of the system of evangelical religion. It was about the year 1535, when this favourable change of his sentiments commenced; but, until 1542, it does not appear that he professed himself a protestant.

As I am now to enter upon that period of Knox's life, in which he renounced the Roman Catholic communion, and commenced reformer, it may not be improper to take a survey of the state of the church and of religion at that time in Scotland. Without an adequate knowledge of this, it is impossible to form a just estimate of the necessity and importance of that Reformation, in the advancement of which he laboured with so great zeal; and nothing has contributed so much to give currency, among Protestants, to prejudices against his character and actions, than ignorance and a superficial consideration of the enormous and almost incredible abuses which reigned in the church. This must be my apology, for what otherwise might be deemed a superfluous and disproportioned digression.

State of religion before the Reformation.

The corruptions by which the Christian religion was universally depraved before the Reformation, had grown to a greater height in Scotland than in any other nation within the pale of the Western church. Superstition and religious imposture, in their grossest forms, gained an easy admission among a rude and ignorant people. By means of these, the clergy attained to an exorbitant degree of opulence and power; which were accompanied, as they always have been, with the corruption of their order, and of the whole system of religion.

The full half of the wealth of the nation belonged to the clergy; and the greater part of this was in the hands of a few of their number, who had the command of the

PERIOD
I.
1505–1542
A.D.

whole body. Avarice, ambition, and the love of secular pomp, reigned among the superior orders. Bishops and abbots rivalled the first nobility in magnificence, and preceded them in honours: they were privy-councillors and Lords of Session, as well as of Parliament, and had long engrossed the principal offices of state. A vacant bishopric or abbacy called forth powerful competitors, who contended for it as for a principality or petty kingdom ; it was obtained by similar arts, and not unfrequently taken possession of by the same weapons. Inferior benefices were openly put to sale, or bestowed on the illiterate and unworthy minions of courtiers; on dice-players, strolling bards, and the bastards of bishops. Pluralities were multiplied without bounds, and benefices given *in commendam* were kept vacant, during the life of the commendatory, sometimes during several lives, to the deprivation of extensive parishes of all provision of religious service ; if a deprivation it could be called, at a time when the cure of souls was no longer regarded as attached to livings, originally endowed for this purpose. There was not such a thing known as for a bishop to preach ; indeed, I scarce recollect a single instance of it, mentioned in history, from the erection of the regular Scottish episcopate, down to the period of the Reformation. The practice was even gone into desuetude among all the secular clergy, and was wholly devolved on the mendicant monks, who employed it for the most mercenary purposes.

Bishops and mendicant monks.

The lives of the clergy, exempted from secular jurisdiction, and corrupted by wealth and idleness, were become a scandal to religion, and an outrage on decency. While they professed chastity, and prohibited, under the severest penalties, any of the ecclesiastical order from contracting lawful wedlock, the bishops set the example of the most shameless profligacy before the inferior clergy ; avowedly kept their harlots ; provided their natural sons with benefices ; and gave their daughters in marriage to the sons of the nobility and principal gentry; many of whom were so mean as to contaminate the blood of their families by such base alliances, for the sake of the rich dowries which they brought.

Through the blind devotion and munificence of princes and nobles, monasteries, those nurseries of superstition and idleness, had greatly multiplied in the nation; and though they had universally degenerated, and were notoriously become the haunts of lewdness and debauchery, it was deemed impious and sacrilegious to reduce their number, abridge their privileges, or alienate their funds. The kingdom swarmed with ignorant, idle, luxurious monks, who, like locusts, devoured the fruits of the earth, and filled the air with pestilential infection: friars, white, black, and grey; canons regular, and of St. Anthony, Carmelites, Carthusians, Cordeliers, Dominicans, Franciscan Conventuals and Observantines, Jacobines, Premonstratensians, monks of Tyrone, and of Vallis Caulium, Hospitallers, and Holy Knights of St. John of Jerusalem; nuns of St. Austin, St. Clare, St. Scholastica, and St. Catherine of Sienna, with canonesses of various clans.

The ignorance of the clergy respecting religion was as gross as the dissoluteness of their morals. Even bishops were not ashamed to confess that they were unacquainted with the canon of their faith, and had never read any part of the sacred Scriptures, except what they met with in their missals. Under such pastors the people perished for lack of knowledge. That book which was able to make them wise unto salvation, and intended to be equally accessible by "Jew and Greek, barbarian and Scythian, bond and free," was locked up from them, and the use of it, in their own tongue, prohibited under the heaviest penalties. The religious service was mumbled over in a dead language, which many of the priests did not understand, and some of them could scarce read; and the greatest care was taken to prevent even catechisms, composed and approved by the clergy, from coming into the hands of the laity.

Scotland, from her local situation, had been less exposed to disturbance from the encroaching ambition, vexatious exactions, and fulminating anathemas of the Vatican court, than the countries in the immediate vicinity of Rome. But from the same cause, it was more easy for the domestic clergy to keep up on the minds of the people that excessive veneration for the Holy See, which could not be long felt by those who had the opportunity of witnessing its vices and worldly politics. The burdens which attended a state of dependence upon a remote foreign jurisdiction, were severely felt. Though the popes did not enjoy the power of presenting to the Scottish prelacies, they wanted not numerous pretexts for interfering with them. The most important causes of a civil nature, which the ecclesiastical courts had contrived to bring within their jurisdiction, were frequently carried to Rome. Large sums of money were annually exported out of the kingdom, for the purchasing of palls, the confirmation of benefices, the conducting of appeals, and for many other purposes, in exchange for which were received leaden bulls, woollen palls, wooden images, plenty of old bones, with similar articles of precious consecrated mummery.

Of the doctrine of Christianity, scarce any thing remained but the name. Instead of being directed to offer up their adorations to one God, the people were taught to divide them among an innumerable company of inferior objects. A plurality of mediators shared the honour of procuring the divine favour, with the " one Mediator between God and man ;" and more petitions were presented to the Virgin Mary and other saints, than to "Him whom the Father heareth always." The sacrifice of the mass was represented as procuring forgiveness of sins to the living and the dead, to the infinite disparagement of the sacrifice by which Jesus Christ expiated sin, and procured everlasting redemption, and the consciences of men were withdrawn from faith in the merits of their Saviour, to a delusive reliance upon priestly absolutions,

PERIOD I. 1505–1542 A.D.

Idolatry of the people.

papal pardons, and voluntary penances. Instead of being instructed to demonstrate the sincerity of their faith and repentance, by forsaking their sins, and to testify their love to God and man, by observing the ordinances of worship authorised by Scripture, and practising the duties of morality, they were taught, that, if they regularly said their *Aves* and *Credos*, confessed themselves to a priest, purchased a mass, went in pilgrimage to the shrine of some celebrated saint, or performed some prescribed act of bodily mortification—if they refrained from flesh on Fridays, and punctually paid their tithes and other church dues, their salvation was infallibly secured in due time : while those who were so rich and pious as to build a chapel or an altar, and to endow it for the support of a priest, to perform masses, obits, and dirges, procured a relaxation of the pains of purgatory for themselves or their relations, according to the extent of their mortifications. It is difficult for us to conceive how empty, ridiculous, and wretched those harangues were, which the monks delivered for sermons. Legendary tales concerning the founder of some religious order, his wonderful sanctity, the miracles which he performed, his combats with the devil, his watchings, fastings, flagellations; the virtue of holy water, chrism, crossing, and exorcism ; the horrors of purgatory, with the numbers released from it by the intercession of some powerful saint ; these, with low jests, table-talk, and fireside scandal, formed the favourite topics of these preachers, and were served up to the people instead of the pure, solid, and sublime doctrines of the Bible.

Rapacity of the priests.

The beds of the dying were besieged, and their last moments disturbed, by avaricious priests, who laboured to extort bequests to themselves or to the church. Not satisfied with the exacting of tithes from the living, a demand was made upon the dead : no sooner had a poor husbandman breathed his last, than the rapacious vicar came and carried off his corps-present, which he repeated as often as death visited the family. Ecclesiastical censures were fulminated against those who were reluctant in making these payments, or who shewed themselves disobedient to the clergy ; and, for a little money, were prostituted on the most trifling occasions. Divine service was neglected ; the churches were deserted (especially after the light of the Reformation had discovered abuses and pointed out a more excellent way) ; so that, except on a few festival days, the places of worship, in many parts of the country, served only as sanctuaries for malefactors, places of traffic, or resorts for pastime.

Persecution, and the suppression of free inquiry, were the only weapons by which its interested supporters were able to defend this system of corruption and imposture. Every avenue by which truth might enter was carefully guarded. Learning was branded as the parent of heresy. The most frightful pictures were drawn of those who had separated from the Romish church, and held up before the eyes of the people, to deter them from imitating their example. If any person who had attained a degree of illumination amidst the general darkness, began to hint dissatisfaction with the conduct of the clergy, and to propose the correction of abuses, he was immediately stigmatised as a heretic, and, if he did not secure his safety by flight, was immured in a dungeon, or committed to the flames. When at last, in spite of all their precautions, the light which was shining around did break in and spread through the nation, they prepared to adopt the most desperate and bloody measures for its suppression.

From this imperfect sketch of the state of religion in this country, we may see how false the representation is which some persons would impose on us; as if popery were a system, erroneous indeed, but purely speculative ; superstitious, but harmless ; provided it had not been accidentally accompanied with intolerance and cruelty. The very reverse is the truth. It may be safely said, that there is not one of its erroneous tenets, or of its superstitious practices, which was not either originally contrived, or artfully accommodated, to advance and support some practical abuse ; to aggrandize the ecclesiastical order, secure to them immunity from civil jurisdiction, sanctify their encroachments upon secular authorities, vindicate their usurpation upon the consciences of men, cherish implicit obedience to the decisions of the church, and extinguish free inquiry and liberal science.

It was a system not more repugnant to the religion of the Bible, than incompatible with the legitimate rights of princes, the independence, liberty, and prosperity of kingdoms ; a system not more destructive to the souls of men, than to social and domestic happiness, and the principles of sound morality. Considerations from every quarter combined in calling aloud for a radical and complete reform. The exertions of all descriptions of persons, of the man of letters, the patriot, the prince, as well as the Christian, each acting in his own sphere for his own interests, with a joint concurrence of all as in a common cause, were urgently required for the extirpation of abuses of which all had reason to complain, and effectuating a revolution, in the advantages of which all would participate. There was, however, no reasonable prospect of accomplishing this, without exposing, in the first place, the falsehood of those notions which have been called speculative. It was principally by means of these that superstition had established its empire over the minds of men ; behind them the Romish ecclesiastics had entrenched themselves, and defended their usurped prerogatives and possessions ; and had any prince or legislature endeavoured to deprive them of these, while the body of the people remained unenlightened, they would soon have found reason to repent the hazardous attempt. To the revival of the primitive doctrines and institutions of Christianity, by the preaching and writings of the reformers, and to those controversies by which the popish errors were confuted from scripture, (for which many modern philosophers seem to have so thorough a contempt,) we are chiefly indebted for the overthrow of superstition, ignorance, and despotism; and for the blessings, political and religious, which we enjoy, all of which may be traced to the reformation from popery.

How grateful should we be to divine Providence for this happy revolution! For those persons do but "sport with their own imaginations," who flatter themselves that it must have taken place in the ordinary course of human affairs, and overlook the many convincing proofs of the superintending direction of superior wisdom, in the whole combination of circumstances which contributed to bring about the Reformation in this country, as well as throughout Europe. How much are we indebted to those men, who, under God, were the instruments in effecting it; who cheerfully jeoparded their lives, to achieve a design which involved the felicity of millions unborn; boldly attacked the system of error and corruption, fortified by popular credulity, custom, and laws, fenced with the most dreadful penalties; and having forced the stronghold of superstition, and penetrated the recesses of its temple, tore aside the veil which concealed that monstrous idol which the whole world had so long worshipped, and dissolving the magic spell by which the human mind was bound, restored it to liberty! How criminal must those be, who, sitting at ease under the vines and fig-trees planted by the unwearied labours, and watered by the blood of these patriots, discover their disesteem of the invaluable privileges which they inherit, or their ignorance of the expense at which they were purchased, by the most unworthy treatment of those to whom they owe them; misrepresent their actions, calumniate their motives, and cruelly lacerate their memories!

> Patriots have toil'd, and in their country's cause
> Bled nobly; and their deeds, as they deserve,
> Receive proud recompense.———
> But fairer wreaths are due, tho' never paid,
> To those who, posted at the shrine of truth,
> Have fallen in her defence.———
> ————————— Their blood is shed.

PERIOD
I.
1505–1542
A.D.

In confirmation of the noblest claim,
Our claim to feed upon immortal truth,
To walk with God, to be divinely free,
To soar, and to anticipate the skies.
Yet few remember them !————————
——————————————With their names
No bard embalms and sanctifies his song;
And history, so warm on meaner themes,
Is cold on this. She execrates indeed
The tyranny that doom'd them to the fire,
But gives the glorious sufferers little praise.

COWPER, Task, Book V.

The reformed doctrine had made considerable progress in Scotland, before it was embraced by Knox. Patrick Hamilton, a youth of noble descent, obtained the honour, not conferred upon many of his rank, of first announcing its glad tidings to his countrymen, and sealing them with his blood. As early as the year 1526, previous to the breach of Henry VIII. with the Romish See, a gleam of light was, by some unknown means, imparted to the mind of that noble youth, amidst the darkness which brooded around him. Guided by this, he directed his course to Wittemberg; and, after conferring with the German Reformer, went to prosecute the study of the Scriptures in the Protestant university of Marpurg, under the direction of Francis Lambert of Avignon. In that retreat, he was seized with such an irresistible desire to communicate to his countrymen the knowledge which he had received, that he left Marpurg, contrary to the remonstrances of his acquaintances, and returned to Scotland. His freedom in exposing the reigning corruptions soon drew upon him the jealousy of the popish clergy, who decoyed him to St. Andrews; where, on the last day of February 1528, he obtained the crown of martyrdom, by the hands of Archbishop Beatoun. The murder of Hamilton was afterwards avenged in the blood of the nephew and successor of his persecutor; and the flames in which he expired were, "in the course of one generation, to enlighten all Scotland; and to consume, with avenging fury, the Catholic superstition, the papal power, and the prelacy itself."

Patrick Hamilton.

1528 A.D.

The cruel death of a person of rank, and the sufferings which he bore with the most undaunted fortitude and Christian patience, excited a general inquiry into his opinions among the learned, as well as the vulgar, in St. Andrews. Under the connivance of John Winram, the sub-prior, they secretly spread among the noviciates of the abbey. Gawin Logie, rector of St. Leonard's college, was so successful in instilling them into the minds of the students, that it became proverbial to say of any one suspected of Lutheranism, that "he had drunk of St. Leonard's well." The clergy, alarmed at the progress of the new opinions, adopted the most rigorous measures for their extirpation. Strict inquisition was made after heretics; the flames of persecution were kindled in all quarters of the country; and, from 1530 to 1540, many innocent and excellent men suffered the most cruel death. Several purchased their lives by recantation. Numbers made their escape to England and the continent; among whom were the following learned men, Gawin Logie, Alexander Setoun, Alexander Aless, John M'Bee, John Fife, John Macdowal, John Mackbray, George Buchanan, James Harrison, and Robert Richardson.

These violent proceedings could not arrest the progress of truth. By means of merchants, especially those of Dundee, Leith, and Montrose, who carried on trade with England and the continent, Tindall's translations of the Scriptures, and many protestant books, were imported, and circulated through the nation. Poetry lent her aid to the opposers of ignorance and superstition, and contributed greatly to the advancement of the Reformation, in this as well as other countries. Sir David Lindsay of the Mount, a favourite of James V. and an excellent poet, lashed the vices of the clergy, and exposed to ridicule many of the absurdities and superstitions of popery, in the most popular and poignant satires. His satirical play, which, though professing to correct the abuses of all estates, was principally levelled against those of the church, was repeatedly acted before the royal family, the court, and vast assemblies of people, to the great mortification, and still greater damage of the clergy; and copies of it were in the hands of ploughmen, artizans, and children. The royal poet was followed by others who wrote in the same strain, but more avowedly asserting the protestant doctrines; and metrical epistles, moralities, and psalms, in the Scottish language, were every where disseminated and read with avidity, notwithstanding prohibitory statutes and prosecutions. In the year 1540, the reformed doctrine could number among its converts, besides a multitude of the common people, many persons of rank and external respectability; as William Earl of Glencairn,

Alexander Lord Kilmaurs, William Earl of Errol, William Lord Ruthven, his daughter Lillias, married to the Master of Drummond, John Stewart, son of Lord Methven, Sir James Sandilands, with his whole family, Sir David Lindsay, Erskine of Dun, Melville of Raith, Balnaves of Halhill, the laird of Lauriston, with William Johnston, and Robert Alexander, advocates. These names deserve more consideration from the early period at which they were enrolled as friends of the reformed religion. It has often been alleged, that the desire of sharing in the rich spoils of the popish church, together with intrigues of the court of England, engaged the Scottish nobles on the side of the Reformation. It is reasonable to think, that, at a later period, this was in so far true. But at the time of which we now speak, the prospect of overturning the established church was too distant and uncertain, to induce persons, merely from cupidity, to take a step by which they exposed their lives and fortunes to the most imminent hazard; nor had the English monarch then extended his influence in Scotland, by the arts which he afterwards employed.

From the year 1540 to the end of 1542, the numbers of the reformed rapidly increased. Twice did the clergy attempt to cut them off by one desperate blow. They presented to the king a list, containing the names of some hundreds, possessed of property and wealth, whom they denounced as heretics; and endeavoured to procure his consent to their condemnation, by flattering him with the immense riches which would accrue to him from their forfeiture. The first time the proposal was made, James rejected it with strong marks of displeasure; but so violent was the antipathy which he at last conceived against his nobility, and so much had he fallen under the influence of the clergy, that it is highly probable he would have yielded to their solicitations, had not that disaster happened, which put an end to his unhappy life.

PERIOD II.

FROM HIS EMBRACING THE REFORMED RELIGION, ANNO 1542, TO HIS RELEASE FROM THE FRENCH GALLEYS, ANNO 1549.

WHILE this fermentation of opinion was spreading through the nation, Knox, from the state in which his mind was, could not remain long unaffected. The reformed doctrines had been imbibed by several of his acquaintances, and they were the topic of common conversation and dispute among the learned and inquisitive at the university. His change of views first discovered itself in his philosophical lectures, in which he began to forsake the scholastic path, and to recommend to his pupils a more rational and useful method of study. Even this innovation excited against him violent suspicions of heresy, which were confirmed, when he proceeded to reprehend the corruptions which prevailed in the church. It was impossible for him, after this, to remain in safety at St. Andrews, which was wholly under the power of Cardinal Beatoun, the most determined supporter of the Romish church, and enemy of all reform. He left that place, and retired to the south, where, within a short time, he avowed his full belief of the protestant doctrine. Provoked by his defection, and alarmed lest he should draw others after him, the clergy were anxious to rid themselves of such an adversary. Having passed sentence against him as a heretic, and degraded him from the priesthood, says Beza, the Cardinal employed assassins to way-lay him, by whose hands he must have fallen, had not providence placed him under the protection of the laird of Langniddrie.

Thomas Gulliaume, or Williams, was very useful to Knox, in leading him to a more perfect acquaintance with the truth. He was a friar of eminence, and along with John Rough, acted as chaplain to the Earl of Arran, during the short time that he favoured the Reformation, at the beginning of his regency, by whom he was employed in preaching in different parts of the kingdom. But the person to whom our Reformer was most indebted, was George Wishart, a gentleman of the house of Pittarow, in Mearns. Being driven into banishment by Cardinal Beatoun, for teaching the Greek New Testament in Montrose, he had resided for some years at the university of Cambridge. In the year 1544, he returned to his native country, in the company of the commissioners who had been sent to negociate a treaty with Henry VIII. of England. Seldom do we meet, in ecclesiastical history, with a character so amiable and interesting as that of George Wishart. Excelling the rest of his countrymen at that period in learning, of the most persuasive eloquence, irreproachable in life, courteous and affable in manners; his fervent piety, zeal, and courage in the cause of truth, were tempered with uncommon meekness, modesty, patience, prudence, and charity. In his tour of preaching through Scotland, he was usually accompanied by some of the principal gentry; and the people, who flocked to hear him, were ravished with his discourses. To this teacher Knox attached himself, and profited greatly by his sermons and private instructions. During his last visit to Lothian, he wait-

PERIOD
II.
1542-1543
A.D.

ed constantly on his person, and bore the sword, which was carried before him, from the time that an attempt was made to assassinate him at Dundee. Wishart was highly pleased with the zeal and talents of Knox, and seems to have presaged his future usefulness, at the same time that he laboured under a strong presentiment of his own approaching martyrdom. On the night in which he was apprehended by Bothwell, at the instigation of the Cardinal, he directed the sword to be taken from him, and while he insisted for liberty to accompany him to Ormiston, dismissed him with this reply, " Nay, returne to your bairnes (meaning his pupils), and God blis you: ane is sufficient for a sacrifice."

Having relinquished all thoughts of officiating in that church which had invested him with clerical orders, Knox had entered as tutor into the family of Hugh Douglas of Longniddrie, a gentleman in East Lothian, who had embraced the reformed doctrines. John Cockburn of Ormiston, a neighbouring gentleman of the same persuasion, also put his son under his tuition. These young men were instructed by him in the principles of religion, as well as of the learned languages. He managed their religious instruction in such a way as to allow the rest of the family, and the people of the neighbourhood, to reap advantage from it. He catechised them publicly in a chapel at Longniddrie, in which he also read to them, at stated times, a chapter of the Bible, accompanied with explanatory remarks. The memory of this has been preserved by tradition, and the chapel, the ruins of which are still apparent, is popularly called John Knox's kirk.

Knox as tutor at Longnid- drie.

It was not to be expected, that he would long be suffered to continue this employment, under a government which was now entirely at the devotion of Cardinal Beatoun, who had gained over to his measures the timid and irresolute regent. But in the midst of his cruelties, and while he was planning still more desperate deeds, the Cardinal was himself suddenly cut off. A conspiracy was formed against his life; and a small, but determined band, (some of whom seem to have been instigated by resentment for private injuries, and the influence of the English court, others animated by a desire to revenge his cruelties, and deliver their country from oppression), on the 29th of May 1546, seized upon the castle of St. Andrews, in which he resided, and put him to death.

The death of Beatoun did not, however, free Knox from persecution. John Hamilton, an illegitimate brother of the Regent, who was nominated to the vacant bishopric, sought his life with as great eagerness as his predecessor. He was obliged to conceal himself, and to remove from place to place, to provide for his safety. Wearied with this mode of living, and apprehensive that he would some day fall into the hands of his enemies, he came to the resolution of leaving Scotland. He had no desire to go to England, because, although "the Pope's name was suppressed" in that kingdom, " his laws and corruptions remained in full vigour." His determination was to visit Germany, and prosecute his studies in some of the Protestant universities, until he should see a favourable change in the state of his native country. The lairds of Longniddrie and Ormiston were extremely reluctant to part with him, and, by their importunities, prevailed with him to take refuge, along with their sons, in the castle of St. Andrews, which continued to be held by the conspirators.

Writers unfriendly to our Reformer have endeavoured to fix an accusation upon him, respecting the assassination of Cardinal Beatoun. Some have ignorantly asserted that he was one of the conspirators. Others, better informed, have argued that he made himself accessory to their crime, by taking shelter among them; with more plausibility, others have appealed to his writings, as a proof that he vindicated the deed of the conspirators as laudable, or at least innocent. I know that some of Knox's vindicators have denied this charge, and maintain that he justified it only in as far as it was the work of God, or a just retribution in Providence for the crimes of which the Cardinal had been guilty, without approving the conduct of those who were the instruments of punishing him. The just judgment of heaven is, I acknowledge, the chief thing to which he directs the attention of his reader; at the same time, I think no one who carefully reads what he has written on this subject, can doubt that he justified the action of the conspirators. The truth is, he held the opinion, that persons who, by the commission of flagrant crimes, had forfeited their lives, according to the law of God, and the just laws of society, such as notorious murderers and tyrants, might warrantably be put to death by private individuals; provided all redress, in the ordinary course of justice, was rendered impossible, in consequence of the offenders having usurped the executive authority, or being systematically protected by oppressive rulers. This was an opinion of the same kind with that of *tyrannocide*, held by so many of the ancients, and defended by Buchanan in his dialogue, *De jure regni apud Scotos*. It is a principle, I confess, of dangerous application, extremely liable to be abused by factious, fanatical, and desperate men, as a pretext for perpetrating the most nefarious deeds. It would be unjust, however, on this account, to confound it with the principle, which, by giving to individuals a liberty to revenge their own quarrels, legitimates assassination, a practice which was exceedingly common in that age. I may add, that there have been instances of persons, not invested with public authority, executing punishment upon flagitious offenders, as to which we may scruple to load the memory of the actors with an aggravated charge of murder, although we cannot approve of their conduct.

Knox entered the castle of St. Andrews, at the time of Easter, 1547, and conducted the education of his pupils after his accustomed manner. In the chapel within the castle, he read to them his lectures on the Scriptures, beginning at the place in the gospel according to John, where he had left off at Longniddrie. He catechised them in the parish church belonging to the city. A number of persons attended both these exercises. Among those who had taken refuge in the castle, (though not engaged in the conspiracy against the Cardinal), were John Rough, who, since his dismissal by the Regent, had lurked in Kyle, Sir David Lindsay of the Mount, and Henry Balnaves of Halhill. These persons were so much pleased with Knox's doctrine and mode of teaching, that they urged him to preach publicly to the people, and to become colleague to Rough, who acted as chaplain to the garrison. But he resisted all their solicitations, assigning as a reason, that he did not consider himself as having a call to this employment, and would not be guilty of intrusion. They did not, however, desist from their purpose; but, having consulted with their brethren, came to a resolution, without his knowledge, that a call should be publicly given him, in the name of the whole, to become one of their ministers.

Accordingly, on a day fixed for the purpose, Rough preached a sermon on the election of ministers, in which he declared the power which a congregation, however small, had over any one in whom they perceived gifts suited to the office, and how dangerous it was for such a person to reject the call of those who desired instruction. Sermon being ended, the preacher turned to Knox, who was present, and addressed him in these words: "Brother, you shall not be offended, although I speak unto you that which I have in charge, even from all those that are here present, which is this: In the name of God, and of his Son Jesus Christ, and in the name of all that presently call you by my mouth, I charge you that you refuse not this holy vocation, but as you tender the glory of God, the increase of Christ's kingdom, the edification of your brethren, and the comfort of me, whom you understand well enough to be oppressed by the multitude of labours, that you take upon you the public office and charge of preaching, even as you look to avoid God's

heavy displeasure, and desire that he shall multiply his
graces unto you." Then addressing himself to the congregation, he said, " Was not this your charge unto me!
and do ye not approve this vocation?" They all
answered, " It was ; and we approve it." Abashed and
overwhelmed by this unexpected and solemn charge,
Knox was unable to speak, but bursting into tears,
retired from the assembly, and shut himself up in his
chamber. " His countenance and behaviour from that
day, till the day that he was compelled to present himself
in the public place of preaching, did sufficiently declare
the grief and trouble of his heart ; for no man saw any
sign of mirth from him, neither had he pleasure to
accompany any man for many days together."

PERIOD
II.
1542–1549
A.D.

Knox in-
stalled in
the minis-
try at St.
Andrews.

This scene cannot fail to interest such as are impressed
with the weight of the ministerial function, and will
awaken a train of feelings in the breasts of those who
have been intrusted with the gospel. It revives the
memory of those early days of the church, when persons
did not rush forward to the altar, nor beg to " be put into
one of the priests' offices, to eat a piece of bread ;" when
men of piety and talents, deeply impressed with the awful
responsibility of the office, and their own insufficiency,
were, with great difficulty, induced to take on those
orders, which they had long desired, and for which they
had laboured to qualify themselves. What a glaring
contrast to this was exhibited in the conduct of the
herd, which at this time filled the stalls of the popish
church ! The behaviour of Knox also reproves those
who become preachers of their own accord ; who, from
vague and enthusiastic desires of doing good, or a fond
conceit of their own gifts, trample upon good order, and
thrust themselves into a sacred public employment,
without any regular call.

We are not, however, to imagine that his distress of
mind, and the reluctance which he discovered in complying with the call which he had now received, proceeded from consciousness of its invalidity, by the defect

PERIOD
II.
1542-1549
A.D.

of certain external formalities which had been usual in the church, or which, in ordinary cases, might be observed with propriety, in the installation of persons into sacred offices. These, as far as warranted by Scripture, or conducive to the preservation of decent order, he did not contemn : his judgment respecting them may be learned from the early practice of the Scottish reformed church, in the organization of which he had so active a share.

Scruples.

In common with all the original reformers, he rejected the necessity of episcopal ordination, as totally unauthorized by the laws of Christ ; nor did he regard the imposition of the hands of presbyters as a rite essential to the validity of orders, or of necessary observance in all circumstances of the church. The papists, indeed, did not fail to declaim on this topic, representing Knox, and other reformed ministers, as destitute of all lawful vocation. In the same strain did many hierarchical writers of the English church afterwards learn to talk, not scrupling, by their extravagant doctrine, of the absolute necessity of ordination by the hands of a bishop, who derived his powers by uninterrupted succession from the apostles, to invalidate and nullify the orders of all the reformed churches, except their own ; a doctrine which has been revived in the present enlightened age, and unblushingly avowed and defended, with the greater part of its absurd, illiberal, and horrid consequences. I will not say that Knox paid no respect whatever to his early ordination in the popish church, (although, if we credit the testimony of his adversaries, this was his opinion) ; but I have little doubt that he looked upon the charge which he received at St. Andrews as principally constituting his call to the ministry.

His grief at the charge imposed upon him.

His distress of mind on the present occasion proceeded from a higher source than the deficiency of some external formalities in his call. He had now very different thoughts as to the importance of the ministerial office, from what he had entertained when ceremoniously invested with orders. The care of immortal souls, of whom he must give an account to the Chief Bishop: the charge of declaring " the whole counsel of God, keeping nothing back," however ungrateful to his hearers, and of " preaching in season and out of season;" the manner of life, afflictions, persecutions, imprisonment, exile, and violent death, to which the preachers of the protestant doctrine were exposed; the hazard of his sinking under these hardships, and " making shipwreck of faith and a good conscience;" these, with similar considerations, rushed into his mind, and filled it with agitation and grief. At length, satisfied that he had the call of God to engage in this work, he composed his mind to a reliance on Him who had engaged to make his " strength perfect in the weakness" of his servants, and resolved, with the apostle, " not to count his life dear, that he might finish with joy the ministry which he received of the Lord, to testify the gospel of the grace of God." Often did he afterwards reflect with lively emotion upon this very interesting step of his life, and never, in the midst of his greatest sufferings, did he see reason to repent the choice which he had so deliberately made.

An occurrence which took place about this time contributed to fix his wavering resolution, and induced an earlier compliance with the call of the congregation than he might otherwise have been disposed to yield Though sound in doctrine, Rough's literary acquirements were moderate. Of this circumstance, the patrons of the established religion in the university and abbey took advantage; among others, one called Dean John Annan, had long proved vexatious to him, by stating objections to the doctrine which he preached, and entangling him with sophisms, or garbled quotations from the fathers. Knox had assisted the preacher with his pen, and by his superior skill in logic and the writings of the fathers, exposed Annan's fallacies, and confuted the popish errors. One day at a public disputation in the parish church, in the presence of a great number of people, Annan being beat from all his defences, fled, as his

Popish errors confuted.

last refuge, to the infallible authority of the church, by which the tenets of the Lutherans being condemned as heretical, all further disputation, he alleged, was unnecessary. To this Knox's reply was, that before they could submit to this summary determination of the matters of controversy, it was previously requisite to ascertain the true church by the marks given in scripture, lest they should blindly receive, as their spiritual mother, a harlot instead of the immaculate spouse of Jesus Christ.

" For," continued he, " as for your Roman church as it is now corrupted, wherein stands the hope of your victory, I no more doubt that it is the synagogue of Satan, and the head thereof, called the Pope, to be that MAN OF SIN, of whom the apostle speaks, than I doubt that Jesus Christ suffered by the procurement of the visible church of Jerusalem. Yea, I offer myself, by word or writing, to prove the Roman church this day farther degenerate from the purity which was in the days of the apostles, than were the church of the Jews from the ordinances given by Moses, when they consented to the innocent death of Jesus Christ." This was a bold charge; but the minds of the people were prepared to listen to the proof. They exclaimed, that if this was true, they had been miserably deceived, and insisted, as they could not all read his writings, that he should ascend the pulpit and give them an opportunity of hearing the probation of what he had so confidenty affirmed. The challenge was not to be retracted, and the request was reasonable. The following Sunday was fixed for making good his promise.

On the day appointed, he appeared in the pulpit of the parish church, and gave out Daniel vii. 24, 25, as his text. After an introduction, in which he explained the vision, and shewed that the four empires, emblematically represented by four different animals, were the Babylonian, Persian, Grecian, and Roman, out of the ruins of the last of which empires, the power described in his text arose, he proceeded to shew that this was applicable to no other power but that of the degenerate Romish church. He compared the parallel passages in the New Testament, and shewed that the king mentioned in his text was the same elsewhere called the Man of Sin, the Antichrist, the Babylonian harlot; and that this did not mean any single person, but a body or multitude of people under a wicked head, including a succession of persons, occupying the same station. In support of his assertion that the papal power was antichristian, he described it under the three heads of life, doctrine, and laws. He depicted the lives of the popes from ecclesiastical history, contrasted their doctrine with that of the New Testament, particularly in the article of justification, and their laws enjoining holidays, abstinence from meats, from marriage, &c. with the laws of Christ. He quoted from the canon law the blasphemous titles and prerogatives ascribed to the Pope, as an additional proof that he was described in his text. In conclusion, he signified, that if any present thought that he had misquoted, or misinterpreted the testimonies which he had produced from the scriptures, history, or writings of the doctors of the church, he was ready upon their coming to him, in the presence of witnesses, to give them satisfaction. There were among the audience, his former preceptor, Major, the members of the university, the subprior of the abbey, and a great number of canons and friars of different orders.

This sermon, delivered with a great portion of that popular eloquence for which Knox was afterwards so celebrated, made great noise, and excited much speculation among all classes. The former reformed preachers, not excepting Wishart, had contented themselves with refuting some of the grosser errors of the established religion. Knox struck at the root of popery, by boldly pronouncing the Pope to be antichrist, and the whole system erroneous and antiscriptural. The report of the sermon, and the effects produced by it, was soon conveyed to the elect bishop of St. Andrews, who wrote to

Winram, the sub-prior and vicar-general during the vacancy of the see, that he was surprised he would allow such heretical and schismatical doctrine to be taught without opposition. Winram was at bottom friendly to the reformed tenets ; but he durst not altogether disregard this admonition, and therefore appointed a convention of the most learned men to be held in St. Leonard's Yards, to which he summoned the preachers. Nine articles drawn from their sermons were exhibited, " the strangeness of which (the sub-prior said) had moved him to call for them to hear their answers."

Knox, when called, expressed his satisfaction at appearing before an auditory so honourable and apparently so modest and grave. As he was not a stranger to the report concerning the private sentiments of Winram, and nothing was more abhorrent to his mind than dissimulation, he, before commencing his defence, obtested him to deal uprightly in a matter of such magnitude ; if he advanced any thing which was contrary to Scripture, he desired the sub-prior to oppose it, that the people might not be deceived, but if he was convinced that what he taught was true and scriptural, it was his duty to give it the sanction of his authority. To this Winram cautiously replied, that he did not come there as a judge, and would neither approve nor condemn ; he wished a free conference, and, if Knox pleased, he would reason with him a little. Accordingly, he proceeded to state some objections to one of the propositions maintained by Knox, " that in the worship of God, and especially in the administration of the sacraments, the rule prescribed in the Scriptures is to be observed without addition or diminution ; and that the church has no right to devise religious ceremonies, and impose significations upon them." After maintaining the argument for a short time, the sub-prior devolved it on a grey-friar, named Arbugkill, who took it up with great confidence, but was soon forced to yield with disgrace. He rashly engaged to prove the divine institution of ceremonies ; and being pushed by his antagonist from the Gospel and Acts to the Epistles, and from one epistle to another, he was driven at last to affirm, "that the apostles had not received the Holy Ghost when they wrote the epistles, but they afterwards received him and ordained ceremonies." "Father!" exclaimed the sub-prior, "what say ye? God forbid that ye say that; for then farewell the ground of our faith!" The friar, abashed and confounded, attempted to correct his error, but in vain. Knox could not afterwards bring him to the argument upon any of the articles. He resolved all into the authority of the church. His opponent urging that the church had no power to act contrary to the express directions of Scripture, which enjoined an exact conformity to the divine laws respecting worship; "if so," said Arbugkill, "you will leave us no church." "Yes," rejoined Knox, sarcastically, "in David I read of the church of malignants, *Odi ecclesiam malignantium;* this church you may have without the word, and fighting against it. Of this church if you will be I cannot hinder you; but as for me, I will be of no other church but that which has Jesus Christ for pastor, hears his voice, and will not hear the voice of a stranger." For purgatory, the friar had no better authority than that of Virgil in the sixth Æneid; and the pains of it according to him were—*a bad wife.*

" Solventur risu tabulæ: tu missus abibis."

Instructed by the issue of this convention, the papists avoided for the future all disputation, which tended only to injure their cause. Had the castle of St. Andrews been in their power, they would soon have silenced these troublesome preachers; but as matters stood, more moderate and crafty measures were necessary. The plan adopted for counteracting the popular preaching of Knox and Rough was politic. Orders were issued, that all the learned men in the abbey and university should preach by turns every Sunday in the parish church. By this

The papists discomfited.

means the reformed preachers were excluded on those days, when the greatest audiences attended ; and it was expected that the diligence of the established clergy would conciliate the affections of the people. To avoid offence or occasion of speculation, they were directed not to touch in their sermons upon any of the controverted points. Knox easily saw through this artifice, but contented himself, in the sermons which he still delivered on week days, with expressing a wish that they would shew themselves equally diligent in places where their labours were more necessary. At the same time, he rejoiced, he said, that Christ was preached, and nothing publicly spoken against the truth ; if any thing of this kind should be advanced, he requested the people to suspend their judgment, until they should have an opportunity of hearing him.

First fruits.

His labours were so successful during the few months that he preached at St. Andrews, that, besides those in the castle, a great number of the inhabitants of the town renounced popery, and made profession of the protestant faith, by participating of the Lord's Supper, which he administered to them in the manner afterwards practised in the reformed church of Scotland. The gratification which he felt in these first fruits of his ministry, was in some degree abated by instances of vicious conduct in those under his charge, some of whom were guilty of those acts of licentiousness too common among soldiery placed in similar circumstances. From the time that he was chosen to be their preacher, he openly rebuked these disorders, and when he perceived that his admonitions failed in putting a stop to them, he did not conceal his apprehensions of the issue of the enterprise in which they were engaged.

A French fleet before St. Andrews.

In the end of June 1547, a French fleet, with a considerable body of land forces, under the command of Leo Strozzi, appeared before St. Andrews, to assist the governor in the reduction of the castle. It was invested both by sea and land ; and being disappointed of the expected aid from England, the besieged, after a brave and vigorous resistance, were under the necessity of capitulating to the French commander on the last day of July. The terms of the capitulation were honourable; the lives of all that were in the castle were to be spared, they were to be transported to France, and if they did not chuse to enter into the service of the French king, were to be conveyed to any other country which they might prefer, except Scotland. John Rough had left the castle previous to the commencement of the siege, and retired to England. Knox, although he did not expect that the garrison would be able to hold out, could not prevail upon himself to desert his charge, and resolved to share with his brethren the hazard of the siege. He was conveyed along with the rest on board the fleet, which, in a few days, set sail for France, arrived at Fecamp, and, going up the Seine, anchored before Rouen. The capitulation was violated, and they were all detained prisoners of war, at the solicitation of the Pope and Scottish clergy. The principal gentlemen were incarcerated in Rouen, Cherburg, Brest, and Mont St. Michel. Knox, with some others, was confined on board the galleys, bound with chains, and treated with all the indignities offered to heretics, in addition to the rigours of ordinary captivity.

Knox on board the fleet conveyed to France.

From Rouen they sailed to Nantes, and lay upon the Loire during the following winter. Solicitations, threatenings, and violence, were all employed to make the prisoners recant their religion, and countenance the popish worship. But so great was their abhorrence of its idolatry, that not a single individual of the whole company, on land or water, could be induced to symbolize in the smallest degree. While the prison-ships lay on the Loire, mass was frequently said, and *Salve Regina* sung on board, or on the shore within their hearing: on these occasions they were brought out and threatened with torture, if they did not give the usual signs of reverence; but instead of complying, they covered their heads as soon as the service began. Knox has related a humour-

3

ous incident which took place on one of these occasions; and although he has not named the person concerned in it, most probably it was himself. One day a fine painted image of the Virgin was brought into one of the galleys, and presented to a Scots prisoner to kiss. He desired the bearer not to trouble him, for such idols were accursed, and he would not touch it. The officers roughly replied, that he should; put it to his face, and thrust it into his hands. Upon this he took hold of the image, and watching his opportunity, threw it into the river, saying, "Lat our Ladie now save hirself: sche is lycht anoughe, lat hir leirne to swime." After this, they were no more troubled in that way.

The galleys returned to Scotland in summer 1548, as near as I can collect, and continued for a considerable time on the east coast, to watch for English vessels.

Knox's health was now greatly impaired by the severity of his confinement, and he was seized with a fever, during which his life was despaired of by all in the ship. But even in this state, his fortitude of mind remained unsubdued, and he comforted his fellow-prisoners with hopes of release. To their anxious desponding inquiries (natural to men in their situation), "if he thought they would ever obtain their liberty," his uniform answer was, "God will deliver us to his glory, even in this life." While they lay on the coast between Dundee and St. Andrews, Mr. (afterwards Sir) James Balfour, who was confined in the same ship, desired him to look to the land, and see if he knew it. Though at that time very sick, he replied, "Yes, I know it well; for I see the steeple of that place where God first opened my mouth in public to his glory; and I am fully persuaded, how weak soever I now appear, that I shall not depart this life, till that my tongue shall glorify his godly name in the same place." This striking reply Sir James repeated, in the presence of many witnesses, a number of years before Knox returned to Scotland, and when there was very little prospect of his words being verified.

We must not, however, think that he possessed this elevation and tranquillity of mind, during the whole time of his imprisonment. When first thrown into cruel bonds, insulted by his enemies, and without any apparent prospect of release, he was not a stranger to the anguish of despondency, so pathetically described by the royal psalmist of Israel. He felt that conflict in his spirit, with which all good men are acquainted; and which becomes peculiarly sharp when joined with corporal affliction. But, having had recourse to prayer, the never-failing refuge of the oppressed, he was relieved from all his fears, and, reposing upon the promise and providence of the God whom he served, attained to "the confidence and rejoicing of hope."

When free from fever, he relieved the tedium of captivity, by committing to writing a confession of his faith, containing the substance of what he had taught at St. Andrews, with a particular account of the disputation which he had maintained in St. Leonard's Yards. This he found means to convey to his religious acquaintances in Scotland, accompanied with an earnest exhortation to persevere in the faith which they had professed, whatever persecutions they might suffer for its sake. To this confession I find him afterwards referring, in the defence of his doctrine before the bishop of Durham. "Let no man think, that because I am in the realm of England, therefore so boldly I speak. No, God hath taken that suspicion from me. For the body lying in most painful bands, in the midst of cruel tyrants, his mercy and goodness provided that the hand should write and bear witness to the confession of the heart, more abundantly than ever yet the tongue spake."

Notwithstanding the rigour of their confinement, the prisoners, who were separated, found opportunities of occasionally corresponding with one another. Henry Balnaves of Halhill composed in his prison a Treatise on Justification, and the Works and Conversation of a Justified Man. This being conveyed to Knox, probably after his

Henry
Balnaves.

second return in the galleys from Scotland, he was so much pleased with it, that he divided it into chapters, added some marginal notes, and a concise epitome of its contents; to the whole he prefixed a recommendatory dedication, intending that it should be published for the use of their brethren in Scotland, as soon as an opportunity offered. The reader will not, I am persuaded, be displeased to breathe a little the spirit which animated this undaunted confessor, when "his feet lay fast in irons," as expressed by him in this dedication; from which I shall quote more freely, as the book is rare.

It is thus described: "John Knox, the bound servant of Jesus Christ, unto his best beloved brethren of the congregation of the castle of St. Andrews, and to all professors of Christ's true evangel, desireth grace, mercy and peace, from God the Father, with perpetual consolation of the Holy Spirit." After mentioning a number of instances in which the name of God was magnified, and the interests of religion advanced, by the exile of those who were driven from their native countries by tyranny, as in the examples of Joseph, Moses, Daniel, and the primitive Christians; he goes on thus: "Which thing shall openly declare this godly work subsequent. The counsel of Satan in the persecution of us, first, was to stop the wholesome wind of Christ's evangel to blow upon the parts where we converse and dwell; and secondly, so to oppress ourselves by corporal affliction and worldly calamities, that no place should we find to godly study. But by the great mercy and infinite goodness of God our Father shall these his counsels be frustrate and vain. For, in despite of him and all his wicked members, shall yet that same word (O Lord! this I speak, confiding in thy holy promise) openly be proclaimed in that same country. And how that our merciful Father, amongst these tempestuous storms, by all men's expectation, hath provided some rest for us, this present work shall testify, which was sent to me in Roane, lying in irons, and some troubled by corporal infirmity, in a galley named Nostre Dame, by an honourable brother, Mr Henry Balnaves of Halhill, for the present holden as prisoner, (though unjustly) in the old palace of Roane. Which work after I had once again read to the great comfort and consolation of my spirit, by counsel and advice of the foresaid noble and faithful man, author of the said work, I thought expedient it should be digested in chapters, &c. Which thing I have done as imbecility of ingine [i. e. genius or wit] and incommodity of place would permit; not so much to illustrate the work (which in the self is godly and perfect) as, together with the foresaid nobleman and faithful brother, to give my confession of the article of justification therein contained. And I beseech you, beloved brethren, earnestly to consider, if we deny any thing presently, (or yet conceal and hide) which any time before we professed in that article. And now we have not the Castle of St. Andrews to be our defence, as some of our enemies falsely accused us, saying, If we wanted our walls, we would not speak so boldly.—But blessed be that Lord whose infinite goodness and wisdom hath taken from us the occasion of that slander, and hath shewn unto us, that the serpent hath power only to sting the heel, that is, to molest and trouble the flesh, but not to move the spirit, from constant adhering to Christ Jesus, nor public professing of his true word. O blessed be thou, Eternal Father, which, by thy only mercy, hast preserved us to this day, and provided that the confession of our faith (which ever we desired all men to have known) should, by this treatise, come plainly to light. Continue, O Lord, and grant unto us, that as now with pen and ink, so shortly we may confess with voice and tongue the same before thy congregation; upon whom look, O Lord God, with the eyes of thy mercy, and suffer no more darkness to prevail. I pray you, pardon me, beloved brethren, that on this manner, I digress; vehemence of spirit (the Lord knoweth I lie not) compelleth me thereto."

The prisoners in Mont St. Michel consulted Knox, as

A prayer.

to the lawfulness of attempting to escape by breaking their prison, which was opposed by some of their number, lest their escape should subject their brethren who remained in confinement to more severe treatment. He returned for answer, that such fears were not a sufficient reason for relinquishing the design, and that they might, with a safe conscience, effect their escape, provided it could be done "without the blood of any shed or spilt: but to shed any man's blood for their freedom, he would never consent." The attempt was accordingly made by them, and successfully executed, "without harm done to the person of any, and without touching any thing that appertained to the king, the captain, or the house."

Knox
regains
his liberty At length, after enduring a tedious and severe imprisonment of nineteen months, Knox obtained his liberty. This happened in the month of February 1549, according to the modern computation. By what means his liberation was procured, I cannot certainly determine. One account says, that the galley in which he was confined, was taken in the channel by the English. According to another account, he was liberated by order of the king of France, because it appeared, on examination, that he was not concerned in the murder of the Cardinal, nor accessory to other crimes committed by those who held the Castle of St. Andrews. Others say, that his acquaintances purchased his liberty, induced by the hopes which they cherished of great things to be accomplished by him. It is not improbable, however, that he owed his liberty to the circumstance of the French Court having now accomplished their great object in Scotland, by the consent of the parliament to the marriage of their young Queen to the Dauphin, and by obtaining possession of her person; after which they felt less inclined to revenge the quarrels of the Scottish clergy.

PERIOD III.

FROM HIS RELEASE FROM THE FRENCH GALLEYS, ANNO 1549, TO HIS DEPARTURE OUT OF ENGLAND, ANNO 1554.

UPON regaining his liberty, Knox immediately repaired to England. The objections which he had formerly entertained against a residence in that kingdom were now in a great measure removed. Henry VIII. died in the year 1547; and Archbishop Cranmer, released from the severe restraint under which he had been held by his tyrannical and capricious master, exerted himself with much zeal in advancing the Reformation. In this he was cordially supported by those who governed the kingdom during the minority of Edward VI. But the undertaking was extensive and difficult, and in carrying it on, he found a great deficiency of ecclesiastical coadjutors. The greater part of the incumbent bishops, though they externally complied with the alterations introduced by authority, remained attached to the old religion, and secretly thwarted, instead of seconding the measures of the Primate. The mass of the people were sunk in wretched ignorance of religion, and from ignorance, were addicted to those superstitions to which they had been always accustomed: while the inferior clergy, in general, were as unwilling as they were unable to undertake their instruction. Cranmer, with the concurrence of the Protector, had invited learned protestants to come from Germany into England, and placed Peter Martyr, Martin Bucer, Paul Fagius, and Emanuel Tremellius, as professors in the universities of Oxford and Cambridge. This was a wise measure, as it secured a future supply of useful preachers, trained up by these able masters. But the necessity was urgent, and demanded immediate provision. For this purpose, it was judged expedient, instead of fixing a number of orthodox and popular preachers in par-

Marginal notes:

PERIOD III.

Cranmer invites learned protestants from Germany

ticular charges, to employ them in itinerating through different parts of the kingdom, where the clergy were most illiterate or disaffected, and the inhabitants most addicted to superstition.

In these circumstances, our zealous countryman did not remain long unemployed. The reputation which he had gained by preaching at St. Andrews was not unknown in England, and his late sufferings recommended him to Cranmer and the Privy Council. He was accordingly, soon after his arrival in England, sent down from London, by their authority, to preach in Berwick; a situation the more acceptable to him, as it afforded him an opportunity to ascertain the state of religion in his native country, to correspond with his friends, and impart to them his advice. The Council had every reason to be pleased with the choice which they had made of a northern preacher. He had long thirsted for the opportunity which he now enjoyed. His captivity, during which he had felt the powerful support which the protestant doctrine yielded to his mind, had inflamed his love to it, and his zeal against popery. He spared neither time nor bodily strength in the instruction of those to whom he was sent. Regarding the worship of the popish church as grossly idolatrous, and its doctrine as damnable, he attacked both with the utmost fervour, and exerted himself in drawing his hearers from them, with as much eagerness as in saving their lives from a devouring flame or flood. Nor were his labours fruitless: during the two years that he continued in Berwick, numbers were, by his ministry, converted from error and ignorance, and a general reformation of manners became visible among the soldiers of the garrison, who had formerly been noted for turbulence and licentiousness.

The popularity and success of a protestant preacher were very galling to the clergy in that quarter, who were, almost to a man, bigotted papists, and enjoyed the patronage of the bishop of the diocese. Tonstal, bishop of Durham, like his friend Sir Thomas More, was one of

those men of whom it is extremely difficult to give a
correct idea, qualities of an opposite kind being apparently
blended in their character. Surpassing all his brethren
in polite learning, he was the patron of bigotry and
superstition. Displaying, in private life, that moderation
and suavity of manners which liberal studies usually
inspire, he was accessory to the public measures of a
reign, disgraced throughout by the most shocking barbarities. Claiming our praise for honesty, by opposing
in Parliament innovations which, in his judgment, he
condemned, he again forfeited it by the most tame
acquiescence and ample conformity ; thereby maintaining his station amidst all the revolutions of religion
during three successive reigns. He had paid little attention to the science immediately connected with his profession, and most probably was indifferent to the controversies then agitated ; but living in an age in which it
was necessary for every man to choose his side, he
adhered to those opinions which had been long established, and were friendly to the power and splendour of
the ecclesiastical order. As if anxious to atone for his
fault, in forwarding those measures which produced a
breach between England and the Roman See, he opposed
in Parliament all the subsequent changes. Opposition
awakened his zeal ; he became at last a strenuous advocate for the popish tenets ; and wrote a book in defence
of transubstantiation, of which, says bishop Burnet, "the
Latin style is better than the divinity."

The labours of Knox within his diocese, who exerted
himself to overthrow what the bishop wished to support,
must have been very disagreeable to Tonstal. As the
preacher acted under the sanction of the protector and
council, he durst not inhibit him ; but he was disposed
to listen to and encourage informations lodged by the
clergy against the doctrine which he taught. Although
the town of Berwick was Knox's principal station during
the years 1549 and 1550, it is probable that he was
appointed to preach occasionally in the adjacent country.

Whether, in the course of his itinerancy, he had, in the
beginning of 1550, gone as far as Newcastle, and preached
in that town, or whether he was called up to it, in consequence of complaints against his sermons delivered at
Berwick, does not clearly appear. It is, however, certain,
that a charge was exhibited against him before the
bishop, for teaching that the sacrifice of the mass was
idolatrous, and a day appointed for him publicly to
assign his reasons for this opinion. Accordingly, on the
4th of April 1550, a great assembly being convened in
Newcastle, among whom were the members of the council, the bishop of Durham, and the learned men of his
Knox in   cathedral, Knox delivered, in their presence, an ample
Newcastle   defence of the doctrine, against which complaints had
been made. After an appropriate exordium, in which
he stated to the audience the occasion and design of his
appearance before them, and cautioned them against the
powerful prejudices of education and custom in favour of
erroneous opinions and practices in religion, he proceeded to establish the doctrine which he had taught.
The mode in which he treated the subject was well
adapted to his auditory, which was composed of the un-
learned as well as the learned. He proposed his arguments in the syllogistic form, according to the practice
of the schools, but illustrated them with a plainness
level to the meanest capacity among his hearers. Passing over the more gross notions, and the shameful traffic
in masses, extremely common at that time, he engaged
to prove that the mass, " in her most high degree, and
most honest garments," was an idol struck from the
inventive brain of superstition, which had supplanted
the sacrament of the Supper, and engrossed the honour
due to the person and sacrifice of Jesus Christ. " Spare
no arrows," was the motto which Knox wore on his
standard ; the authority of scripture, and the force of
reasoning, grave reproof, and pointed irony, were in their
turn employed by him. In the course of this defence, he
did not restrain those sallies of raillery, which the fool-

cries of the popish superstition irresistibly provoke, even
from those who are deeply impressed with its pernicious
tendency.   Before concluding, he adverted to certain
doctrines which had been taught in that place on the pre-
·ceding Sunday, the falsehood of which he was prepared
to demonstrate ; but he would, in the first place, he said,
submit to the preacher the notes of the sermon which
he had taken down, that he might correct them as he
saw proper ; for his object was not to misrepresent or
captiously entrap a speaker, by catching at words unad-
visedly uttered, but to defend the truth, and warn his
hearers against errors destructive to their souls.

PERIOD
III.
1549–1554
A.D.

This defence had the effect of extending Knox's fame
through the north of England, while it completely silenced the bishop and his lea..ned suffragans. He continued to preach at Berwick during the remaining part
of this year, and in the following was removed to Newcastle, and placed in a sphere of greater usefulness. In
December 1551, the Privy Council conferred on him a
mark of their approbation, by appointing him one of
king Edward's chaplains in ordinary. "It was appointed,"
says his majesty, in a journal of important transactions
which he wrote with his own hand, "that I should have
six chaplains in ordinary, of which two ever to be present,
and four absent in preaching ; one year two in Wales,
two in Lancashire and Derby; next year two in the
marches of Scotland, and two in Yorkshire; the third
year two in Norfolk and Essex, and two in Kent and
Sussex. These six to be Bill, Harle, Perne, Grindal,
Bradford, and——." The name of the sixth has been
dashed out of the journal, but the industrious Strype has
shewn that it was Knox. "These it seems," says bishop
Burnet, "were the most zealous and readiest preachers.
who were sent about as itinerants, to supply the defects
of the greatest part of the clergy, who were generally very
faulty." An annual salary of £40 was allotted to each of
the chaplains.

Knox ap-
pointed a
chaplain
in ordin-
ary to Ed-
ward VI.

In the course of the year, Knox was consulted about

the Book of Common Prayer, which was undergoing a review. On that occasion it is probable that he was called up to London for a short time. Although the persons who had the chief direction of ecclesiastical affairs were not disposed, or did not think it yet expedient, to introduce that thorough reform which he judged necessary, in order to reduce the worship of the English church to the scripture model, his representations were not altogether disregarded. He had influence to procure an important change on the communion office, completely excluding the notion of the corporeal presence of Christ in the sacrament, and guarding against the adoration of the elements, too much countenanced by the practice of kneeling at their reception, which was still continued. Knox speaks of these amendments with great satisfaction, in his Admonition to the Professors of Truth in England. "Also God gave boldness and knowledge to the court of parliament to take away the *round clipped god*, wherein standeth all the holiness of the Papists, and to command common bread to be used at the Lord's table, and also to take away most part of superstitions (kneeling at the Lord's table excepted) which before prophaned Christ's true religion." These alterations gave great offence to the Papists. In a disputation with Latimer, after the accession of queen Mary, the Prolocutor, Dr. Weston, complained of our countryman's influence in procuring them. "A runagate Scot did take away the adoration or worshipping of Christ in the sacrament, by whose procurement that heresie was put into the last communion book; so much prevailed that one man's authoritie at that time." In the following year, he was employed in revising the Articles of Religion previous to their ratification by parliament.

Miss Marjory Bowes. During his residence at Berwick, Knox had formed an acquaintance with Miss Marjory Bowes, a young lady who afterwards became his wife. She belonged to the honourable family of Bowes, and was nearly allied to Sir Robert Bowes, a distinguished courtier during the reigns of Henry VIII. and his son Edward. Before he left Berwick, he had paid his addresses to this young lady, and met with a favourable reception. Her mother was also friendly to the match ; but, owing to some reason, most probably the presumed aversion of her father, it was deemed prudent to delay the consummating of the union. But having come under a formal promise to her, he considered himself as sacredly bound, and, in his letters to Mrs. Bowes, always addressed her by the name of Mother.

Without derogating from the praise justly due to those worthy men, who were at this time employed in disseminating religious truth through England, I may say that our countryman was not behind the first of them, in the unwearied assiduity with which he laboured in the stations assigned to him. From an early period, his mind seems to have presaged, that the golden opportunity enjoyed would not be of long duration. He was eager to " redeem the time," and indefatigable both in his studies and teaching. In addition to his ordinary services on Sabbath, he preached regularly on week days, frequently on every day of the week. Besides the portion of time which he allotted to study, he was often employed in conversing with persons who applied to him for advice on religious subjects. The Council were not insensible to the value of his services, and conferred on him several marks of approbation. They wrote different letters to the governors and principal inhabitants of the places where he preached, recommending him to their notice and protection. They secured him in the regular payment of his salary, until such time as he should be provided with a benefice. It was also out of respect to him, that, in September 1552, they granted a patent to his brother William Knox, a merchant, giving him liberty, for a limited time, to trade to any port of England, in a vessel of a hundred tons burden.

Knox an itinerant preacher.

But the things which recommended Knox to the Council, drew upon him the hatred of a numerous and powerful party in the northern counties, who remained ad-

dicted to Popery.   Irritated by his boldness and success
in attacking their superstition, and sensible that it would
be vain, and even dangerous, to prefer an accusation
against him on that ground, they watched for an opportunity of catching at something in his discourses or behaviour, which they might improve to his disadvantage.
He had long observed with great anxiety, the impatience
with which the papists submitted to the present government, and their eager desires for any change which might
lead to the overthrow of the Protestant religion; desires
which were expressed by them in the north, without
that reserve which prudence dictated in places adjacent
to the seat of authority.   He had witnessed the joy with
which they received the news of the Protector's fall, and
was no stranger to the satisfaction with which they circulated prognostications as to the speedy demise of the
king.   In a sermon preached by him about Christmas
1552, he gave vent to his feelings on this subject; and,
lamenting the obstinacy of the papists, asserted that such
as were enemies to the gospel, then preached in England,
were secret traitors to the crown and commonwealth,
thirsted for nothing more than his majesty's death, and
cared not who should reign over them, provided they got
their idolatry again erected.   This free speech was immediately laid hold on by his enemies, and transmitted,
with many aggravations, to some great men about court,
secretly in their interest, who therefore preferred a charge
against him, for high offences, before the Privy Council.

In taking this step, they were not a little encouraged
by their knowledge of the sentiments of the Duke of
Northumberland, who had lately come down to his charge
as warden-general of the northern marches.   This ambitious and unprincipled nobleman had employed his affected zeal for the reformed religion, as a stirrup to mount
to the highest preferment in the state, which he had recently procured by the ruin of the Duke of Somerset, the Protector of the kingdom.   Knox had offended him by publicly lamenting the fall of Somerset, as threatening dan-

ger to the Reformation, of which he had always shewn himself a zealous friend, whatever his other faults might have been. Nor could the freedom which the preacher used, in reproving from the pulpit the vices of great as well as small, fail to be displeasing to a man of Northumberland's character. On these accounts, he was desirous to have Knox removed from that quarter, and had actually applied for this, by a letter to the Council, previous to the occurrence just mentioned; alleging, as a pretext, the great resort of Scotsmen unto him: as if any real danger was to be apprehended from this intercourse with a man, of whose fidelity the existing government had so many strong pledges, and who uniformly employed all his influence to remove the prejudices of his countrymen against England.

In consequence of the charges exhibited against him to the Council, he received a citation to repair immediately to London, and answer for his conduct. The following extract of a letter, addressed, "to his sister," will shew the state of his mind on receiving the summons: "Urgent necessity will not suffer that I testify my mind to you. My Lord of Westmoreland has written to me this Wednesday, at six of the clock at night, immediately thereafter to repair unto him, as I will answer at my peril. I could not obtain licence to remain the time of the sermon upon the morrow. Blessed be God who does ratify and confirm the truth of his word from time to time, as our weakness shall require! Your adversary, sister, doth labour that you should doubt whether this be the word of God or not. If there had never been testimonial of the undoubted truth thereof before these our ages, may not such things as we see daily come to pass prove the verity thereof? Doth it not affirm, that it shall be preached, and yet contemned and lightly regarded by many; that the true professors thereof shall be hated by father, mother, and others of the contrary religion; that the most faithful shall be persecuted? And cometh not all these things to pass in ourselves? Rejoice, sister, for the same word that forespeaketh trouble doth certify us of the glory consequent. As for myself, albeit the extremity should now apprehend me, it is not come unlooked for. But, alas! I fear that yet I be not ripe nor able to glorify Christ by my death; but what lacketh now, God shall perform in his own time. Be sure I will not forget you and your company, so long as mortal man may remember earthly creature."

Upon reaching London he found that his enemies had been uncommonly industrious in exciting prejudices against him, by transmitting the most false and injurious information. But the Council, after hearing his defences, were convinced of their malice, and honourably acquitted him. He was employed to preach before the court, and gave great satisfaction, particularly to his Majesty, who contracted a favour for him, and was very desirous to have him promoted in the church. It was resolved by the Council that he should preach in London, and the southern counties, during the year 1553; but he was allowed to return for a short time to Newcastle, either to settle his affairs, or as a public testimony of his innocence. In a letter to his sister, dated Newcastle, 23d March 1553, we find him writing as follows: "Look further of this matter in the other letter, written unto you at such a time as many thought I should never write after to man. Heinous were the delations laid against me, and many are the lies that are made to the Council. But God one day shall destroy all lying tongues, and shall deliver his servants from calamity. I look but one day or other to fall in their hands; for more and more rageth the members of the devil against me. This assault of Satan has been to his confusion, and to the glory of God. And therefore, sister, cease not to praise God, and to call for my comfort; for great is the multitude of enemies, whom every one the Lord shall confound. I intend not to depart from Newcastle before Easter."

The vigour of his constitution had been greatly im-

He is acquitted.

Letter to his sister.

paired by his confinement in the French galleys, which, together with his labours in England had brought on a gravel. In the course of the year 1553 he endured several violent attacks of this acute disorder, accompanied with severe pain in his head and stomach. "My daily labours must now increase," says he, in the letter last quoted, "and therefore spare me as much as you may. My old malady troubles me sore, and nothing is more contrarious to my health than writing. Think not that I weary to visit you; but unless my pain shall cease, I will altogether become unprofitable. Work, O Lord, even as pleaseth thy infinite goodness, and relax the troubles, at thy own pleasure, of such as seeketh thy glory to shine. Amen." In another letter to the same correspondent, he writes—"the pain of my head and stomach troubles me greatly. Daily I find my body decay; but the providence of my God shall not be frustrate. I am charged to be at Widrington on Sunday, where I think I shall also remain Monday. The Spirit of the Lord Jesus rest with you. Desire such faithful as with whom ye communicate your mind, to pray that, at the pleasure of our good God, my dolour both of body and spirit may be relieved somewhat; for presently it is very bitter. Never found I the Spirit, I praise my God, so abundant where God's glory ought to be declared; and therefore I am sure there abides something that yet we see not." "Your messenger," says he in another letter, "found me in bed, after a sore trouble and most dolorous night; and so dolour may complain to dolour when we two meet. But the infinite goodness of God, who never despiseth the petitions of a sore troubled heart, shall, at his good pleasure, put end to these pains that we presently suffer, and in place thereof shall crown us with glory and immortality for ever. But, dear sister, I am even of mind with faithful Job, yet most sore tormented, that my pain shall have no end in this life. The power of God may, against the purpose of my heart, alter such things as appear not to be altered, as he did unto Job;

but dolour and pain, with sore anguish, cries the contrary. And this is more plain than ever I spake, to let
you know ye have a fellow and companion in trouble,
and thus rest in Christ, for the head of the serpent is
already broken down, and he is stinging us upon the
heel."

About the beginning of April 1553, he returned to
London. In the month of February preceding, archbishop Cranmer had been desired by the Council to present him to the vacant living of All-Hallows in that city.
This proposal, which originated in the personal favour of
the young King, was very disagreeable to Northumberland, who exerted himself privately to hinder his preferment. His interference was, however, unnecessary on
the present occasion; for when the living was offered to
him, Knox declined it, and when questioned as to his
reasons, readily acknowledged, that he had not freedom
in his mind to accept of a fixed charge, in the present
state of the English church. His refusal, with the reason assigned, having given offence, he was, on the 14th of
April, called before the Privy Council. There were present the archbishop of Canterbury, Goodrick, bishop of
Ely and Lord Chancellor, the Earls of Bedford, North-
ampton, and Shrewsbury, the Lords Treasurer and Cham-
berlain, with the two Secretaries. They asked him, why
he had refused the benefice provided for him in London?
He answered, that he was fully satisfied that he could be
more useful to the church in another situation. Being
interrogated, If it was his opinion, that no person could
lawfully serve in ecclesiastical ministrations, according to
the present laws of that realm? he frankly replied, That
there were many things which needed reformation, without which ministers could not, in his opinion, discharge
their office conscientiously in the sight of God; for no
minister, according to the existing laws, had power to
prevent the unworthy from participating of the sacraments, "which was a chief point of his office." He was
asked, If kneeling at the Lord's table was not indiffer-

ent? He replied that Christ's action was most perfect, and in it no such posture was used; that it was most safe to follow his example; and that kneeling was an addition and an invention of men. On this article there was a smart dispute between him and some of the Lords of the Council. After long reasoning he was told, that they had not sent for him with any bad design, but were sorry to understand that he was of a contrary judgment to the common order. He said, he was sorry that the common order was contrary to Christ's institution. They dismissed him with soft speeches, advising him to endeavour to bring his mind to communicate according to the established rites.

If honours and emoluments could have biassed the independent mind of our countryman, he must have been induced to become a full conformist to the English church At the special request of Edward VI., and with the concurrence of his council, he was offered a bishopric ; but the same reasons which prevented him from accepting the living of All-Hallows, determined him to reject this more tempting offer. The fact is attested by Beza, who adds, that his refusal was accompanied with a censure of the Episcopal office, as destitute of divine authority, and not even exercised in England according to the ecclesiastical canons. Knox himself speaks in one of his treatises of the " high promotions offered to him by Edward ;" and we shall find him at a later period of his life expressly asserting that he had refused a bishopric.

Offer of a
bishopric
rejected.

It may be proper, in this place, to give a more particular account of Knox's sentiments respecting the English church. It is well known that the reformation of religion was conducted in England in a very different way from what was afterwards adopted in Scotland, both as to worship and ecclesiastical polity. In England, the papal supremacy was transferred to the prince ; the hierarchy being subjected to the civil power, was suffered to remain, and the principal forms of the ancient wor-

ship, after removing the grosser superstitions, were retained; whereas, in Scotland all of these were discarded,
as destitute of divine authority, unprofitable, burdensome, or savouring of Popery; and the worship and
government of the church were reduced to the primitive
standard of Scriptural simplicity. The influence of
Knox in recommending this establishment to his countrymen, is universally allowed, but, as he officiated for
a considerable time in the Church of England, and on this
account was supposed to have been pleased with its constitution, it has been usually said that he contracted a
dislike to it during his exile on the continent, after the
death of Edward VI., and having then imbibed the sentiments of Calvin, carried them along with him to his
native country, and organised the Scottish Church after
the Genevan model. This statement is inaccurate. His
objections to the English liturgy were increased and
strengthened during his residence on the continent, but
they existed before that time. His judgment respecting
ecclesiastical government and discipline was matured
during that period, but his radical sentiments on these
heads were formed long before he saw Calvin, or had any
intercourse with the foreign reformers. At Geneva he
saw a church, which, upon the whole, corresponded with
his idea of the divinely authorised pattern; but he did
not indiscriminately approve, nor servilely imitate either
that, or any other existing establishment.

An in-
accurate
statement

As early as the year 1547, he taught, in his first
sermons at St. Andrews, that no mortal man could be
head of the church; that there were no true bishops, but
such as preached personally without a substitute; that in
religion men are bound to regulate themselves by divine
laws, and that the sacraments ought to be administered
exactly according to the institution and example of
Christ. We have seen that, in a solemn disputation in
the same place, he maintained that the church has no
authority, on pretext of decorating divine service, to
devise ceremonies, and impose significations upon them.

This position he also defended in the year 1550 at New-castle, and in his late appearance before the Privy Council at London. It was impossible that the English church, in any of the shapes which it assumed, could stand the test of these principles. The ecclesiastical supremacy, the various orders and dependencies of the hierarchy, crossing in baptism, and kneeling in the eucharist, with other ceremonies; the theatrical dress, the mimical gestures, the vain repetitions used in religious service, were all cashiered and repudiated by the cardinal principle to which he steadily adhered, that in the church of Christ, and especially in the acts of worship, every thing ought to be arranged and conducted, not by the pleasure and appointment of men, but according to the dictates of inspired wisdom and authority.

He rejoiced that liberty and encouragement were given to preach the pure word of God throughout the extensive realm of England; that idolatry and gross superstition were suppressed; and that the rulers were disposed to support the Reformation, and even to carry it farther than had yet been done. Considering the character of the greater part of the clergy, the extreme paucity of useful preachers, and other hinderances to the introduction of the primitive order and discipline of the church, he acquiesced in the authority exercised by a part of the bishops, under the direction of the Privy Council, and endeavoured to strengthen their hands, in the advancement of the common cause, by painful preaching in the stations which were assigned to him. But he could not be induced to contradict or conceal his decided sentiments, and cautiously avoided coming under engagements, by which he would have approved what he was convinced to be unlawful, or injurious to the interests of religion. Upon these principles, he never submitted to the unlimited use of the liturgy, during the time that he was in England, refused to become a bishop, and declined accepting a fixed charge. When he perceived that progress in Reformation was arrested, by the influence of a

PERIOD III.
1549-1554
A D

Idolatry suppress'd in England.

popish faction and the dictates of a temporising policy;
that abuses, which had formerly been acknowledged,
began to be vindicated and stiffly maintained; above all,
when he saw, after the accession of Elisabeth, that a
retrograde course was taken, and a yoke of ceremonies,
more grievous than that which the most sincere Protestants had formerly complained of, was imposed and enforced by arbitrary statutes, he judged it necessary to
speak in a tone of more decided and severe reprehension.

Among other things which he censured in the English
ecclesiastical establishment, were the continuing to employ a great number of ignorant and insufficient priests,
who had been accustomed to nothing but saying mass,
and singing the litany; the general substitution of the
reading of homilies, the mumbling of prayers, or the
chaunting of matins or even-song, in the place of preaching; the formal celebration of the sacraments, unaccom-
panied with instruction to the people; the scandalous
prevalence of pluralities; and the total want of ecclesiastical discipline. He was of opinion that the clergy ought
not to be entangled, and diverted from the duties of
their offices, by holding civil places; that the bishops
should lay aside their secular titles and dignities; that
the bishoprics should be divided, so that in every city
or large town, there might be placed a godly and learned
man, with others joined with him for the management of

Schools
proposed
to be
erected
through-
out En-
gland.

ecclesiastical matters; and that schools for the education
of youth should be universally erected through the
nation.

Nor did the principal persons who were active in
effecting the English Reformation differ widely from
Knox in these sentiments; although they might not
have the same conviction of their importance, and the
expediency of reducing them to practice. We will mistake exceedingly, if we suppose that they were men of
the same principles and temper with many who succeeded
to their places, that they were satisfied with the pitch
to which they had carried the Reformation of the English

church, and regarded it as a paragon and perfect pattern to other churches. They were strangers to those extravagant and illiberal notions which were afterwards adopted by the fond admirers of the hierarchy and liturgy. They would have laughed at the man who would have seriously asserted, that the ceremonies constituted any part of " the beauty of holiness," or that the imposition of the hands of a bishop was essential to the validity of ordination; they would not have owned that person as a Protestant who would have ventured to insinuate, that where this was wanting, there was no Christian ministry, no ordinances, no church, and perhaps—no salvation! Many things which their successors have applauded they barely tolerated, and they would have been happy if the circumstances of their time would have permitted them to introduce alterations, which have since been cried down as puritanical innovations. Strange as it may appear to some, I am not afraid of exceeding the truth when I say, that if the first English reformers, including the Protestant bishops, had been left to their own choice, if they had not been held back by the dead weight of a large mass of popishly-affected clergy in the reign of Edward, and restrained by the supreme civil authority on the accession of Elisabeth, they would have brought the government and worship of the Church of England nearly to the pattern of the other reformed churches.

Such, in particular, was the earnest wish of his Majesty Edward VI. a prince who, besides his other rare qualities, had an unfeigned reverence for the word of God, and a disposition to comply with its prescriptions in preference to custom and established usages, who showed himself uniformly inclined to give relief to his conscientious subjects, and sincerely bent on promoting the union of all the friends of the reformed religion at home and abroad. Of his intentions on this head, there remain the most unquestionable and satisfactory documents. Had his life been spared, there is every reason to think that he would have accomplished the rectification of those evils in the English church, which the most steady and enlightened protestants have lamented. Had his sister Elisabeth been of the same spirit with him, and prosecuted the plan which he laid down, she would have united all the friends of the Reformation, the great support of her authority; she would have weakened the interest of the Roman Catholics, whom all her accommodating measures could not gain, nor prevent from repeatedly conspiring against her life and crown; she would have put an end to those dissensions among her protestant subjects which continued during the whole of her reign, which she bequeathed as a legacy to her successors, and which, being fomented and exasperated by the severities employed for their suppression, at length burst forth to the temporary overthrow of the hierarchy, and of the monarchy, which patronized its exorbitancies, and resisted a reform, which had been previously attempted upon sober and enlightened principles; dissensions which subsist to this day, and, though softened by the partial lenitive of a toleration, have gradually alienated from the communion of that church a large proportion of the population of the nation, and which, if a timeous and salutary remedy be not applied, may ultimately undermine the foundations of the English establishment.

Knox in London interviews the court.

During the time that Knox was in London, he had full opportunity for observing the state of the court; and the observations which he made filled his mind with the most anxious forebodings. Of the piety and sincerity of the young king, he entertained not the smallest doubt. Personal acquaintance heightened the idea which he had conceived of his character from report, and enabled him to add his testimony to the tribute of praise, which all who knew that prince have so cheerfully paid to his uncommon virtues and endowments. But the principal courtiers by whom he was at that time surrounded, were persons of a very different description, and gave proofs, too unequivocal to be mistaken of indifference to all religion, and readiness to fall in with and forward the re-establishment of the ancient superstition, whenever this might be required upon a change of rulers. The health of Edward, which had long been declining, growing gradually worse, so that no hope of his recovery remained, they were eager only about the aggrandizing of their families, and providing for the security of their places and fortunes.

The royal chaplains were men of a very different stamp from those who have usually occupied that place in the courts of princes. They were no time-serving, supple, smooth-tongued parasites; they were not afraid of forfeiting their pensions, or of alarming the consciences, and wounding the delicate ears of their royal and noble auditors, by denouncing the vices which they committed, and the judgments of Heaven to which they exposed themselves. The freedom used by the venerable Latimer is well known from his printed sermons, which for their homely honesty, artless simplicity, native humour, and genuine pictures of the manners of the age, continue still to be read with interest. Grindal, Lever, and Bradford, who were superior to him in learning, evinced the same fidelity and courage. They censured the ambition, avarice, luxury, oppression, and irreligion which reigned in the court. As long as their sovereign was able to give personal attendance on the sermons, the preachers were treated with exterior decency and respect; but after he was confined to his chamber by a consumptive cough, the resentment of the courtiers vented itself openly in the most contumelious speeches and insolent behaviour. Those who are acquainted with our countryman's character, will readily conceive that the sermons delivered by him at court, were not less bold and free than those of his colleagues. We may form a judgment of them, from the account which he has given of the last sermon which he preached before his Majesty, in which he directed several piercing glances of reproof at the haughty premier, and his crafty relation, the Marquis of Winchester

PERIOD
III.
1549–1554
A.D.

Lord High Treasurer, both of whom were among his hearers.

On the 6th of July 1553, Edward VI. departed this life, to the unspeakable grief of all the lovers of learning, virtue, and the protestant religion; and a black cloud spread over England, which, after hovering a while, burst into a dreadful hurricane, that raged during five years with the most destructive fury. Knox was at this time in London. He received the afflicting tidings of his Majesty's decease with becoming fortitude, and resignation to the sovereign will of Heaven. The event did not meet him unprepared: he had long anticipated it, with its probable consequences; the prospect had produced the keenest anguish in his breast, and drawn tears from his eyes; and he had frequently introduced the subject into his public discourses and confidential conversations with his friends. Writing to Mrs. Bowes, some time after this, he says: "How oft have you and I talked of these present days, till neither of us both could refrain tears, when no such appearance then was seen of man! How oft have I said unto you, that I looked daily for trouble, and that I wondered at it, that so long I should escape it! What moved me to refuse (and that with displeasure of all men, even of those that best loved me) those high promotions that were offered by him whom God hath taken from us for our offences! Assuredly the foresight of trouble to come. How oft have I said unto you, that the time would not be long that England would give me bread! Advise with the last letter that I wrote unto your brother-in-law, and consider what is therein contained."

Letter
to Mrs.
Bowes.

He remained in London until the 19th of July, when Mary was proclaimed queen, only nine days after the same ceremony had been performed in that city, for the amiable and unfortunate Lady Jane Grey. He was so affected with the thoughtless demonstrations of joy given by the inhabitants at an event which threatened such danger to the religious faith which they still avowed, that

"Bloody
Mary."

he could not refrain from publicly testifying his displeasure, and warning them in his sermons of the calamities
which they might look for.   Immediately after this, he
seems to have withdrawn from London, and retired to the
north, being justly apprehensive of the measures which
might be pursued by the new government.

To induce the protestants to submit peaceably to her
government, Mary amused them for some time with proclamations, in which she promised not to do violence to
their consciences.   Though aware of the bigotry of the
queen, and the spirit of the religion to which she was devoted, the protestant ministers reckoned it their duty to
improve this respite.   In the month of August, Knox
returned to the south, and resumed his labours.   It seems
to have been at this time that he composed the Confession
and Prayer, which he commonly used in the congregations to which he preached, in which he prayed for Queen
Mary by name, and for the suppression of such as meditated rebellion.   While he itinerated through Buckinghamshire, he was attended by large audiences, which
his popularity and the alarming crisis drew together ;
especially at Amersham, a borough formerly noted for
the general reception of the doctrines of Wickliffe, the
precursor of the Reformation in England, and from which
the seed sown by his followers had never been altogether
eradicated.   Wherever he went, he earnestly exhorted
the people to repentance under the tokens of divine displeasure, and to a steady adherence to the faith which
they had embraced.   He continued to preach in Buckinghamshire and Kent during the harvest months, although the measures of government daily rendered his
safety more precarious ; and in the beginning of November, returned to London, where he resided in the houses
of Mr. Locke and Mr. Hickman, two respectable merchants
of his acquaintance.

While the measures of the new government threatened
danger to all the protestants in the kingdom, and our
countryman was under daily apprehensions of imprison-

ment, he met with a severe trial of a private nature. I have already mentioned his engagements to Miss Bowes. At this time, it was judged proper by both parties to avow the connection, and to proceed to solemnize the union. This step was opposed by the young lady's father; and his opposition was accompanied with circumstances which gave much distress to Knox, Mrs. Bowes, and her daughter. His refusal seems to have proceeded from family pride; but I am inclined to think that it was also influenced by religious considerations; as from different hints dropped in the correspondence, Mr. Bowes appears to have been, if not inclined to Popery in his judgment, at least resolved to comply with the religion now favoured by the court. We find Knox writing to Mrs. Bowes on this subject from London, in a letter, dated 20th September 1553: " My great labours, wherein I desire your daily prayers, will not suffer me to satisfy my mind touching all the process between your husband and you, touching my matter with his daughter. I praise God heartily, both for your boldness and constancy. But I beseech you, mother, trouble not yourself too much therewith. It becomes me now to jeopard my life for the comfort and deliverance of my own flesh, as that I will do, by God's grace, both fear and friendship of all earthly creatures laid aside. I have written to your husband, the contents whereof I trust our brother Harry will declare to you and to my wife. If I escape sickness and imprisonment, [you may] be sure to see me soon."

His wife and mother-in-law were very anxious that he should settle in Berwick, or the neighbourhood of it, where he might perhaps be allowed to reside peaceably, although in a more private way than formerly. But for this purpose some pecuniary provision was requisite. Since the accession of Queen Mary, the payment of the salary allotted to him by government had been stopped. Indeed, he had not received any part of it for the last twelvemonths. His wife's relations were abundantly able to give him a sufficient establishment, but their dissatisfaction with the marriage rendered them averse. Induced by the importunity of his mother-in-law, he applied to Sir Robert Bowes at London, and attempted, by a candid explanation of all circumstances, to remove any umbrage which he had conceived against him, and procure an amicable settlement of the whole affair. He communicated the unfavourable issue of this interview, in a letter to Mrs. Bowes, of which the following is an extract.

"Dear Mother, so may and will I call you, not only for the tender affection I bear unto you in Christ, but also for the motherly kindness ye have shewn unto me at all times since our first acquaintance, albeit such things as I have desired (if it had pleased God), and ye and others have long desired, are never like to come to pass, yet shall ye be sure that my love and care toward you shall never abate, so long as I can care for any earthly creature. Ye shall understand that this 6th of November, I spake with Sir Robert Bowes, on the matter ye know, according to your request, whose disdainful, yea, despiteful words, hath so pierced my heart, that my life is bitter unto me. I bear a good countenance with a sore troubled heart; while he that ought to consider matters with a deep judgment is become not only a despiser, but also a taunter of God's messengers. God be merciful unto him. Among other his most unpleasing words, while that I was about to have declared my part in the whole matter, he said, 'Away with your rhetorical reasons, for I will not be persuaded with them.' God knows I did use no rhetoric or coloured speech, but would have spoken the truth, and that in most simple manner. I am not a good oratour in my own cause. But what he would not be content to hear of me, God shall declare to him one day to his displeasure, unless he repent. It is supposed that all the matter comes by you and me. I pray God that your conscience were quiet, and at peace, and I regard not what country consume this my wicked carcase. And were [it] not that no man's unthankfulness shall move me (God supporting my infirmity) to cease to do profit unto Christ's congregation, those days should be few that England would give me bread. And I fear that, when all is done, I shall be driven to that end; for I cannot abide the disdainful hatred of those, of whom not only I thought I might have craved kindness, but also to whom God hath been by me more liberal than they be thankful. But so must men declare themselves. Affections does trouble me at this present: yet I doubt not to overcome by him, who will not leave comfortless his afflicted to the end: whose omnipotent Spirit rest with you. Amen."

He refers to the same disagreeable affair in another letter written about the end of this year. After mentioning the bad state of his health, which had been greatly increased by distress of mind, he adds, "It will be after the 12th day before I can be at Berwick; and almost I am determined not to come at all. Ye know the cause. God be more merciful unto some, than they are equitable unto me in judgment. The testimony of my conscience absolves me, before his face who looks not upon the presence of man." These extracts shew us the heart of the writer; they discover the sensibility of his temper, the keenness of his feelings, and his pride and independence of spirit struggling with affection to his relations, and a sense of duty.

Returns
to New-
castle.

About the end of November, or beginning of December, he returned from the south to Newcastle. The Parliament had by this time repealed all the laws made in favour of the Reformation, and restored the Roman Catholic religion; but liberty was reserved, to such as pleased, to observe the Protestant worship, until the 20th of December. After that period they were thrown out of the protection of the law, and exposed to the pains decreed against heretics. Many of the bishops and ministers were committed to prison; others had escaped

beyond sea. Knox could not however prevail on himself
either to flee the kingdom, or to desist from preaching.
Three days after the period limited by the statute had
elapsed, he says in one of his letters, " I may not answer
your places of Scripture, nor yet write the exposition of
the 6th psalm, for every day of this week must I preach,
if this wicked carcase will permit."

His enemies, who had been defeated in their attempts
to ruin him under the former government, had now access
to rulers sufficiently disposed to listen to their informations. They were not dilatory in improving the opportunity. In the end of December 1553, or beginning of
January 1554, his servant was seized as he carried letters
from him to his wife and mother-in-law, and the letters
taken from him, with the view of finding in them some
matter of accusation against the writer. As they contained merely religious advices, and exhortations to
constancy in the faith which they professed, which he was
prepared to avow before any court to which he might be
called, he was not alarmed at their interception. But,
being aware of the uneasiness which the report would
give to his friends at Berwick, he set out immediately
with the design of visiting them. Notwithstanding the
secrecy with which he conducted this journey, the
rumour of it quickly spread ; and some of his wife's
relations who had joined him, persuaded that he was in
imminent danger, prevailed on him, greatly against his
own inclination, to relinquish his design of proceeding to
Berwick, and to retire to a place of safety on the coast,
from which he might escape by sea, provided the search
after him was continued. From this retreat he wrote to
his wife and mother, acquainting them with the reasons
of his absconding, and the little prospect which he had of
being able at that time to see them. His brethren, he
said, had, " partly by admonition, partly by tears, compelled him to obey," somewhat contrary to his own
mind ; for " never could he die in a more honest quarrel,"
than by suffering as a witness for that truth of which

God had made him a messenger. Notwithstanding this state of his mind, he promised, if providence prepared the way, to " obey the voices of his brethren, and give place to the fury and rage of Satan for a time."

Having ascertained that the apprehensions of his friends were too well founded, and that he could not elude the pursuit of his enemies, if he remained in England, he procured a vessel, which, on the 28th of January 1554, landed him safely at Dieppe, a port of Normandy, in France.

PERIOD IV.

FROM HIS DEPARTURE OUT OF ENGLAND, ANNO 1554, TO HIS INVITATION INTO
SCOTLAND, BY THE PROTESTANT NOBILITY, ANNO 1557.

PROVIDENCE, which had more important services in reserve for Knox, made use of the urgent importunities of his friends to hurry him away from the danger to which, had he been left to the determination of his own mind, his zeal and fearlessness would have prompted him to expose himself. No sooner did he reach a foreign shore than he began to regret the course which he had been induced to take. When he thought upon his fellow-preachers, whom he had left behind him immured in dungeons, and the people lately under his charge, now scattered abroad as sheep without a shepherd, and a prey to ravening wolves, he felt an indescribable pang, and an almost irresistible desire to return and share in the hazardous but honourable conflict. Although he had only complied with the divine direction, " when they persecute you in one city, flee ye unto another," and in his own breast stood acquitted of cowardice, he found it difficult to divest his conduct of the appearance of that weakness, and was afraid it might operate as a discouragement to his brethren in England, or an inducement to them to make sinful compliances with the view of saving their lives.

On this subject we find him unbosoming himself to Mrs. Bowes in his letters from Dieppe. "The desire that I have to hear of your continuance with Christ Jesus, in the day of this his battle (which shortly shall end to the confusion of his proud enemies), neither by tongue nor by pen can I express, beloved mother. Assuredly, it is such, that it vanquisheth and overcometh all remembrance and solicitude which the flesh useth to take for feeding and defence of herself. For, in every realm and nation, God will stir up some one or other to minister those things that appertain to this wretched life; and, if men will cease to do their office, yet will he send his ravens: so that in every place, perchance, I may find some fathers to my body. But, alas! where I shall find children to be begotten unto God, by the word of life, that can I not presently consider; and therefore the spiritual life of such as sometime boldly professed Christ (God knoweth), is to my heart more dear than all the glory, riches, and honour in earth; and the falling back of such men as I hear daily to turn back to that idol again, is to me more dolorous than, I trust, the corporal death shall [be,] whenever it shall come at God's appointment. Some will ask then, Why did I flee? Assuredly I cannot tell. But of one thing I am sure, the fear of death was not the chief cause of my fleeing. I trust that one cause hath been to let me see with my corporal eyes, that all had not a true heart to Christ Jesus, that, in the day of rest and peace, bare a fair face. But my fleeing is no matter: by God's grace I may come to battle before that all the conflict be ended. And haste the time, O Lord! at thy good pleasure, that once again my tongue may yet praise thy holy name before the congregation, if it were but in the very hour of death."— "I would not bow my knee before that most abominable idol for all the torments that earthly tyrants can devise, God so assisting

me as his holy Spirit presently moveth me to write unfeignedly. And albeit that I have, in the beginning of
this battle, appeared to play the faint-hearted and feeble
soldier (the cause I remit to God), yet my prayer is, that
I may be restored to the battle again. And blessed be
God, the Father of our Lord Jesus Christ, I am not left so
bare without comfort, but my hope is to obtain such mercy, that, if a short end be not made of all my miseries by fi-
nal death, which to me were no small advantage, that yet,
by Him who never despiseth the sobs of the sore afflicted,
I shall be so encouraged to fight, that England and Scotland shall both know, that I am ready to suffer more
than either poverty or exile, for the profession of that
doctrine, and that heavenly religion, whereof it has pleased his merciful providence to make me, among others, a
simple soldier and witness-bearer unto men. And therefore, mother, let no fear enter into your heart, as that I,
escaping the furious rage of these ravening wolves, that
for our unthankfulness are lately loosed from their bands,
do repent any thing of my former fervency. No, mother; for a few sermons by me to be made within England,
my heart at this hour could be content to suffer more
than nature were able to sustain; as by the grace of the
most mighty and most merciful God, who only is God
of comfort and consolation through Christ Jesus, one
day shall be known."

Reflec-
tions.

In his present sequestered situation, he had full leisure to meditate upon the various and surprising turns
of providence in his lot, during the last seven years; his
call to the ministry and employment at St. Andrews,
his subsequent imprisonment and release, the sphere of
usefulness in which he had been placed in England, with
the afflicting manner in which he was excluded from it,
and driven to seek refuge as an exile in that country to
which he had formerly been carried as a prisoner. The
late events seemed in a special manner to summon him
to a solemn review of the manner in which he had discharged the sacred trust committed to him, as a "stew-

ard of the mysteries of God." It will throw light on
his character, and may not be without use to such as occupy the same station, to exhibit the result of his reflections on this subject. He could not, without ingratitude
to Him who had called him to be his servant, deny, that
his qualifications for the ministry had been in no small
degree improved since he came to England; and he had
the testimony of his own conscience, in addition to that
of his numerous auditors, that he had not altogether
neglected the gifts bestowed on him, but had exercised
them with some measure of fidelity and painfulness. At
the same time, he found reason for self-accusation on
different grounds. Having mentioned, in one of his letters, the reiterated charge of Christ to Peter, "Feed my
sheep, feed my lambs," he exclaims, "O alas! how small
is the number of pastors that obeys this commandment.
But this matter will I not deplore, except that I (not
speaking of others) will accuse myself that do not, I confess, the uttermost of my power in feeding the lambs
and sheep of Christ. I satisfy, peradventure, many men
in the small labours I take; but I satisfy not myself.
I have done somewhat, but not according to my duty."
In the discharge of private duties, he acknowledges, that
shame, and the fear of incurring the malignant scandal
of the world, had hindered him from visiting the ignorant and distressed, and administering to them the instruction and comfort which they craved. In public ministrations, he had been deficient in fervency and fidelity,
in impartiality, and in diligence. He could not charge
himself with flattery, and his " rude plainness" had given
offence to some; but his conscience now accused him of
not having been sufficiently plain in admonishing offenders. His custom was to describe the vices of which his hearers were guilty, in such colours that they might read their
own image; but being " unwilling to provoke all men
against him," he restrained himself from particular ap-
plications. Though his " eye had not been much set on
worldly promotion," he had sometimes been allured, by

affection for friends and familiar acquaintances, to reside too long in particular places, to the neglect of others. That day he thought he had not sinned, if he had not been idle; now he was convinced that it was his duty to have considered how long he should remain in one place, and how many hungry souls were starving elsewhere. Sometimes, at the solicitation of friends, he had spared himself, and spent the time in worldly business, or in bodily recreation and exercise, when he ought to have been employed in the discharge of his official duties. "Besides these," says he, "I was assaulted, yea infected, with more gross sins; that is, my wicked nature desired the favours, the estimation, and praise of men: against which, albeit that sometimes the Spirit of God did move me to fight, and earnestly did stir me (God knoweth I lie not) to sob and lament for these imperfections; yet never ceased they to trouble me, when any occasion was offered; and so privily and craftily did they enter into my breast, that I could not perceive myself to be wounded, till vain-glory had almost got the upper hand. O Lord! be merciful to my great offence; and deal not with me according to my iniquity, but according to the multitude of thy mercies."

Such was the strict scrutiny which Knox made into his ministerial conduct. To many the offences of which he accused himself will appear slight and venial; others will perceive in them nothing worthy of blame. But they struck his mind in a very different light, in the hour of adversity and solitary meditation. If he had such reason for self-condemnation, whose labours were so abundant as to appear to us excessive, how few are there in the same station who may not say, I do remember my faults this day.

He did not, however, abandon himself to melancholy and unavailing complaints. One of his first cares, after arriving at Dieppe, was to employ his pen in writing suitable advices to those whom he could no longer instruct by his sermons and conversation. With this view he transmitted to England two short treatises. The *one* was an exposition of the sixth psalm, which he had begun to write in England, at the request of Mrs. Bowes, but had not found leisure to finish. It is an excellent practical discourse upon that portion of Scripture, and will be read with peculiar satisfaction by those who have been trained to religion in the school of adversity. The other treatise was a large letter, addressed to those in London and other parts of England, among whom he had been employed as a preacher. The drift of it was to warn them against defection from the religion which they had professed, or giving countenance to the idolatrous worship erected among them. The conclusion is a most impressive and eloquent exhortation, in which he addresses their consciences, their hopes, their fears, their feelings, and adjures them by all that is sacred, and all that is dear to them, as men, as parents, and as Christians, not to start back from their good profession, and plunge themselves and their posterity into the gulf of ignorance and idolatry. the reader of this letter cannot fail to be struck with its animated strain, when he reflects, that it proceeded from a foreign exile, in a strange country, without a single acquaintance, and ignorant where he would find a place of abode or the means of subsistence.

PERIOD IV. 1554–1557 A.D.

An earnest exhortation.

On the last day of February 1554, he set out from Dieppe, like the Hebrew patriarch of old, "not knowing whither he went;" and "committing his way to God," travelled through France, and came to Switzerland. A correspondence had been kept up between some of the English reformers and the most noted divines of the Helvetic church. The latter had already heard, with the sincerest grief, of the overthrow of the Reformation in England, and the dispersion of its friends. Upon making himself known, Knox was cordially received by them, and treated with the most Christian hospitality. He spent some time in Switzerland, visiting the particular churches, and conferring with the

Visits Switzerland.

learned men. Certain difficult questions, suggested by
the present conjuncture of affairs in England, which he
had revolved in his mind, he propounded to them for advice, and was confirmed in his own judgment by the coin-
cidence of their views.

In the beginning of May he returned to Dieppe, to
receive information from England, a journey which he
repeated at intervals as long as he remained on the continent.   The kind reception which he had met with, and
the agreeable company which he enjoyed, during his short
residence in Switzerland, had helped to dissipate the
cloud which hung upon his spirits when he landed in
France, and to open his mind to more pleasing prospects
as to the issue of the present afflicting providences.   This
appears from a letter written by him at this time, and
addressed " To his afflicted brethren."   After discoursing of the situation of the disciples of Christ, during the
time that he lay in the grave, and the sudden transition
which they experienced, from the depth of sorrow to
the summit of joy, upon the reappearance of their Master; he adds: " The remembrance thereof is unto my
heart great matter of consolation.   For yet my good
hope is, that one day or other, Christ Jesus, that now is
crucified in England, shall rise again, in despite of his
enemies, and shall appear to his weak and sore troubled
disciples (for yet some he hath in that wretched and
miserable realm); to whom he shall say, 'Peace be unto
you : it is I ; be not afraid.' "

His spirit was also refreshed, at this time, by the information which he received of the constancy with which
his mother-in-law adhered to the protestant faith.   It
appears that her husband had expected that she and the
rest of her family had consciences equally accommodating with his own.   It was not until she had evinced,
in the most determined manner, her resolution to forsake friends and native country, rather than sacrifice her
religion, that she was released from his importunities to
comply with the Roman Catholic religion.   Before he

went to Switzerland, Knox had signified his intention, if his life was spared, of visiting his friends at Berwick. When he returned to Dieppe, he had not relinquished the thoughts of this enterprise. His friends, by their letters, would, it is likely, dissuade him from this; and, after cool consideration, he resolved to postpone an attempt, by which he must have risked his life, without any prospect of doing good.

PERIOD IV. 1554–1557 A.D.

Wherefore, setting out again from Dieppe, he repaired to Geneva. It was on this occasion that he first became personally acquainted with the celebrated Calvin, and formed that intimate friendship which subsisted between them till the death of the latter, in 1564. They were nearly of the same age ; and there was a striking similarity in their sentiments, and in the prominent features of their character. The Genevan Reformer was highly pleased with the piety and talents of Knox, who, in his turn, entertained a greater esteem and deference for Calvin than for any other of the reformers. As Geneva was an eligible situation for prosecuting study, and he approved much of the religious order established in it, he resolved to make that city the ordinary place of his residence during the continuance of his exile.

Knox and Calvin.

But no prospect of personal safety or accommodation could banish from his mind the thoughts of his persecuted brethren. In the month of July he undertook another journey to Dieppe, to inform himself accurately of their situation, and learn if he could do any thing for their comfort. On this occasion he received tidings, which tore open those wounds which had begun to close. The severities used against the Protestants of England daily increased ; and, what was still more afflicting to him, many of those who had embraced the truth under his ministry had been induced to recant, and go over to popery. In the agony of his spirit he wrote to them, setting before them the destruction to which they exposed their immortal souls by such cowardly desertion, and earnestly calling them to repent. Under his present

Backsliding in England.

impressions, he repeated his former admonitions to his
mother-in-law, including his wife; over whose religious
constancy he was tenderly jealous. "By pen will I
write, because the bodies are put asunder to meet again
at God's pleasure, that which by mouth, and face to
face, ye have heard. That if man or angel labour to
bring you back from the confession that once you have
given, let them in that behalf be accursed. If any
trouble you above measure, whether they be magistrates
or carnal friends, they shall bear their just condemnation, unless they speedily repent. But now, mother,
comfort you my heart (God grant ye may) in this my
great affliction and dolorous pilgrimage; continue stoutly
to the end, and bow you never before that idol, and so
will the rest of worldly troubles be unto me more tolerable. With my own heart I oft commune, yea, and, as
it were, comforting myself, I appear to triumph, that
God shall not suffer you to fall in that rebuke. Sure I
am, that both ye would fear and eshame to commit that
abomination in my presence, who am but a wretched
man, subject to sin and misery like to yourself. But, O
mother! though no earthly creature should be offended
with you, yet fear ye the presence and offence of Him,
who, present in all places, searcheth the very heart and
reins, whose indignation, once kindled against the inobedient,—and no sin more inflameth his wrath than idolatry doth,—no creature in heaven nor in earth is able to
appease."

An admo-
nition.

The sin of
idolatry.

He was in this state of mind when he composed the
Admonition to England, which was published about the
end of this year. Those who have censured him, as
indulging in an excessive vehemence of spirit and bitterness of language, usually refer to this tract in support of
the charge. It is true that he there paints the persecuting papists in the blackest colours, and holds them up
as objects of human execration and divine vengeance. I
do not stop here to inquire whether he was chargeable
with transgressing the bounds of moderation prescribed

by religion and the gospel, in the expression of his indignation and zeal; or whether the censures pronounced
by his accusers, and the principles upon which they proceed, do not involve a condemnation of the temper and
language of the most righteous men mentioned in Scripture, and even of our Saviour himself. But I ask, Is
there no apology for his severity to be found in the
characters of the persons against whom he wrote, and in
the state of his own feelings, lacerated, not by personal
sufferings, but by sympathy with his suffering brethren,
who were driven into prisons by their unnatural countrymen, "as sheep for the slaughter," to be brought forth
and barbarously immolated to appease the Roman Mo-
loch? Who could suppress indignation in speaking of
the conduct of men, who, having raised themselves to
honour and affluence by the warmest professions of
friendship to the reformed religion under the preceding
reign, now abetted the most violent proceedings against
their former brethren and benefactors? What terms
were too strong for stigmatizing the execrable system of
persecution coolly projected by the dissembling, vindictive Gardiner, the brutal barbarity of the bloody Bonner,
or the unrelenting, insatiable cruelty of Mary, who,
having extinguished the feelings of humanity, and di-
vested herself of the tenderness which characterises her
sex, issued orders for the murder of her subjects, until
her own husband, bigotted and unfeeling as he was,
turned with disgust from the spectacle, and continued to
urge to fresh severities the willing instruments of her
cruelty, after they were sated with blood!

PERIOD
IV.
1554-1557
A.D.

Apostasy
and perse-
cution in
England.

> On such a theme 'tis impious to be calm;
> Passion is reason, transport temper here.—YOUNG.

"Oppression makes a wise man mad;" but, to use the
words of a modern orator, with a more just application, "the distemper is still the madness of the wise,
which is better than the sobriety of fools. Their cry is
the voice of sacred misery, exalted, not into wild raving,

but into the sanctified phrensy of prophecy and inspiration."

Knox returned to Geneva, and applied himself to
study with all the ardour of youth, although his age
now bordered upon fifty. It was about this time that
he seems to have made some proficiency in the knowledge
of the Hebrew language, which he had no opportunity
of acquiring in early life. It is natural to enquire, by
what funds he was supported during his exile. However much inclined his mother-in-law was to relieve his
necessities, the disposition of her husband seems to have put
it greatly out of her power. Any small sum which his
friends had advanced to him, before his sudden departure
from England, was exhausted; and he was at this time
very much straitened for money. Being unwilling to
burden strangers, he looked for assistance to the voluntary contributions of those among whom he had laboured.
In a letter to Mrs. Bowes, he says, " My own estate I
cannot well declare; but God shall guide the footsteps
of him that is wilsome, and will feed him in trouble
that never greatly solicited for the world. If any collection might be made among the faithful, it were no
shame for me to receive that which Paul refused not in
the time of his trouble. But all I remit to His providence, that ever careth for his own." I find from his
letters, that remittances were made to him by particular
friends, both in England and Scotland, during his residence on the continent.

Remit-
tances
from En-
gland and
Scotland.

In the mean time, the persecution growing hot in England, great numbers of the protestants made their escape, and sought refuge in foreign countries. Before
the close of the year 1554, it was computed that there
were no fewer than eight hundred learned Englishmen,
besides others of different conditions, on the continent.
The foreign reformed churches exhibited, on this occasion, an amiable proof of the spirit of their religion, and
amply recompensed the kindness which many foreigners
had experienced in England, during the reign of Edward.

They emulated one another in exertions to accommodate, and alleviate the sufferings, of the unfortunate refugees who were dispersed among them. The principal places in which they obtained settlements, were Zurich, Basle, Geneva, Arrow, Embden, Wezel, Strasburgh, Duysburgh, and Frankfort.

Frankfort on the Maine was a rich imperial city of Germany, which, at an early period, had embraced the Reformation, and befriended protestant refugees from all countries, as far as this could be done without coming to an open breach with the Emperor, who watched their conduct with a jealous eye. There was already a church of French protestants in that city. On the 14th of July 1554, the English exiles who had come to Frankfort, obtained from the magistrates the joint use of the place of worship allotted to the French, with liberty to perform religious service in their own language. This was granted upon the condition of their conforming as nearly as possible to the form of worship used by the French church, a prudent precaution which their political circumstances dictated. The offer was gratefully accepted by the English, who came to an unanimous agreement, that in using the English liturgy they would omit the litany, the audible responses, the surplice, with other ceremonies, which, " in those reformed churches would seem more than strange," or which were " superstitious and superfluous." Having settled this point in the most harmonious manner, elected a pastor and deacons, *pro tempore*, and agreed upon some rules for discipline, they wrote a circular letter to their brethren scattered in different places, inviting them to Frankfort, to share with them in their accommodations, and unite their prayers for the afflicted church of England. The exiles at Strasburgh, in their reply, recommended to them certain persons as most fit for the offices of superintendent and pastors; a recommendation not asked by the congregation at Frankfort, who did not think a superintendent requisite in their situation, and meant to have two or three pastors of equal authority. They, accordingly, proceeded to make choice of three, one of whom was Knox, who received information of his election, by the following letter from the congregation delivered to him in Geneva.

"We have received letters from our brethren off Strausbrough, but not in suche sorte and ample wise as we looked for; whereupon we assembled together in the H. Goaste (we hope), and have, with one voice and consent, chosen yow so particulerly to be one off the ministers off our congregation here, to preache unto us the moste lively worde of God, accordinge to the gift that God hathe geven yow; for as muche as we have here, throughe the mercifull goodnes off God, a churche to be congregated together in the name of Christe, and be all of one body, and also beinge of one nation, tonge, and countrie. And at this presente, having need of such a one as yow, we do desier yow and also require yow, in the name of God, not to deny us, nor to refuse theis oure requests; but that yow will aide, helpe, and assiste us with your presence in this our good and godlie enterprise, which we have taken in hand, to the glorie off God and the profit off his congregation, and the poore sheepe off Christ dispersed abroad, who, withe your and like presences, woulde come hither and be of one folde, where as nowe they wander abroad as loste sheepe withowte anie gide. We mistruste not but that you will joifully accepte this callinge. Fare ye well from Franckford this 24. of September."

Knox was averse to undertake this charge, either from a desire to continue his studies at Geneva, or from an apprehension of difficulties which he might meet with at Frankfort. By the persuasion of Calvin, he was, however, induced to comply with the call, and, repairing to Frankfort in the month of November, commenced his ministry with the universal consent and approbation of the congregation. But previous to his arrival, the harmony, which at first subsisted among that people, had been disturbed. In reply to their circular letter, the exiles at Zurich had signified that they would not come to Frankfort, unless they obtained security that the church there would "use the same order of service concerning religion, which was, in England, last set forth by King Edward;" for they were fully determined "to admit and use no other." By varying from that service, they alleged, they would give occasion to their adversaries to charge their religion with imperfection and mutability, and condemn their brethren in England, who were now sealing it with their blood. To these representations the brethren at Frankfort replied, that they had obtained the liberty of a place of worship, upon condition of their accommodating as much as possible to the form used by the French church; that there were a number of things in the English service-book which would be offensive to the protestants among whom they resided, and had been occasion of scruple to conscientious men at home; that, by the variations which they had introduced no reflection was made upon the ordinances of their late sovereign and his council, who had themselves altered many things, and had resolved on greater alterations, without thinking that they gave any handle to their popish adversaries; far less did they detract from the credit of the martyrs, who, they were persuaded, shed their blood in confirmation of more important things than mutable ceremonies of human appointment. This answer did not satisfy the learned men at Zurich, though it induced them to lower their tone; not contented with forming their own resolution, they instigated their brethren at Strasburgh to urge the same request, and, by letters and messengers, fomented dissension in the congregation at Frankfort.

When Knox arrived, he found that the seeds of animosity had already sprung up among them. From his sentiments respecting the English service-book we may be sure that the eagerness manifested by those who wished to impose it was very displeasing to him. But so sensible was he of the pernicious and discreditable effects of division among brethren exiled for the same faith, that he resolved to act as a moderator between the two parties, and to avoid, as far as possible, every thing which tended to widen or continue the breach. Accordingly, when the congregation had agreed to the order of the Genevan church, and requested him to proceed to administer the communion according to it, (although, in his judgment, he approved of that order), he declined to use it, until their learned brethren in other places were consulted. At the same time, he signified that he had not freedom to administer the sacraments agreeably to the English liturgy. If he could not be allowed to perform this service in a manner more consonant to scripture, he requested that some other might be employed in this duty, and he would willingly confine himself to preaching: if neither of these could be granted, he besought them to release him altogether from his charge. To this last request they would by no means consent.

Fearing that if these differences were not speedily accommodated, they would burst into a flame of contention, Knox, along with some others, was employed to draw up a summary of the Book of Common Prayer, and having translated it into Latin, to send it to Calvin for his opinion and advice. Calvin replied in a letter, dated January 20, 1555; he lamented the unseemly contentions which prevailed among them; signified, that he had always recommended moderation respecting external ceremonies, but could not but condemn the obstinacy of those who would consent to no change of old customs; in the liturgy of England he had found many tolerable fooleries, (*tolerabiles ineptias*), he meant things which might be tolerated at the beginning of a reformation, but ought afterwards to be removed; he thought that the present condition of the English warranted them to attempt this, and to agree upon an order more conducive to edification; and, for his part, he could not understand what those meant who discovered such fondness for Popish dregs.

This letter, being read to the congregation, had a great
effect in repressing the keenness of such as had urged
the unlimited use of the liturgy; and a committee was
appointed to draw up a form which might accommodate
all differences. When this committee met, Knox told
them that he was convinced it was necessary for one of
the parties to relent before they could come to an amicable settlement; he would therefore state, he said, what
he judged most proper, and having exonered himself,
would allow them without opposition to determine as
they should answer to God and the church. They accordingly agreed upon a form of worship, in which some
things were taken from the English liturgy, and others
added, which were thought suitable to their circumstances. This was to continue in force until the end of
April next; if any dispute arose in the interval, it was
to be referred to five of the most celebrated foreign divines. This agreement was subscribed by all the members of the congregation; thanks were publicly returned
to God for the restoration of harmony; and the communion was received as a pledge of union, and the burial
of all past offences.

But this agreement was soon after violated, and the
peace of that unhappy congregation again broken, in the
most wanton and scandalous manner. On the 13th of
March, Dr. Cox, who had been preceptor to Edward VI.,
came from England to Frankfort, with some others in
his company. The first day that they attended public
worship after their arrival, they broke through the established order, by answering aloud after the minister in
the time of divine service. Being admonished by some
of the elders to refrain from that practice, they insolent-
ly replied: "That they would do as they had done in
England; and they would have the face of an English
church." On the following Sabbath, one of the number
intruded himself into the pulpit, without the consent of
the pastors or the congregation, and read the litany,

PERIOD
IV.
1554–1557
A.D.

Dr Cox
and others
admon-
ished.

Cox and the other accomplices echoing the responses. This offensive behaviour was aggravated by the consideration, that some of them, before leaving England, had been guilty of compliances with Popery, for which they had as yet given no satisfaction.

Such an insult upon the whole body, and outrage upon all decency and order, could not be passed over in silence. It was Knox's turn to preach on the afternoon of the last mentioned Sabbath. In the course of lecturing through Genesis, he had come to the narration of the behaviour of Ham to his father Noah when he lay exposed in his tent. Having discoursed from this of the infirmities of brethren which ought to be concealed, he remarked that there were other things, which, as they tended to the open dishonouring of God, and disquieting of his church, ought to be disclosed and publicly re-

Cox and
his friends
rebuked
by Knox. buked. He then reminded them of the contention which had existed in the congregation, and of the happy manner in which, after long and painful labour, it had been ended, to the joy of all, by the solemn agreement which had that day been flagrantly violated. This, he said, it became not the proudest of them to have attempted. Nothing which was destitute of a divine warrant ought to be obtruded upon any Christian church. In that book, for which some entertained such an overweening fondness, he would undertake to prove publicly, that there were things imperfect, impure, and superstitious; and, if any would go about to burden a free congregation with such things, he would not fail, as often as he occupied that place, (provided his text afforded occasion), to oppose their design. As he had been forced to enter upon that subject, he would say further, that, in his judgment, slackness in reforming religion, when time and opportunity were granted, was one cause of the divine displeasure against England. He adverted to the trouble which Bishop Hooper had suffered for refusing some of the ceremonies, to the want of discipline, and to e well known fact that three, four, or five benefices had been occupied by one man, to the depriving of the ck of Christ of their necessary food.

This free reprimand was much stomached by those ainst whom it was levelled, especially by such as had ld pluralities in England, who complained that the eacher had slandered their mother church. Loud nplaints being made against the sermon, a special eting was appointed to consider them. At this meet-, instead of prosecuting their complaints, the friends the liturgy began with insisting, that Dr. Cox and his ends should be admitted to a vote. This was resisted the great majority; because they had not yet sub-ibed the discipline of the church, nor given satisfac-n for their late disorderly conduct, and for their sin-compliances in England. The behaviour of our untryman, on this occasion, was more remarkable for deration and magnanimity, than for prudence. Al-ugh aware of their hostility to himself, and that they ght admission chiefly to overpower him by numbers, was so confident of the justice of his cause, and cious to remove prejudices, that he entreated and pre-led with the meeting to yield, and admit them pre-tly to a vote. This disinterestedness was thrown ay on the opposite party: no sooner were they ad-ited, and had obtained a majority of voices, than x, although he had no authority in the congregation, charged Knox from preaching, and from all interfer-e with congregational affairs.

Knox dismissed by Cox.

The great body of the congregation were indignant at se proceedings; and there was some reason to fear t their mutual animosity would break out into some graceful disorder. A representation of the circum-nces having been made to the magistrates of Frank-t, they, after in vain recommending a private accom-dation, issued an order that the congregation should form exactly to the worship used by the French rch, as nothing but confusion had ensued since they

departed from it; if this was not complied with, th
threatened to shut up their place of worship. To t
peremptory injunction the Coxian faction pretende
cheerful submission, while they clandestinely concer
measures for obtaining its revocation, and enforcing th
favourite liturgy upon their reclaiming brethren.

Perceiving the influence which our countryman h
in the congregation, and despairing to carry their p
into execution, as long as he was among them, th
determined in the first place to get rid of him.
accomplish this, they had recourse to one of the ba
and most unchristian arts ever employed to ruin
adversary. Two of them, in concurrence with oth

went privately to the magistrates, and accused Knox
high treason against the Emperor of Germany, his
Philip, and Queen Mary of England; putting into th
hands a copy of a book which he had lately publish
in which the passages upon which the charge was foun
were marked! " O Lord God !" says Knox, when n
rating this step, " open their hearts to see their wick
ness ; and forgive them, for thy manifold mercies. A
I forgive them, O Lord, from the bottom of mine hea
But that thy message sent by my mouth may not
slandered, I am compelled to declare the cause of
departing, and to utter their follies, to their amendme
I trust, and the example of others, who in the sa
banishment can have so cruel hearts as to persec
their brethren."   The book which the accusers left w
the magistrates was his Admonition to England ; and
passage upon which they principally fixed, as subst
tiating the charge of treason against the Emperor, v
the following, originally spoken to the inhabitants
Amersham in Buckinghamshire, on occasion of the
moured marriage of Queen Mary with Philip, the
and heir of Charles V., a match which was at that ti
dreaded even by many of the English Catholics.
England, England, if thou obstinately wilt return i
Egypt, that is, if thou contract marriage, confederacy

gue with such princes as do maintain and advance
latry ; such as the Emperor, who is no less enemy to
rist than ever was Nero : if for the pleasure of such
nces thou return to thy old abominations before used
der papistry, then assuredly, O England, thou shalt
plagued and brought to desolation, by the means of
ose whose favour thou seekest." The other passages
ated to the cruelty of Queen Mary of England.

The magistrates, in consequence of this accusation,
t for Whittingham, a respectable member of the
glish congregation, and interrogated him concerning
ox's character. He told them that he was "a learned,
ve, and godly man." They then acquainted him
th the serious accusation which had been lodged
ainst him by some of his countrymen, and, giving
n the book, charged him, *sub pœna pacis*, to bring
em an exact Latin translation of the passages which
re marked. This being done, they commanded Knox
desist from preaching, until their pleasure should be
own. "Yet," says he, in his narrative, "being desirous
hear others, I went to the church next day, not
nking that my company would have offended any.
t as soon as my accusers saw me, they, with —— and
ers, departed from the sermon ; some of them protest-
 with great vehemence, that they would not tarry
ere I was." The magistrates were extremely per-
xed how to act in this delicate business : on the one
nd, they were satisfied of the malice of Knox's accu-
s ; on the other, they were afraid that information of
 charge would be conveyed to the Emperor's Council,
ich sat at Augsburgh, and that they might be obliged
deliver up the accused to them, or to the Queen of Eng-
d. In this dilemma, they desired Whittingham to ad-
 his friend privately, to retire of his own accord from
ankfort. At the same time, they did not dissemble their
estation of the unnatural conduct of the informers,
o, waiting upon them to know the result of their delib-
tions, were dismissed from their presence with frowns.

On the 25th of March, Knox delivered a very cons
atory discourse to about fifty members of the congre
tion, who assembled at his lodgings in the eveni
Next day they accompanied him some miles on his jo
ney from Frankfort, and, with heavy hearts and ma
tears, committed him to God, and took their leave.

No sooner was Knox gone, than Cox, who had priva
ly concerted the plan with Dr. Glauberg, a civilian, a
nephew of the chief magistrate, procured an order fr
the Senate for the unlimited use of the English litur,
by means of the false representation, that it was now u
versally acceptable to the congregation. The next s
was the abrogation of the discipline, and then the
pointment of a bishop, or superintendent over the p
tors. Having accomplished these important impro
ments, they could now boast that they had "the face
an English church." Yes! they could now raise th
heads above all the reformed churches who had the h
our of entertaining them; who, though they might ha
all the office-bearers and ordinances instituted by Chr
had neither bishop, nor litany, nor surplice! Th
could now lift up their faces in the presence of 1
church of Rome herself, and claim——But let me ⁣
forget, that the men of whom I write were at this ti
suffering exile for the protestant religion, and that th
really detested the body of popery, though childish
and superstitiously attached to its attire, and gestu⁣
and language.

The sequel of the transactions, in the English cong
gation at Frankfort, does not properly belong to this m
moir. I shall only add, that after some ineffectual
tempts to obtain satisfaction for the breach of 1
church's peace, and the injurious treatment of th
minister, a considerable number of the members left 1
John Fox city; some of them, as Fox the celebrated martyrolog
repairing to Basil, the greater part to Geneva, where th
obtained a place of worship, and lived in great harmo
and love, until the storm of persecution in England bl

er, at the death of Queen Mary; while those who reained at Frankfort, as if to expiate their offence against
nox, continued a prey to endless contention. Cox and
s learned colleagues, having accomplished their favour-
object, soon left them to compose the strife which
ey had excited, and provided themselves elsewhere
th a less expensive situation for carrying on their
dies.

I have been the more minute in the detail of these
nsactions, not only because of the share which the
bject of this memoir had in them, but because they
row light upon the controversy between the conformists
d nonconformists, which runs through the succeeding
riod of the ecclesiastical history of England. "The
ubles at Frankfort" present, in miniature, a striking
ture of that contentious scene which was afterwards
hibited on a larger scale in the mother-country. The
ue of that affair augured ill as to the prospect of an
icable adjustment of the litigated points. It had been
ual to urge conformity to the obnoxious ceremonies,
m the respect due to the authority by which they
re enjoined. But here there was no authority enjoin-
g them, but rather the contrary. If they were urged
th such intolerant importunity in a place where the
ws and customs were repugnant to them, what was to
expected in England, where law and custom were on
ir side? The divines, who were advanced in the church
the accession of Elizabeth, professed that they desired
removal of those grounds of strife, but could not ob-
n it from the Queen: and I am disposed to give many
them credit for the sincerity of their professions. But
they shewed themselves so stiff and unyielding when
matter was wholly in their own power; as some
them were so eager in wreathing a yoke about the
sciences of their brethren, that they urged reluc-
t magistrates to rivet it; is it any wonder that their
plications for relief were cold and ineffectual, when
de to rulers who were disposed to make the yoke still

The
troubles
at Frank-
fort and
in En-
gland con-
trasted.

more severe, and to "chastise with scorpions those who
they had chastised with whips?" I repeat it; when
consider the transactions at Frankfort, I am not surpris
at the defeating of every subsequent attempt to advan
the Reformation in England, or to procure relief to tho
who scrupled to yield conformity to some of the eccle
astical laws. I know it is pleaded, that the things co1
plained of are matters of indifference, not prohibited
scripture, not imposed as essential to religion, or necessa
to salvation, matters that can affect no well inform
conscience; and that such as refuse them, when enact
by authority, are influenced by unreasonable scrupulo
ty, conceited, pragmatical, opinionative, and what n
This has been the usual language of a ruling party, wh
imposing upon the consciences of the minority.   But r
to urge here the danger of allowing to any class of rule
civil or ecclesiastical, a power of enjoining indiffere
things in religion; nor the undeniable fact, that t
burdensome system of ceremonial observances, by whi
religion was corrupted under the papacy, was gradua
introduced under these and similar pretexts; nor tl
the things in question, when complexly and forma
considered, are not really matters of indifference; not
insist at present, I say, upon these topics, the answer

Divisions
at Frank-
fort.

the above plea is short and decisive. "These things a
pear matters of conscience and importance to the scru
lers: you say they are matters of indifference. W
then violate the sacred peace of the church, and perp
uate division; why silence, deprive, harass, and stal
men of acknowledged learning and piety, and drive fr
communion a sober and devout people; why tortu
their consciences, and endanger their souls by the imp
sition of things which, in your judgment, are indiffere
not necessary, and unworthy to become subjects of co
tention?"

Dic——, et eris mihi magnus Apollo

Upon retiring from Frankfort, Knox went directly

eneva. He was cordially welcomed back by Calvin. his advice had great weight in disposing Knox to mply with the invitation from Frankfort, he felt uch hurt at the treatment which had obliged him to ave it. In reply to an apologetic epistle which he reived from Dr. Cox, Calvin, although he restrained himf from saying any thing which might revive or increase e flame, could not conceal his opinion, that Knox had en used in an unbrotherly, unchristian manner, and at it would have been better for the accuser to have reained at home, than to have brought a firebrand into a reign country to inflame a peaceable society.

It appeared from the event, that providence had disgaged Knox from his late charge, to employ him on more important service. From the time that he was rried prisoner into France, he had never lost sight of otland, nor relinquished the hope of again preaching his native country. His constant employment, dur-g the five years which he spent in England, occupied s mind, and lessened the regret which he felt, at seeing e great object of his desire apparently at as great a stance as ever. Upon leaving England, his attention is more particularly directed to his native country; d, soon after returning from Frankfort, he was informthat matters began to assume a more favourable aparance there than they had worn for a number of ars. After the surrender of the castle of St. Andrews, d the banishment of the protestants who had taken fuge in it, an irrecoverable blow seemed to have been ven to the reformed cause in Scotland. The clergy umphed in their victory, and flattered themselves that ey had stifled the voice of opposition. There were ll many protestants in the kingdom; but they satisd themselves with retaining their sentiments in secret, thout exposing their lives to certain destruction by owing them, or exciting the suspicions of their enemies private conventicles. An event which threatened

the extinction of the Reformation in Britain proved t
means of reviving it in Scotland. Several of those w
were driven from England by the persecution of Ma
took refuge in this country, and were overlooked,
consequence of the security into which the Scotti
clergy had been lulled by success. Travelling from pla
to place, they instructed many, and fanned the late
zeal of those who had formerly received the knowled
of the truth.

William Harlow.

William Harlow, whose zeal and knowledge of the do
trines of the gospel compensated for the defects of his ed
cation, was the first preacher who came. After him arriv
John Willock, in summer 1555, being charged with
commission from the Duchess of Embden to the Quee
Regent. Willock became afterwards the chief co-adj

John Willock.

tor of Knox, who entertained the highest esteem and a
fection for him. The union of their talents and pec
liar qualities was of great advantage to the Reformatio
Willock was not inferior to Knox in learning: and a
though he did not equal him in intrepidity and e
quence, surpassed him in affability, prudence, and addres
by which means he was sometimes able to maintain h
station and accomplish his purposes, when his colleag
could not act with safety or success. He was a nati
of Ayrshire, and had worn the monastic habit; but,
an early period, he embraced the reformed opinio
and fled into England. During the severe persecuti
for the six articles, he was, in 1541, thrown into t
prison of the Fleet. He was afterwards chaplain to t
Duke of Suffolk, the father of Lady Jane Grey; and up
the accession of Queen Mary, he retired to East Frieslar

Although Knox did not know what it was to fe
danger, and was little accustomed to consult his perso
al ease, when he had the prospect of being useful in h
Master's service, none of his enterprises were undertak
rashly, and without serious deliberation upon the ca
which he had to engage in them. On the present occ

sion, he felt at first averse to a journey into Scotland, notwithstanding some encouraging circumstances in the intelligence which he had received from that quarter. He had been so much tossed about of late, that he felt a peculiar relish in the learned leisure which he at present enjoyed, and was desirous to prolong. His anxiety to see his wife, after an absence of nearly two years, and the importunity with which his mother-in-law, in her letters, urged him to visit them, determined him at last to undertake the journey. Setting out from Geneva in the month of August 1555, he came to Dieppe, and, sailing from that port, landed on the east coast, near the boundaries between Scotland and England, about the end of harvest. He repaired immediately to Berwick, where he had the satisfaction of finding his wife and her mother in comfortable circumstances, enjoying the happiness of religious society with several individuals in that city, who, like themselves, had not "bowed the knee" to the established idolatry, nor submitted to "receive the mark" of Antichrist.

Having remained some time with them, he set out secretly to visit the Protestants in Edinburgh, intending, after a short stay, to return to Berwick. But he found employment which detained him beyond his expectation. In Edinburgh he lodged with James Syme, a respectable and religious burgess, to whose house the friends of the reformed doctrine repaired, to attend his instructions, as soon as they were informed of his arrival. Among these were John Erskine of Dun, and William Maitland, younger of Lethington, afterwards Secretary to Mary Queen of Scots. John Willock was also in Edinburgh at this time. Those who heard him, being exceedingly gratified with his doctrine, brought their friends and acquaintances along with them, and his audiences daily increased. Being confined to a private house, he was obliged to preach to successive assemblies; and was almost unremittingly employed, by night as well as by day, in communicating instruction to persons

PERIOD
IV.
1554-15
A.D.

Knox arrives at Berwick.

Visits Edinburgh.

who demanded it with extraordinary avidity. The following letter written by him to Mrs. Bowes, to excuse himself for not returning so soon as he had purposed, will convey the best idea of his employment and feelings on this occasion.

"The wayis of man ar not in his awn power. Albeit my journey toward Scotland, belovit mother, was maist contrarious to my awn judgement, befoir I did interpryse the same; yet this day I prais God for thame wha was the cause externall of my resort to theis quarteris; that is, I prais God in yow and for yow, whome hie maid the instrument to draw me frome the den of my awn eas, (you allane did draw me from the rest of quyet studie,) to contemplat and behald the fervent thrist of oure brethrene, night and day sobbing and gronyng for the breid of lyfe. Gif I had not sene it with my eis, in my awn contry, I culd not have beleveit it! I praisit God, when I was with you, perceaving that, in the middis of Sodome, God had mo Lottis than one, and ma faithfull dochteris than tua. But the fervencie heir dioth fer exceid all utheris that I have seen. And thairfoir ye sall pacientlie bear, altho' I spend heir yet sum dayis; for depart I cannot unto sic tyme as God quenche their thrist a litill. Yea, mother, thair fervencie doith sa ravische me, that I can not but accus and condemp my sleuthfull coldnes. God grant thame thair hartis desyre; and I pray yow adverteis [me] of your estait, and of thingis that have occurit sence your last wrytting. Comfort your self in Goddis promissis, and be assureit that God steiris up mo friendies than we be war of. My commendation to all in your company. I commit you to the protectioun of the Omnipotent. In great haist; the 4. of November 1555. From Scotland. Your sone, Johne Knox."

When he arrived in Scotland, he found that the friends of the reformed doctrine, in general, continued to attend the Popish worship, and even the celebration of mass; principally with the view of avoiding the scandal which they would otherwise incur. This was very disagreeable

to Knox, who, in his sermons and conversation, disclosed
the impiety of that service, and the danger of symbolis-
ing with it. A meeting being appointed for the express
purpose of discussing this question, Maitland defended
the practice with all that ingenuity and learning for
which he was distinguished ; but his arguments were so
satisfactorily answered by Knox, that he yielded the
point as indefensible, and agreed with the rest of his
brethren, to abstain for the future from such temporising
conduct. Thus was a formal separation made from the
Popish church in Scotland, which may justly be regarded
as an important step in the Reformation.

Mr. Erskine prevailed on Knox to accompany him to
his family seat of Dun, in Angus, where he continued a
month, preaching every day. The principal persons in
that neighbourhood attended his sermons. After he returned to the south, he resided for the most part in
Calder-house, with Sir James Sandilands. Here he was
attended by Lord Lorn, afterwards Earl of Argyle, the
Master of Mar, afterwards Earl of Mar, and Lord James
Stewart, natural son of James V., and prior of St. Andrews,
afterwards Earl of Murray ; the two last of whom Knox
lived to see Regents of Scotland. These noblemen were
highly pleased with the doctrine which he taught. In
the beginning of the year 1556, he was conducted by
Lockhart of Bar, and Campbell of Kineancleugh, to
Kyle, the ancient receptacle of the Scottish Lollards,
where there were a number of adherents to the reformed
doctrine. He preached in the houses of Bar, Kineancleugh, Carnell, Ochiltree, and Gadgirth, and in the town
of Ayr. In several of these places, he also dispensed the
sacrament of our Lord's Supper. A little before Easter,
the Earl of Glencairn sent for him to his manor of Finlayston, in which, after preaching, he also dispensed the
sacrament ; the Earl, his lady, and two of their sons,
with some friends assembled for that purpose, participating of the sacred feast. From Finlayston he returned to
Calder-house, and soon after paid a second visit to Dun,

during which he preached more openly than before. The most of the gentlemen of Mearns did at this time make profession of the reformed religion, by sitting down at the Lord's Table ; and entered into a solemn and mutual bond, in which they renounced the Popish communion, and engaged to maintain the true preaching of the gospel, according as providence should favour them with opportunities. This seems to have been the first of those religious bonds or covenants, by which the confederation of the Protestants in Scotland was so frequently ratified.

The dangers to which Knox and his friends had been accustomed, had taught them to conduct matters with such secrecy, that he had preached for a considerable time and in different places, before the clergy knew that he was in the kingdom. Concealment was, however, impracticable after his audiences became so numerous. His preaching in Ayr was reported to the Court, and formed the topic of conversation in the presence of the Queen Regent. Some affirmed that the preacher was an Englishman ; "a prelate not of the least pride (probably Beatoun, Archbishop of Glasgow,) said, Nay ; no Englishman, but it is *Knox*, that *knave*." " It was my Lord's pleasure," says Knox, "so to baptize a poor man ; the reason whereof, if it should be required, his rochet and mitre must stand for authority. What further liberty he used in defining things like uncertain to him, to wit, of my learning and doctrine, at this present I omit. For what hath my life and conversation been, since it hath pleased God to call me from the puddle of Papistry, let my very enemies speak ; and what learning I have, they may prove when they please." Interest was at this time made by the bishops for his apprehension ; but the Queen Regent discouraged the application.

After his last journey to the north, the friars flocked from all quarters to the bishops, and instigated them to adopt speedy and decisive measures for checking the alarming effects of his preaching. In consequence of this, Knox was summoned to appear before a convention of the clergy, in the church of the black friars at Edinburgh, on the 15th of May. This diet he resolved to keep, and with that view came to Edinburgh, before the day appointed, accompanied by Erksine of Dun, and several other gentlemen. The clergy had never dreamed of his attendance; when apprised of his design, being afraid to bring matters to extremity, and unassured of the regent's decided support, they met beforehand, cast the summons under pretence of some informality, and deserted the diet against him. On the day on which he should have appeared as a pannel, Knox preached in the bishop of Dunkeld's large lodging, to a far greater audience than had before attended him in Edinburgh. During the ten following days, he preached in the same place, forenoon and afternoon; none of the clergy making the smallest attempt to disturb him. In the midst of these labours, he wrote the following hasty line to Mrs. Bowes:

" Belovit mother, with my maist hartlie commendation in the Lord Jesus, albeit I was fullie purpoisit to have visitit yow befoir this tyme, yet hath God laid impedimentis, whilk I culd not avoyd. Thay ar suche as I dout not ar to his glorie, and to the comfort of many heir. The trumpet blew the ald sound thrie dayis together, till privat houssis, of indifferent largenes, culd not conteane the voce of it. God, for Chryst his Sonis sake, grant me to be myndfull, that the sobbis of my hart hath not bene in vane, nor neglectit, in the presence of his majestie. O! sweet war the death that suld follow sic fourtie dayis in Edinburgh as heir I have had thrie. Rejose, mother; the tyme of our deliverance aproacheth: for, as Sathan rageth, sa dois the grace of the Halie Spreit abound, and daylie geveth new testimonyis of the everlasting love of oure mercifull Father. I can wryt na mair to you at this present. The grace of the Lord Jesus rest with you. In haste—this Monunday. Your sone, John Knox."

About this time, the Earl Marishal, at the desire of the Earl of Glencairn, attended an evening exhortation delivered by Knox. He was so much pleased with it, that he joined with Glencairn, in urging the preacher to write a letter to the Queen Regent, which they thought, might have the effect of inclining her to protect the reformed preachers, if not also to give a favourable ear to their doctrine. With this request he was induced to comply.

As a specimen of the manner in which this letter was written, I shall give the following quotation, in the original language. "I dout not, that the rumouris, whilk haif cumin to your Grace's earis of me, haif bene such, that (yf all reportis wer trew) I wer unworthie to live in the earth. And wonder it is, that the voces of the multitude suld not so have inflamed your Grace's hart with just hatred of such a one as I am accuseit to be. that all acces to pitie suld have bene schute up. I am traduceit as ane heretick, accusit as a fals teacher, and seducer of the pepill, besydis uther opprobries, whilk (affirmit be men of warldlie honour and estimatioun) may easelie kendill the wrath of majestratis, whair innocencie is not knawin. But blissit be God, the Father of our Lord Jesus Chryst, who, by the dew of his heavenlie grace, hath so quenchit the fyre of displeasure as yit in your Grace's hart, (whilk of lait dayis I have understaud) that Sathan is frustrat of his interpryse and purpois. Whilk is to my hart no small comfort; not so muche (God is witnes) for any benefit that I can resave in this miserable lyfe, by protectioun of any earthlie creature, (for the cupe whilk it behoveth me to drink is apoyntit by the wisdome of him whois consallis ar not changeable) as that I am for that benefit whilk I am assurit your Grace sall resave; yf that ye continew in lyke moderatioun and clemencie towardis utheris, that maist unjustlie ar and sal be accusit, as that your Grace hath begun towardis me, and my most desperat cause." An orator, he continued, might justly require of her Grace a motherly pity towards her subjects, the execution of justice upon murderers and oppressors, a heart free from avarice and partiality, a mind studious of the public welfare, with other virtues which heathen as well as inspired writers required in rulers. But, in his opinion, it was vain to crave reformation of manners, when religion was so much corrupted. He could not propose, in the present letter, to lay open the sources, progress, and extent of those errors and corruptions which had overspread and inundated the church; but, if her majesty would grant him an opportunity and liberty of speech, he was ready to undertake this task. In the mean time, he could not refrain from calling her attention to this important subject, and pointing out to her the fallacy of some general prejudices, by which she was in danger of being deceived. She ought to beware of thinking, that the care of religion did not belong to magistrates, but was devolved wholly on the clergy; that it was a thing incredible that religion should be so universally depraved; or that true religion was to be judged of by the majority of voices, custom, the laws and determinations of men, or any thing but the infallible dictates of inspired Scripture. He knew that innovations in religion were deemed hazardous; but the urgent necessity and immense magnitude of the object ought, in the present case, to swallow up the fear of danger. He was aware that a public reformation might be thought to exceed her authority as regent; but she could not be bound to maintain idolatry and manifest abuses, not to suffer the fury of the clergy to rage in murdering innocent men, merely because they worshipped God according to his word.

Though Knox's pen was not the most smooth nor delicate, and he often irritated by the plainness and severity of his language, the letter to the Queen Regent is far from being uncourtly. It seems to have been written with great care; and, in point of language, it may be compared with any composition of that period, for

PERIO IV. 1554-15 A.D.

A courtly letter.

simplicity and forcible expression. Its strain was well calculated for stimulating the inquiries, and confirming the resolutions of one who was impressed with a conviction of the reigning evils in the church, or who, though not resolved in judgment as to the matters in controversy, was determined to preserve moderation between the contending parties. Notwithstanding her imposing manners, the Regent was not a person of this description. The Earl of Glencairn delivered the letter into her hand; she glanced at it with a careless air, and gave it to the archbishop of Glasgow, saying, Please you, my Lord to read a pasquil. The report of this induced Knox, after he retired from Scotland, to publish the letter, with additions, in which he used a more pointed and severe style.

While he was thus employed in Scotland, he received letters from the English congregation at Geneva, stating that they had made choice of him as one of their pastors, and urging him to come and take the inspection of them. He judged it his duty to comply with this invitation, and began immediately to prepare for the journey. His wife and mother-in-law had by this time joined him at Edinburgh; and Mrs. Bowes, being now a widow, resolved to accompany her daughter and her husband to Geneva. Having sent them before him in a vessel to Dieppe, Knox again visited and took his leave of the brethren in the different places where he had preached. Campbell of Kinneancleugh conducted him to the Earl of Argyle, and he preached for some days in Castle Campbell. Argyle, and the laird of Glenorchy urged him to remain in Scotland, but he resisted all their importunities. "If God so blessed their small beginnings," he said, "that they continued in godliness, whensoever they pleased to command him, they should find him obedient. But once he must needs visit that little flock, which the wickedness of men had compelled him to leave." Accordingly, in the month of July 1556, he left Scotland, and, arriving at Dieppe, proceeded with his family to Geneva.

No sooner did the clergy understand that he had quitted the kingdom, than they, in a dastardly manner, renewed the summons against him, which they had deserted during his presence, and, upon his noncompearance, passed sentence against him, adjudging his body to the flames, and his soul to damnation. As his person was out of their reach, they caused his effigy to be ignominiously burned at the cross of Edinburgh. Against this sentence, he drew up his Appellation, which he afterwards published, with a supplication and exhortation, directed to the nobility and commonalty of Scotland. It may not be improper here to subjoin his summary of the doctrine taught by him, during his late visit to Scotland, which was declared to be so execrable, and subjected the preacher to such horrible pains. He taught, that there was no other name by which men could be saved but that of Jesus, and that all reliance on the merits of any other was vain and delusive; that He, having by his one sacrifice, sanctified and reconciled to God those who should inherit the promised kingdom, all other sacrifices which men pretended to offer for sin were blasphemous; that all men ought to hate sin, which was so odious before God that no other sacrifice could satisfy for it, except the death of his Son; that they ought to magnify their heavenly Father, who did not spare the substance of his glory, but gave him up to suffer the ignominious and cruel death of the cross for us; and that those who were washed from their former sins were bound to lead a new life, fighting against the lusts of the flesh, and studying to glorify God by good works. In conformity with the certification of his Master, that he would deny and be ashamed of those who should deny and be ashamed of him and his words before a wicked generation, he further taught, that it was incumbent on those who hoped for life everlasting, to avoid idolatry, superstition, and all vain religion, in one word, every way of worship which was destitute of authority from the word of God. This doctrine he did believe so con-

Doctrine taught by Knox.

formable to God's holy scriptures, that he thought no creature could have been so impudent as to deny any point or article of it; yet him as an heretic, and his doctrine as heretical, had the false bishops and ungodly clergy damned, pronouncing against him the sentence of death, in testification of which, they had burned his picture: from which sentence he appealed to a lawful and general council, to be held, agreeably to ancient laws and canons; humbly requiring the nobility and commons of Scotland, until such time as these controversies were decided, to take him, and others accused and persecuted, under their protection, and to regard this his plain appellation as of no less effect, than if it had been made with greater solemnity and ceremonies.

The late visit of our Reformer (for so he may now be fitly designed) was of vast consequence. The foundations of that noble edifice, which he was afterwards so instrumental in rearing, were, on this occasion, properly laid. Some may be apt to blame him for relinquishing too precipitately, an undertaking which he had so auspiciously begun. But, without pretending to ascertain the train of reflections which occurred to his own mind, we may trace, in his determination, the wise arrangement of that providence which watched over the infant Reformation, and guided the steps of the Reformer. His absence was now no less conducive to the preservation of the cause, than his presence and personal labours had

The seed sown, and taking root. lately been to its advancement. Matters were not yet ripened for a general Reformation in Scotland; and the clergy would never have suffered so zealous and able a champion of the new doctrines to live in the country. By timely withdrawing, he not only preserved his own life, and reserved his labours to a more fit opportunity, but he averted the storm of persecution from the heads of his brethren. Deprived of their teachers, their adversaries became less jealous of them; while, in their private meetings, they continued to confirm one another in the doctrine which they had received, and

the seed lately sown had time to take root and to
spread.

Before he took his departure, Knox was careful to
give his brethren such directions as he judged most
necessary for them, particularly for promoting mutual
edification, when they were deprived of the benefit of
pastors. Not satisfied with communicating these orally,
he committed them to writing in a common letter, which
he either left behind him, or sent from Dieppe, to be
circulated in the different quarters where he had preached. In this letter, he warmly recommended the exercises of worship and religious instruction in every family.
He advised, that those belonging to different families
should meet together, if possible, once every week. In
these assemblies, they should begin with confession of
sins, and invocation of the divine blessing. After a
portion of Scripture had been read, if any brother had
any exhortation, interpretation, or doubt, he might
speak ; but this ought to be done with modesty, and a
desire to edify, or to be edified; "multiplication of
words, perplexed interpretation, and wilfulness in reasoning," being carefully avoided. If any difficulties, which
they could not solve, occurred in the course of reading
or conference, he advised them to commit these to
writing, before they dismissed, that they might submit
them to the judgment of the learned. He signified his
own readiness to give them his advice and opinion, whenever it should be required. Their assemblies ought
always to be closed, as well as opened, by prayer.
There is every reason to conclude, that these directions
were punctually complied with ; this letter may, therefore, be viewed as an important document regarding the
state of the Protestant church in Scotland, previous to
the establishment of the Reformation.

Among his letters are several answers to questions
which they had transmitted to him for advice. The
questions are such as might be supposed to arise in the
minds of serious persons lately made acquainted with

the Scripture, difficulted with particular expressions, and at a loss how to apply some of its directions to their situation. They discover an inquisitive and conscientious disposition; and at the same time, illustrate the disadvantages under which ordinary Christians labour when deprived of the assistance of learned teachers. Our Reformer's answers display an intimate acquaintance with Scripture, dexterity in expounding it, with prudence in giving advice in cases of conscience, so as not to encourage a dangerous laxity on the one hand, or scrupulosity and excessive rigidity on the other.

Knox reached Geneva before the end of harvest, and took upon him the charge of the English congregation there, among whom he laboured during the two following years. This short period was the most quiet of his life.

In the bosom of his own family, he experienced that soothing care to which he had hitherto been a stranger, and which his frequent bodily ailments required. Two sons were born to him in Geneva. The greatest cordiality among themselves, and affection to him, subsisted in the small flock under his charge. With his colleague, Christopher Goodman, he lived as a brother; and was happy in the friendship of Calvin and the other pastors of Geneva. So much was he pleased with the purity of religion established in that city, that he warmly recommended it to his religious acquaintances in England, as the best Christian asylum to which they could flee. "In my heart," says he, in a letter to his friend Mr. Locke, "I could have wished, yea, and cannot cease to wish, that it might please God to guide and conduct yourself to this place, where I neither fear nor eshame to say, is the most perfect school of Christ that ever was in the earth, since the days of the apostles. In other places I confess Christ to be truly preached; but manners and religion so sincerely reformed, I have not yet seen in any other place beside."

But neither the enjoyment of personal accommodations, nor the pleasure of literary society, nor the endearments of domestic happiness, could subdue our Reformer's ruling passion, or unfix his determination to return to Scotland, as soon as an opportunity should offer for advancing the Reformation among his countrymen. In a letter written to some of his friends in Edinburgh, March 16, 1557, we find him expressing himself thus: "My own motion and daily prayer is, not only that I may visit you, but also that with joy I may end my battle among you. And assure yourself of that, that whenever a greater number among you shall call upon me than now hath bound me to serve them, by his grace it shall not be the fear of punishment, neither yet of the death temporal, that shall impede my coming to you." A certain heroic confidence, and assurance of ultimate success have often been displayed by those whom providence has raised up to achieve great revolutions in the world; by which they have been borne up under discouragements which would have overwhelmed men of ordinary spirits, and emboldened to face dangers from which others would have shrunk appalled. This enthusiastic heroism (I use not the epithet in a bad sense) often blazed forth in the conduct of the great German Reformer. Knox possessed no inconsiderable portion of the same spirit. "Satan, I confess, rageth," says he, in a letter nearly of the same date with that last quoted; "but potent is He that promised to be with us, in all such enterprises as we take in hand at his commandment, for the glory of his name, and for maintenance of his true religion. And therefore the less fear we any contrary power: yea, in the boldness of our God, we altogether contemn them, be they kings, emperors, men, angels, or devils. For they shall never be able to prevail against the simple truth of God which we openly profess: by the permission of God, they may appear to prevail against our bodies; but our cause shall triumph in despite of Satan."

Within a month after he wrote the letter last quoted but one, James Syme, who had been his host at Edinburgh, and James Barron, another burgess of the same

Invited to Scotland.

city, arrived at Geneva with a letter, and credence, from the Earl of Glencairn, Lords Lorn, Erskine, and James Stewart, informing him that those who had professed the reformed doctrine remained stedfast, that its adversaries were daily losing credit in the nation, and that those who possessed the supreme authority, although they had not yet declared themselves friendly, still refrained from persecution; and inviting him in their own name, and in that of their brethren, to return to Scotland, where he would find them all ready to receive him, and to spend their lives and fortunes in advancing the cause which they had espoused.

PERIOD V.

FROM HIS INVITATION INTO SCOTLAND, BY THE PROTESTANT NOBILITY, ANNO 1557, TO HIS SETTLEMENT AS MINISTER OF EDINBURGH, UPON THE ESTABLISH-MENT OF THE REFORMATION ANNO 1560.

PERIOD
V.

THIS invitation Knox laid before his congregation, and also submitted to Calvin and his colleagues. The latter delivered it as their opinion, "that he could not refuse the call, without shewing himself rebellious to God, and unmerciful to his country." His congregation agreed to sacrifice their particular interest to the greater good of the church; and his own family silently acquiesced. Upon this, he returned an answer to the letter of the nobility, signifying, that he meant to visit them with all reasonable expedition. Accordingly, after seeing the congregation agreeably provided with a pastor in his room, and settling his other affairs, he took an affectionate leave of his friends at Geneva, and went to Dieppe, in the beginning of October. While he waited there for a vessel, he received letters from Scotland, written in a very different strain from the former. These informed him, that new consultations had been held; that some began to

Knox
leaves
Geneva.

repent of the invitation which they had given him to
return to Scotland; and that the greater part seemed irresolute and faint-hearted.

This intelligence exceedingly disconcerted and embar-
rassed him. He instantly dispatched a letter to the nobility who had invited him, upbraiding them for their
timidity and inconstancy. The information, which he
had just received, had, he said, confounded and pierced
him with sorrow. After taking the advice of the most
learned and godly in Europe, for the satisfaction of
his own conscience and theirs respecting this enterprise,
the abandonment of it would reflect disgrace upon
either him or them : it would argue either that he had
been marvellously forward and vain, or else that they
had betrayed great imprudence and want of judgment
in their invitation. To some it might appear a small
matter, that he had left his poor family destitute of
a head, and committed the care of his small but dear-
ly beloved flock to another; but, for his part, he could
not name the sum that would induce him to go through
the same scene a second time, and to behold so many
grave men weeping at his departure. What answer could
he give, on his return, to those who enquired, why he
did not prosecute his journey? He could take God to
witness, that the personal inconveniences to which he
had been subjected, or the mortification which he felt at
the disapointment, was not the chief cause of his grief.
But he was alarmed at the awful consequences which
would ensue, at the bondage and misery, spiritual and
temporal, which they would entail upon themselves and
their children, their subjects and their posterity, if they
neglected the present opportunity of introducing the gospel into their native country. In conscience, he could
except from blame in this matter, none that bare the
name of nobility in Scotland. His words might seem
sharp and indiscreet; but charity would construe them
in the best sense, and wise men would consider that a
true friend cannot flatter, especially in a case which in-

His up-
braiding.

volved the salvation of body and soul, not of a few persons, but of a whole realm. "What are the sobs, and what is the affliction of my troubled heart, God shall one day declare. But this will I add to my former rigour and severity; to wit, if any persuade you, for fear of dangers to follow, to faint in your former purpose, be he esteemed never so wise and friendly, let him be judged of you both foolish, and your mortal enemy.—I am not ignorant that fearful troubles shall ensue your enterprise; as in my former letters I did signify unto you. But, O! joyful and comfortable are those troubles and adversities which man sustaineth for accomplishment of God's will revealed in his word. For how terrible that ever they appear to the judgment of natural men, yet are they never able to devour nor utterly to consume the sufferers; for the invisible and invincible power of God sustaineth and preserveth according to his promise, all such as with simplicity do obey him.—No less cause have ye to enter in your former enterprise, than Moses had to go to the presence of Pharaoh; for your subjects, yea, your brethren, are oppressed; their bodies and souls holden in bondage: and God speaketh to your consciences, (unless ye be dead with the blind world), that ye ought to hazard your own lives, be it against kings or emperors, for their deliverance. For, only for that cause are ye called princes of the people, and receive honour, tribute, and homage at God's commandment, not by reason of your birth and progeny, (as the most part of men falsely do suppose), but by reason of your office and duty; which is, to vindicate and deliver your subjects and brethren from all violence and oppression, to the uttermost of your power."

Having sent off this letter, with others, written in the same strain, to Erskine of Dun, Wishart of Pittarrow, and some other gentlemen of his acquaintance, he resolved to spend some time in the interior of France, hoping to receive in a little more favourable accounts from Scotland. The reformed doctrine had been early introduced into the kingdom of France; it had been watered with the blood of many martyrs; and all the violence and barbarity which had been employed, had not been able to extirpate it, or prevent it from spreading among all ranks. The Parisian protestants were at present smarting under the effects of one of those massacres which so often disgraced the Roman Catholic religion in that country, before as well as after the commencement of the civil wars. Not satisfied with assaulting them when peaceably assembled for worship in a private house, and treating them with great barbarity, their adversaries, in imitation of their pagan predecessors, invented the most diabolical calumnies against them, and circulated every where, that they were guilty of committing the most flagitious crimes in their assemblies. The innocent sufferers had drawn up an apology, vindicating themselves from this atrocious charge, and Knox having got a copy of this, translated it into English, and wrote a preface and additions to it, intending to publish it for the use of his countrymen.

PERIOD
V.
1557–1560
A.D.

Having acquired the French language, and formed an acquaintance with many of the protestants, he occasionally preached to them in passing through the country. It seems to have been on the present occasion, that he preached in the city of Rochelle, when, having introduced the subject of his native country, he told his audience that he expected, within a few years, to preach in the church of St. Giles, in Edinburgh. There is nothing in our Reformer's letters from which I can learn whether he found any protestants in Dieppe, a place which he so often visited during his exile: it is probable he did; for at an early period of the following century they had a very numerous church in that town.

Passing through the country preaching.

Having received no intelligence of an encouraging nature, Knox determined to relinquish for the present his design of proceeding to Scotland. This resolution does not accord with the usual firmness of our Reformer, and is not sufficiently accounted for in the common histories. The protestant nobles had not retracted their invitation ; the discouraging letters which he had received were written by individuals, without any commission from them ; and if their zeal and courage had begun to flag, there was the more need of his presence to recruit them. His private letters to his familiar acquaintances enable me to state more fully the motives by which he was actuated in taking this retrograde step. He was perfectly aware of the struggle which would be necessary in effectuating the Reformation ; that his presence in Scotland would excite the rage of the clergy, who would make every effort to crush their adversaries, and maintain the lucrative system of corruption ; and that civil discord, confusion, and bloodshed might be expected to ensue. The prospect of these things rushed into his mind, and (regardless of public tranquillity as some have pronounced him to be) staggered his resolution in prosecuting an undertaking which his judgment approved as lawful, laudable and necessary. "When," says he, "I heard such troubles as appeared in that realm, I began to dispute with myself as followeth : 'Shall Christ, the author of peace, concord, and quietness, be preached where war is proclaimed, sedition engendered, and tumults appear to rise? Shall not his evangel be accused as the cause of all this calamity, which is like to follow? What comfort canst thou have to see the one half of the people rise up against the other, yea, to jeopard the one, to murder and destroy the other! But, above all, what joy shall it be to thy heart, to behold with thy eyes thy native country betrayed in [to] the hands of strangers, which to no man's judgment can be avoided ; because that those who ought to defend it, and the liberty thereof, are so blind, dull, and obstinate, that they will not see their own destruction?'" To "these and more deep cogitations" (which continued to distract his mind for several months after he returned to Geneva) he principally imputed his abandonment of the journey to Scotland. At the same time, he was convinced that they were not sufficient to justify his desisting from an undertaking, recommended by so many powerful considerations. "But alas!" says he, "as the wounded man, be he never so expert in physic or surgery, cannot suddenly mitigate his own pain and dolour; no more can I the fear and grief of my heart, although I am not ignorant of what is to be done. It may also be, that the doubts and cold writing of some brethren did augment my dolour, and somewhat discourage me that before was more nor [than] feeble. But nothing do I so much accuse as myself." Whatever were the secondary causes of this step, I cannot but again direct the reader's attention to the wisdom of Providence, in throwing impediments in his way, by which his return to Scotland was protracted to a period, before which it might have been injurious, and at which it was calculated to be in the highest degree useful to the great cause which he had at heart.

Before he left Dieppe, he transmitted two long letters to Scotland: the one, dated 1st December 1557, was addressed to the protestants in general, the other, dated the 17th of the same month, was directed to the nobility. In judging of Knox's influence in advancing the Reformation, we must take into view not only his personal labours, but also the epistolary correspondence which he maintained with his countrymen. By this, he instructed them in his absence, communicated his own advice, and that of the learned among whom he resided, upon every difficult case which occurred, and animated them to constancy and perseverance. The letters which he wrote at this time deserve particular attention in this view. In both of them he prudently avoids any reference to his late disappointment.

In the first letter he strongly inculcates purity of morals, and warns all who professed the reformed religion against those irregularities of life, which were improved to the disparagement of their cause, by two classes of persons; by the papists, who, although the same vices prevailed in a far higher degree among themselves, represented them as the native fruits of the protestant doc-

trine ; and by a new sect, who were enemies to superstition, and had belonged to their own society, but having
deserted it, had become scarcely less hostile to them than
the papists.   The principal design of this letter was to
put them on their guard against the arts of this class of
persons, and to expose their leading errors.

The persons to whom he referred were those who went
under the general name of Anabaptists, a sect which
sprung up in Germany, soon after the commencement of
the Reformation under Luther, broke out into the greatest excesses, and produced the most violent commotions
in different places.   Being suppressed in Germany, it
spread through other countries, and secretly made converts by high pretensions to seriousness and Christian
simplicity ; the spirit of turbulence and wild fanaticism,
which at first characterised the sect, gradually subsiding
after the first effervescence.   Ebullitions of a similar kind
have not infrequently accompanied great revolutions ;
when the minds of men, dazzled by a sudden irradiation,
and released from the galling fetters of despotism, civil
or ecclesiastical, have been disposed to fly to the opposite extreme of anarchy and extravagance.   Nothing
proved more vexing to the original reformers than this ;
it was improved by the defenders of the old system as a
popular argument against all mutation ; and many who
had declared themselves friendly to reform, alarmed, or
pretending to be alarmed, at this hideous spectre, drew
back, and sheltered themselves within the sacred pale of
the Catholic church.

Sect of
Anabap-
tists.

The radical error of this sect, according to the more
improved system held by them at the time of which I
write, was a fond conceit of a certain ideal perfection and
spirituality which belonged to Christians and the Christian church, by which they differed essentially, and *toto
cælo*, from the Jewish church, which they looked upon
as a carnal, worldly society.   By this, they were naturally
led to abridge the rule of faith and manners, by confining
themselves almost entirely to the New Testament and to

adopt their other opinions, concerning the unlawfulness of infant baptism, civil magistracy, national churches, oaths, and defensive war. But besides these notions, the anabaptists were, at this period, generally infected with the Arian and Pelagian heresies, and united with the papists in loading the doctrines maintained by the reformers, respecting predestination and grace, with the most odious charges.

Our Reformer had occasion to meet with some of these sectaries both in England and on the continent, and had ascertained their extravagant and dangerous principles. He was apprised that they were creeping into Scotland, and was afraid that they would insidiously instil their poison into the minds of some of his brethren. He refuted their opinion respecting church-communion, by shewing that they required such purity as was never found in the church, either before or since the completion of the canon of Scripture. In opposition to their Pelagian tenets, he gave the following statement of his sentiments. "If there be any thing which God did not predestinate and appoint, then lacked he wisdom and free regimen; or, if any thing was ever done, or yet after shall be done in heaven or in earth, which he might not have impeded, if so had been his godly pleasure, then is he not omnipotent; which three properties, to wit, wisdom, free regimen, and power, denied to be in God, I pray you what rests in his godhead? The wisdom of our God we acknowledge to be such, that it compelleth the very malice of Satan, and the horrible iniquity of such as be drowned in sin, to serve to his glory and to the profit of his elect. His power we believe and confess to be infinite, and such as no creature in heaven or earth is able to resist. And his regimen we acknowledge to be so free, that none of his creatures dare present them in judgment, to reason, or demand the question, Why hast thou done this or that? But the fountain of this their damnable error,

Anabaptist opinions refuted.

which is, that in God they can acknowledge no justice except that which their foolish brain is able to comprehend, at more opportunity, God willing, we shall entreat."

He assigns his reasons for warning them so particularly against the seduction of these erroneous teachers. Under the cloak of mortification, and the colour of a godly life, they " supplanted the dignity of Christ," and " were become enemies to free justification by faith in his blood." The malice of their Popish adversaries was now visible to all the world. The hypocrisy of mercenary teachers and ungodly professors would soon discover itself. Seldom was open tyranny able to suppress the true religion, when once earnestly embraced by the body of any nation or province. "But deceivable and false doctrine is a poison and venom, which, once drunken, and received, with great difficulty can afterward be purged." Accordingly, he obtested them to " try the spirits" which came unto them, and to suffer no man to take the office of preacher upon him, of his own accord, without trial, and to assemble the people in privy conventions; else Satan would soon have his emissaries among them, who would "destroy the plantation of our heavenly Father." His admonitions, on this head, were not without effect; and the Protestants of Scotland were not distracted with these opinions, but remained united in their views, as to doctrine, worship, and discipline.

Advice to Protestants.

His letter to the Protestant lords breathes a spirit of ardent and noble piety. He endeavours to purify their minds from selfish and worldly principles; to raise, sanctify, and Christianize their motives, by exhibiting and recommending to them the spirit and conduct of the princes and heroes, celebrated, not in profane, but sacred story. The glory of God, the advancement of the kingdom of Jesus Christ, the salvation of themselves and their brethren, the emancipation of their country from spiritual and civil thraldom; these, and not their own honour and aggrandisement, or the revenging of their petty, private quarrels, were the objects which they ought to keep steadily and solely in view.

In this letter, he also communicates his advice on the delicate question of resistance to supreme rulers. They had consulted him on this question, and he had submitted it to the judgment of the most learned on the continent. Soon after the marriage of their young Queen to the Dauphin of France, the Scots began to be jealous of the designs of the French court against their liberties and independence. Their jealousies increased after the Regency was transferred to the Queen Dowager, who was wholly devoted to the interests of France, and had contrived, under different pretexts, to keep a body of French troops in the kingdom. It was not difficult to excite to resistance the independent and haughty barons of Scotland, accustomed to yield but a very limited and precarious obedience even to their native princes. They had lately given a proof of this, by their refusal to co-operate in the war against England, which they considered as undertaken merely for French interests. How did our Reformer act upon this occasion? Did he lay hold on this occurrence, and attempt to inflame the irascible minds of the nobility? Did he persuade them to join with the Earl of Arran and others, who were discontented with the measures of government, and to endeavour in this way to advance their cause? No; on the contrary, he wrote, that rumours were circulated on the continent, that a rebellion was intended in Scotland; and he solemnly charged all that professed the Protestant religion to avoid all accession to it, and to beware of countenancing those who, for the sake of worldly promotion, and other private ends, sought to disturb the government. The nobility were the guardians of the national liberties, and there were limits, beyond which obedience was not due; but recourse ought not to be had to resistance, until matters were tyrannically driven to extremity. It was incumbent on

On the duty of subjects.

them to be very circumspect in all their proceedings, that their adversaries might have no reason to allege, that they covered a seditious and rebellious design with the cloak of religion. His advice to them, therefore, was that, by dutiful and cheerful obedience to all lawful commands, and by humble and repeated requests, they should endeavour to recommend themselves to the supreme authority, and procure its favour in promoting, or, at least, not persecuting the cause in which they were embarked. If all their endeavours failed, and the Regent refused to consent to a public Reformation, they ought to provide that the gospel should be preached, and the sacraments administered to themselves and their brethren; and if attempts were made to crush them by tyrannical violence, it was lawful for them, nay, it was a duty incumbent upon them, in their high station, to stand up in defence of their brethren. "For a great difference there is betwixt lawful obedience, and a fearful flattering of princes, or an unjust accomplishment of their desires, in things which be required, or devised, for the destruction of a commonwealth."

The Geneva Bible, 1558 A.D.

Knox returned to Geneva in the end of the year 1557. During the following year, he was engaged, along with several learned men of his congregation, in making a new translation of the Bible into English; which, from the place where it was composed and first printed, obtained the name of the Geneva Bible. It was at this time that he published his Letter to the Queen Regent, and his Appellation and Exhortation; both of which were transmitted to Scotland, and contributed not a little to the spread of the reformed opinions. I have already given an account of the first of these tracts, which was chiefly intended for removing the prejudices of Catholics. The last was more immediately designed for instructing and animating such as were friendly to the reformed religion. Addressing himself to the nobility and estates, he shews that the care and reformation of religion belonged to civil rulers, and constituted one of the primary duties of their office. This was a dictate of nature as well as revelation; and he would not insist long upon that topic, lest he should seem to suppose them " lesse careful over God's true religion, than were the Ethnikes over their idolatrie." Inferior magistrates, within the sphere of their jurisdiction, the nobles and estates of a kingdom, as well as kings and princes, were bound to attend to this high duty. He then addresses himself to the commonalty of Scotland, and points out their duty and interest, with regard to the important controversy in agitation. They were rational creatures, formed after the image of God; they had souls to be saved; they were accountable for their conduct; they were bound to judge of the truth of religion, and to make profession of it, as well as kings, nobles, or bishops. If idolatry was maintained, if the gospel was suppressed, if the blood of the innocent was shed, how could they be exculpated, provided they kept silence, and did not exert themselves to prevent these evils.

PERIOD
V.
1557–1560
A.D.

But the most singular treatise published this year by Knox, and that which made the greatest noise, was, The first Blast of the Trumpet against the monstrous Regiment of Women; in which he attacked, with great vehemence, the practice of admitting females to the government of nations. There is some reason to think that his mind was struck with the incongruity of this practice, as early as Mary's accession to the throne of England. This was probably one of the points on which he had conferred with the Swiss divines in 1554. It is certain, from a letter written by him in 1556, that his sentiments respecting it were then fixed and decided. He continued, however, to retain them to himself; and refrained for a considerable time from publishing them, out of deference to the opinions of others. But at last, provoked by the tyranny of the Queen of England, and wearied out with her increasing cruelties, he applied the Trumpet to his mouth, and uttered a terrible blast. "To promote a woman to bear rule, superiority, dominion, or empire,

First Blast of the Trumpet.

above any realm, nation or city, is repugnant to nature, contumely to God, a thing most contrarious to his revealed will and approved ordinance; and, finally, it is the subversion of all equity and justice." Such is the first sentence and principal proposition of the work. The arguments by which he endeavours to establish it are, that nature intended the female sex for subjection, not superiority to the male, as appears from their infirmities, corporeal and mental (he excepts, however, such as God, "by singular privilege, and for certain causes, exeemed from the common rank of women"); that the divine law, announced at the creation of the first pair, had expressly assigned to man the dominion over woman, and commanded her to be subject to him; that female government was not permitted among the Jews; is contrary to apostolical injunctions; and leads to the perversion of government, and many pernicious consequences.

Knox's theory on this subject was far from being novel. In confirmation of his opinion, he could appeal to the constitutions of the free states of antiquity, and to the authority of their legislators and philosophers. In the kingdom of France, females were, by an express law, excluded from succeeding to the crown. Edward VI. some time before his death, had proposed to the Privy Council the adoption of this law in England; but the motion, not suiting the ambitious views of the Duke of Northumberland, was overruled. Though his opinion was sanctioned by such high authorities, he was by no means sanguine in his expectations as to the reception of this performance. He tells us, in his preface, that he laid his account not only with the indignation of those interested in the support of the reprobated practice, but with the disapprobation of such gentle spirits among the learned, as would be alarmed at the boldness of the attack. He did not doubt, that he would be called "curious, despiteful, a sower of sedition, and one day perchance attainted for treason:" but, in uttering a truth of which he was deeply convinced, he was determined to

Females
excluded
from suc-
ceeding
to the
crown.

"cover his eyes and shut his ears" from these dangers
and obloquies. He was not disappointed in his apprehensions. It exposed him to the resentment of two queens,
during whose reign it was his lot to live; the one his native princess, and the other exercising a sway in Scotland, scarcely inferior to that of any of its monarchs.
Several of the exiles approved of his opinion, and few of
them would have been displeased at seeing it reduced to
practice, at the time when the Blast was published. But
queen Mary dying soon after it appeared, and her sister
Elizabeth succeeding her, they raised a great outcry
against it. John Fox wrote a letter to the author, in
which he expostulated with him, in a very friendly manner,
as to the impropriety of the publication, and the severity
of its language. Knox, in his reply, did not excuse his
"rude vehemency and inconsiderate affirmations, which
might appear rather to proceed from choler than of zeal
and reason;" but signified, that he was still persuaded of
the principal proposition which he had maintained.

His original intention was to blow his Trumpet thrice,
and to publish his name with the last Blast, to prevent
the odium from falling on any other person. But, finding that it gave offence to many of his brethren, and
being desirous to strengthen rather than invalidate the
authority of Elizabeth, he relinquished the design of
prosecuting the subject. He retained his sentiments to
the last, but abstained from any further declaration of
them, and from replying to his opponents; although
he was provoked by their censures and triumph, and, in
his private letters, sometimes hinted that he would break
silence, if they did not study greater moderation.

In the course of the following year, an answer to the
Blast appeared, under the title of An Harborow for
Faithful Subjects. Though anonymous, like the book
to which it was a reply, it was soon declared to be the
production of John Aylmer, one of the English refugees
on the continent, who had been archdeacon of Stowe,
and tutor to Lady Jane Grey. It was not undertaken

John
Aylmer.

PERIOD
V.
1557–1560
A.D.
———

until the accession of Elizabeth, and was written (as Aylmer's biographer informs us) " upon a consultation holden among the exiles, the better to obtain the favour of the new queen, and to take off any jealousy she might conceive of them, and of the religion which they professed."   This, with some other circumstances, led Knox to express his suspicion, that the author had accommodated his doctrine to the times, and courted the favour of the reigning princess, by flattering her vanity and love of power.   It is certain, that if Knox is entitled to the praise of boldness and disinterestedness, Aylmer carried away the palm for prudence: the latter was advanced to the bishopric of London; the former could, with great difficulty, obtain leave to set his foot again upon English ground.   As Knox's Trumpet would never have sounded its alarm, had it not been for the tyranny of Mary, there is reason to think that Aylmer's " Harborow" would never have been opened " for faithful subjects," but for the auspicious succession of Elizabeth.

Hanc veniam petimusque, damusque vicissim.

This, however, is independent of the merits of the question, which I do not feel inclined to examine minutely.   The change which has taken place in the mode of administering government, in modern times, renders it of less practical importance than it was formerly, when so much depended upon the personal talents and activity of the reigning prince.   It may be added, that the evils incident to a female reign will be less felt under such a constitution as that of Britain, than under a pure and absolute monarchy.   This last consideration is urged by Aylmer; and here his reasoning is most satisfactory. The Blast bears the marks of hasty composition.   The Harborow has been written with great care ; it contains a good collection of historical facts bearing on the question; and though more distinguished for rhetorical exaggeration than logical precision, the reasoning is ingeniously conducted, and occasionally enlivened by strokes

The Harborow.

of humour. It is, upon the whole, a curious as well as rare work.

After all, it is easier to vindicate the expediency of continuing the practice, where it has been established by laws and usuage, than to support the affirmative, when the question is propounded as a general thesis on government. It may fairly be questioned, if Aylmer has refuted the principal arguments of his opponent; and had Knox deemed it prudent to rejoin, he might have exposed the fallacy of his arguments in different instances. In replying to the argument from the apostolical canon (1 Tim. ii. 11—14), the archdeacon is not a little puzzled. Distrusting his distinction between the greater office, " the ecclesiastical function," and the less, " extern policy;" he argues, that the apostle's prohibition may be considered as temporary, and peculiarly applicable to the women of his own time; and he insists that his clients shall not, *in toto*, be excluded from teaching and ruling in the church, any more than in the state. " Me thinke," says he very seriously, "even in this poynte, we must use ἐπιείκεια, a certain moderacion, not absolutely, and in every wise, to debar them herein (as it shall please God) to serve Christ. Are there not, in England, women, think you, that for their learninge and wisdom, could tell their housholde and neighbouris as good a tale as the best Sir Jhone there?" Who can doubt, that the learned Lady Elizabeth, who could direct the Dean of her chapel to " keep to his text," was able to make as good a sermon as any of her clergy? or that she was better qualified for the other parts of the duty, when she composed a book of prayers for herself, while they were obliged to use one made to their hands? In fact, the view which the archdeacon gave of the text was necessary to vindicate the authority of his queen, who was head, or supreme governor of the church as well as the state. She who, by law, had supreme authority over all archbishops, bishops, &c. in the land, with power to superintend, suspend, and controul them in all their ecclesiastical functions ; who, by her injunctions, could direct the primate himself when to preach, and how to preach ; who could licence and silence ministers at her pleasure, had certainly the same right to assume the personal exercise of the office, if she chused to do so ; and must have been bound very moderately indeed, by the apostolical prohibition, " I suffer not a woman to teach, nor to usurp authority over the man, but to be in silence."

There are some things in the Harborow which might have been unpalatable to the queen, if the author had not taken care to sweeten them with that personal flattery, which was as agreeable to Elizabeth as to others of her sex and rank ; and which he administered in sufficient quantities before concluding his work. The ladies will be ready to excuse a slight slip of the pen in the good archdeacon, in consideration of the handsome manner in which he has defended their right to rule ; but they will scarcely believe that the following description of the sex could proceed from him. " Some women," says he, " be wiser, better learned, discreater, constanter, than a number of men." But others, (his biographer says, " the most part") he describes as " fond, foolish, wanton, flibbergibs, tatlers, triffling, wavering, witles, without counsel, feable, carles, rashe, proud, daintie, nise, tale-bearers, eves-droppers, rumour-raisers, evil tongued, worse-minded, and, in every wise, doltified with the dregges of the devil's doungehill!!!" The rude author of the monstrous Blast never spake of the sex in terms half so disrespectful as these. One would suppose that Aylmer had already renounced the character of advocate of the fair sex, and recanted his principles on that head ; as he did respecting the titles and revenues of bishops, which he inveighed against before his return from exile, but afterwards accepted with little scruple ; and, when reminded of the language which he formerly used, apologised for himself, by saying, " When I was a child, I thought as a child ; but when I became a man, I put

away childish things."—But it is time to return, from
this digression, to the narrative.

Our Reformer's letter to the Protestant Lords in Scotland produced its intended effect, in re-animating their
drooping courage. At a consultative meeting held at
Edinburgh, in December 1557, they unanimously resolved to adhere to one another, and exert themselves for the advancement of the Reformation. Having subscribed a solemn bond of mutual assurance,
they renewed their invitation to Knox; and being
afraid that he might hesitate on account of their former
irresolution, they wrote to Calvin, to employ his influence to induce him to comply. Their letters did
not reach Geneva until November 1558. By the same
conveyance Knox received from Scotland letters of later
date, communicating the most agreeable intelligence,
respecting the progress which the reformed cause had
made, and the flourishing appearance which it continued
to wear.

Through the exertions of our Reformer, during his
residence among them in the beginning of the year 1556,
and in pursuance of the instructions which he left
behind him, the Protestants had formed themselves into
congregations which met in different parts of the country
with greater or less privacy, according to the opportunities which they enjoyed. Having come to the resolution of withdrawing from the popish worship, they
endeavoured to provide for their religious instruction
and mutual edification, in the best manner that their
circumstances permitted. As there were no ministers
among them, they continued for some time to be deprived of the dispensation of the sacraments; but certain
intelligent and pious men of their number were chosen,
to read the Scriptures, exhort, and offer up prayers, in
their assemblies. Convinced of the necessity of order
and discipline in their societies, and desirous to have
them organized, as far as within their power, agreeably
to the institution of Christ, they next proceeded to

PERIOD
v.
1557–1560
A.D.

Protest-
ant con-
gregations
formed in
Scotland.

chuse elders, for the inspection of their manners, to whom they promised subjection; and deacons, for the collection and distribution of alms to the poor. Edinburgh was the first place in which this order was established; Dundee the first town in which a reformed church was completely organized, provided with a regular minister, and the dispensation of the sacraments.

During the war with England, which began in autumn 1556, and continued through the following year, the Protestants enjoyed considerable liberty; and, as they improved it with the utmost assiduity, their numbers rapidly increased. William Harlow, John Douglas, Paul Methven, and John Willock, who had again returned from Embden, now began to preach, with greater publicity, in different parts of the country. The Popish clergy were not indifferent to these proceedings, and wanted not inclination to put a stop to them. They prevailed on the Queen Regent to summon the Protestant preachers; but the interposition of the gentlemen of the west country obliged her to abandon the process against them. At length, the clergy determined to revive those cruel measures which, since the year 1550, had been suspended by the political circumstances of the kingdom, more than by their clemency or moderation. On the 28th of April 1558, the Archbishop of St. Andrews committed to the flames Walter Milne, an aged priest, of the most inoffensive manners, and summoned several others to appear, on a charge of heresy, before a convention of the clergy at Edinburgh.

Walter
Milne,
1558 A.D.

This barbarous and illegal execution produced effects of the greatest importance. It raised the horror of the nation to an incredible pitch; and as it was believed, at that time, that the regent was not accessory to the deed, their indignation was directed wholly against the clergy. Throwing aside all fear, and those restraints which prudence, or a regard to established order, had hitherto imposed on them, the people now assembled openly to join in the reformed worship, and avowed

their determination to adhere to it at all hazards. The PERIOD
V.
1557–1560
A.D.
Protestant leaders laid their complaints, in a regular and
respectful manner, before the regent, and repeated their
petition, that she would, by her authority, and in concurrence with the Parliament, restrain the tyrannical
proceedings of the clergy, correct the flagrant and insufferable abuses which prevailed in the church, and
grant to them and their brethren the liberty of religious
instruction and worship, at least according to a restricted
plan, which they laid before her, and to which they
were willing to submit, until such time as their grievances were deliberately examined and redressed. The
Regent's reply was such as to persuade them that she
was friendly to their proposals: she promised that she
would take measures for carrying them legally into
effect, as soon as it was in her power; and that, in the
mean time, they might depend on her protection.

It did not require many arguments to persuade Knox
to comply with an invitation which was accompanied
with such gratifying intelligence; and he began immediately to prepare for his journey to Scotland. The future
settlement of the congregation under his charge occupied
him for some time. Information being received of the Return-
ing from
exile.
death of Mary, queen of England, and the accession of
Elizabeth, the Protestant refugees hastened to return to
their native country. The congregation at Geneva,
having met to return thanks to God for this deliverance,
agreed to send one of their number with letters to their
brethren in different places of the continent, particularly
at Frankfort, congratulating them on the late happy
change, and requesting a confirmation of the mutual
reconciliation which had already been effected, the burial
of all past offences, with a brotherly co-operation, in
endeavouring to obtain such a settlement of religion in
England as would be agreeable to all the sincere well-
wishers of the Reformation. A favourable return to
their letters being obtained, they took leave of the hospi-
table city, and set out for their native country. By them

Knox sent letters to some of his former acquaintances, who were now in the court of Elizabeth, requesting permission to travel through England, on his way to Scotland.

In the month of January 1559, our Reformer took his leave of Geneva, for the last time. In addition to former marks of respect, the republic, before his departure, conferred on him the freedom of the city. He left his wife and family behind him, until he should ascertain that they could live with safety in Scotland. Upon his arrival at Dieppe, in the middle of March, he received information, that the English government had refused to grant him liberty to pass through their dominions. The request had appeared so reasonable in his own mind, considering the station which he had held in that country, and the object of his present journey, that he once thought of proceeding to London, without waiting a formal permission; yet it was not without some difficulty that those who presented it escaped imprisonment.

Knox
refused
liberty
to pass
through
England.

This impolitic severity was occasioned by the informations of some of the exiles, who had not forgotten the old quarrel at Frankfort, and had accused of disloyalty and disaffection to the queen, not only Knox, but all those who had been under his charge at Geneva, whom they represented as proselytes to the opinion which he had published against female government. There was not an individual who could believe that Knox had the most distant eye to Elizabeth in publishing the obnoxious book; nor a person of judgment who could seriously think that her government was exposed to the slightest danger from him or his associates, who felt no less joy at her auspicious accession than the rest of their brethren. If he had been imprudent in that publication, if he had " swerved from the particular question to the general," his error (to use the words of his respondent) " rose not of malice, but of zeal, and by looking more to the present cruelty than to the inconveniencies that after might follow ;" and it was the part of generosity and policy to overlook the fault. Instead of this, Elizabeth and her counsellors took up the charge in a serious light; and the accused were treated with such harshness and disdain, that they repented of leaving their asylum, to return to their native country. This conduct was the more inexcusable, as numbers who had been instrumental in the cruelties of the preceding reign, were admitted to favour, or allowed to remain unmolested; and even Bonner was allowed to present himself at court, and to retire with a simple frown.

> De nobis, post hæc, tristis sententia fertur:
> Dat veniam corvis, vexat censura columbas.
>
> JUVENAL, Sat. ii.

The refusal of his request, and the harsh treatment of his flock, touched to the quick the irritable temper of our Reformer; and it was with some difficulty that he suppressed the desire, which he felt rising in his breast, to prosecute a controversy which he had resolved to abandon. But greater designs occupied his mind and engrossed his attention. It was not for the sake of personal safety, nor from vanity of appearing at court, that he desired to pass through England. He felt the natural wish to visit his old acquaintances in that country, and was anxious for an opportunity of addressing once more those to whom he had preached, especially at Newcastle and Berwick. But there was another object which he had still more at heart, in which the welfare of both England and Scotland were concerned.

Notwithstanding the flattering accounts which he received from his countrymen of the favourable disposition of the queen regent, and the directions which he sent them to cultivate this, he always entertained suspicions of the sincerity of her professions. But, since he left Geneva, they had been confirmed; and the information which he had procured, in travelling through France, conspired with the intelligence which he had lately received from Scotland, in convincing him, that the immediate suppression of the Reformation in his native country, and its consequent suppression in the neighbouring kingdom, were intended.   The plan projected by the gigantic ambition of the princes of Lorrain, brothers of the queen regent of Scotland, has been developed, and described with great accuracy and ability, by a celebrated modern historian.   Suffice it to say here, that the court of France, under their influence, had resolved to set up the claim of the young queen of Scots to the crown of England; to attack Elizabeth, and wrest the sceptre from her hands as a bastard and a heretic; and, as Scotland was the only avenue by which this attack could be successfully made, to begin by suppressing the Reformation, and establishing their power in that country. Knox, in the course of his journies through France, had formed an acquaintance with some persons about the court; and, by their means, had gained some knowledge of the plan.   He was convinced that the Scottish reformers were unable to resist the power of France, which was to be directed against them; and that it was the interest as well as duty, of the English court, to afford them the most effectual support.   But he was afraid that a selfish and narrow policy might prevent them from doing this, until it was too late; and was therefore anxious to call their attention to this subject at an early period, and to put them in possession of the facts that had come to his knowledge.   The assistance which Elizabeth granted to the Scottish protestants, in 1559 and 1560, was dictated by the soundest policy.   It baffled and defeated the designs of her enemies at the very outset; it gave her an influence over Scotland, which all her predecessors could not obtain by the terror of their arms, nor the influence of their money; it secured the stability of her government, by extending and strengthening the protestant interest, the principal pillar on which it rested.   And it reflects not a little credit on our Reformer's sagacity, that he had formed this plan in his mind at so early a period, was the first person who proposed it, and persisted (as we shall see) to urge its adoption, until his endeavours were crowned with success.

Deeply impressed with these considerations, he resolved, although he had already been twice repulsed, to brook the mortification, and make another attempt to obtain an interview with some confidential agent of the English government. With this view, he, on the 10th of April, wrote a letter to Secretary Cecil, with whom he had been personally acquainted during his residence in London. Adverting to the treatment of the exiles who had returned from Geneva, he exculpated them from all responsibility as to the offensive book which he had published, and assured him that he had not consulted with one of them previous to its publication. As for himself, he did not mean to deny that he was the author, nor was he yet prepared to retract the leading sentiment which it contained. But he was not, on that account, less friendly to the person and government of Elizabeth, in whose exaltation he cordially rejoiced; although he rested the defence of her authority upon grounds different from the common. This was the third time that he had craved liberty to pass through England. He had no desire to visit the court, nor to remain long in the country; but he was anxious to communicate to him, or some other trusty person, matters of importance, which it was not prudent to commit to writing, nor to entrust to an ordinary messenger. If his request was refused, it would turn out to the disadvantage of England.

The situation in which he stood, at this time, with the court of England, was so well known, that it was with difficulty that he could find a messenger to carry the letter; and, either despairing of the success of his application, or hastened by intelligence received from Scotland, he sailed from Dieppe on the 22d of April, and landed safely at Leith in the beginning of May.

Knox
lands at
Leith.

On his arrival, he found matters in the most critical state in Scotland. The queen regent had thrown off the mask which she had long worn, and avowed her determination forcibly to suppress the Reformation. As long as she stood in need of the assistance of the protestants to support her authority against the Hamiltons, and procure the matrimonial crown for her son-in-law, the Dauphin of France, she courted their friendship, listened to their plans of reform, professed dissatisfaction with the corruption and tyranny of the ecclesiastical order, and her desire of correcting them as soon as a fit opportunity offered, and flattered them, if not with the hopes of her joining their party, at least with assurances that she would shield them from the fury of the clergy. So completely were they duped by her consummate address and dissimulation, that they complied with all her requests, restrained some of their preachers from teaching in public, and desisted from presenting to the late Parliament a petition which they had prepared ; nor would they believe her insincere, even after different parts of her conduct had afforded strong grounds for suspicion. But, having accomplished the great objects which she had in view, she at last, in conformity with instructions from France, and secret engagements with the clergy, adopted measures which completely undeceived them, and discovered the gulph into which they were ready to be precipitated.

A deputation of leaders wait upon Mary of Guise.

Some of the protestant leaders having waited on her to intercede in behalf of their preachers, who had been summoned by her, she told them in plain terms, that, " in spite of them, they should be all banished from Scotland, although they preached as truly as ever St. Paul did :" and when they reminded her of the repeated promises of protection that she had given them, she unblushingly replied, that " it became not subjects to burden their princes with promises, farther than they pleased to keep them." They told her that, if she violated the engagements which she came under to her subjects, they would consider themselves as released from allegiance to her, and warned her very freely of the dangerous consequences; upon which she adopted milder language, and engaged to prevent the trial. But soon after, upon hearing that the exercise of the reformed religion had been introduced into the town of Perth, she renewed the process, and summoned all the preachers to appear at Stirling, on the tenth of May, to undergo a trial.

The state of our Reformer's mind, upon receiving this information, will appear from the following letter, hastily written by him on the day after he landed in Scotland.

"The perpetual comfort of the Holy Ghost for salutation.

"These few lines are to signify unto you, dear sister, that it hath pleased the merciful providence of my heavenly Father to conduct me to Edinburgh, where I arrived the 2d of May: uncertain as yet what God shall further work in this country, except that I see the battle shall be great. For Satan rageth even to the uttermost, and I am come, I praise my God, even in the brunt of the battle. For my fellow preachers have a day appointed to answer before the Queen Regent, the 10th of this instant, when I intend (if God impede not) also to be present; by life, by death, or else by both, to glorify his godly name, who thus mercifully hath heard my long cries. Assist me, sister, with your prayers, that now I shrink not, when the battle approacheth. Other things I have to communicate unto you, but travel after travel doth so occupy me, that no time is granted me to write. Advertise my brother, Mr. Goodman, of my estate; as, in my other letter sent unto you from Dieppe, I willed you. The grace of our Lord Jesus Christ rest with you. From Edinburgh, in haste, the 3d of May."

Although his own cause was prejudged, and sentence already pronounced against him, he did not hesitate a moment in resolving to present himself voluntarily at Stirling, to assist his brethren in their defence, and share in their danger. Having rested only a single day at Edinburgh, he hurried to Dundee, where he found the principal protestants in Angus and Mearns already assembled, determined to attend their ministers to the place of trial, and to avow their adherence to the doctrines for which they were accused. The providential arrival of such an able champion of the cause, at this crisis, must have been very encouraging to the assembly; and the liberty of accompanying them, which he requested, was readily granted.

Lest the unexpected approach of such a multitude, though unarmed, should alarm or offend the regent, the CONGREGATION (for so the protestants began at this time to be called) agreed to stop at Perth, and sent Erskine of Dun before them to Stirling, to acquaint her with the peaceable object and manner of their coming. Apprehensive that their presence would disconcert her measures, the regent had again recourse to dissimulation. She persuaded Erskine to write to his brethren to desist from their intended journey, and authorised him to promise, in her name, that she would put a stop to the trial. The Congregation testified their pacific intentions by a cheerful compliance with this request, and the greater part, confiding in the royal promise, returned to their homes. But when the day of trial came, the summons was called by the orders of the queen, the accused were outlawed for not appearing, and all were prohibited, under the pain of rebellion, from harbouring or assisting them.

Escaping from Stirling, Erskine brought to Perth the intelligence of this disgraceful transaction, which could not fail to incense the Protestants. It happened that, on the same day on which the news came, Knox, who remained at Perth, preached a sermon, in which he exposed the idolatry of the mass, and of image worship. Sermon being ended, the audience quietly dismissed; a few idle persons only loitered in the church, when an imprudent priest, wishing either to try the disposition of the people, or to shew his contempt of the doctrine which had been just delivered, uncovered a rich altarpiece, decorated with images, and prepared to celebrate mass. A boy, having uttered some expressions of disapprobation, was struck by the priest. He retaliated by throwing a stone at the aggressor, which, falling on the altar, broke one of the images. This operated like a signal upon the people present, who had taken part with the boy; and, in the course of a few minutes, the altar, images, and all the ornaments of the church were torn down, and trampled under foot. The noise soon collected a mob, who, finding no employment in the church, by a sudden and irresistible impulse, flew upon the monasteries; nor could they be restrained by the authority of the magistrates and the persuasions of the preachers, who assembled as soon as they heard of the riot, until the houses of the grey and black friars, with the costly edifice of the Carthusian monks, were laid in ruins. None of the gentlemen or sober part of the Congregation were concerned in this unpremeditated tumult; it was wholly confined to the baser inhabitants, or, as Knox designs them, "the rascall multitude."

The demolition of the monasteries having been represented as the first-fruits of our Reformer's labours on this occasion, it was necessary to give this minute account of the causes which produced that event. Whatever his sentiments were as to the destruction of the instruments and monuments of idolatry, he wished this to be accomplished in a regular manner; he was sensible that such tumultuary proceedings were prejudicial to the cause of the reformers in present circumstances; and, instead of instigating, he exerted himself in putting a stop to the ravages of the mob. If it must be traced to a remote cause, we must impute it to the wanton and dishonourable perfidy of the queen.

In fact, nothing could be more favourable to the designs of the regent than this riot. By her recent conduct, she had forfeited the confidence of the Protestants, and even exposed herself in the eyes of the sober and moderate of her own party. This occurrence afforded her an opportunity of turning the public indignation from herself, and directing it against the Congregation. She did not fail to improve it with her usual address.

PERIOD
V.
1557–1560
A.D.

Having assembled the nobility, she magnified the accidental tumult into a dangerous and designed rebellion. To the Catholics she dwelt upon the sacrilegious overthrow of those venerable structures which their ancestors had dedicated to the service of God. To the Protestants who had not joined those at Perth, she complained of the destruction of the royal foundation of the charter-house, protested that she had no intention of offering violence to their consciences, and promised her protection, provided they assisted her in punishing those who had been guilty of this violation of public order. Having inflamed the minds of all against them, she advanced to Perth with an army, threatening to lay waste the town with fire and sword, and to inflict the most exemplary vengeance on all who had been instrumental in producing the riot.

The Protestants of the north were not insensible of their danger, and did all in their power to appease the rage of the queen; they wrote to her, to the commanders of the French troops, to the Popish nobles, and to those of their own persuasion: they solemnly disclaimed all rebellious intentions; they protested their readiness to yield all due obedience to the government; they obtested and admonished all to refrain from offering violence to peaceable subjects, who sought only the liberty of their consciences. But finding all their endeavours fruitless, they resolved not to suffer themselves and their brethren to be massacred, and prepared for a defence of the town against an illegal and furious assault. So prompt and vigorous were their measures, that the regent, when she approached, deemed it imprudent to attack them, and proposed overtures of accommodation, to which they readily acceded.

The
queen
regent,
with an
army,
before
Perth.

While the two armies lay before Perth, and negociations were going on between them, our Reformer obtained an interview with the prior of St. Andrews and the young Earl of Argyle, who adhered to the regent; he reminded them of the solemn engagements which they had contracted, and charged them with violating PERIOD v. 1557–1560 A.D. these, by abetting measures which tended to the suppression of the reformed religion, and the enslaving of their native country. The noblemen assured him that they held their engagements sacred ; the regent had requested them to use their best endeavours to bring the present differences to an amicable termination ; if, however, she violated the present treaty, they promised, that they would no longer adhere to her, but would openly take part with the rest of the Congregation. The queen was not long in affording them the opportunity of verifying this promise.

Convinced, by numerous proofs, that the queen regent had formed a systematical plan for suppressing the Reformation, the lords of the Congregation renewed their bond of union, and concerted measures for counteracting her designs. For a full account of the interesting struggle that ensued, which was interrupted by treaties artfully proposed and perfidiously violated by the regent, and at last broke out into an open, though not very bloody, civil war, I must refer to the general histories of the period. The object of the present work does not admit of entering into a detail of this, except in as far as our Reformer was immediately engaged in it, or as may be requisite for illustrating his conduct.

Bond of union renewed.

The protestant leaders had frequently supplicated the regent, to employ her authority and influence for removing those corruptions in religion, which could no longer be palliated or concealed. They had made the same application to the clergy, but without success. "To abandon usurped power, to renounce lucrative error, are sacrifices which the virtue of individuals has, on some occasions, offered to truth ; but from any society of men no such effort can be expected. The corruptions of a society, recommended by common utility, and justified by universal practice, are viewed by its members without shame or horror ; and reformation never proceeds from themselves, but is always forced upon them by some foreign hand." The scandalous lives of the clergy, their total neglect of the religious instruction of the people, and the profanation of Christian worship by gross idolatry, were the most glaring abuses. A great part of the nation loudly demanded their correction; and if regular measures had not been adopted for this purpose, the popular indignation would have effected the work. The lords of the Congregation now resolved to introduce a reformation, in those places to which their authority or influence extended, and where the greater part of the inhabitants were friendly, by abolishing the Popish superstition, and setting up the Protestant worship in its room. The feudal ideas respecting the jurisdiction of the nobility, which at that time prevailed in Scotland, in part justified this step: the urgent and extreme necessity of the case forms its best vindication.

St. Andrews was the place fixed on for beginning these operations. With this view, Lord James Stewart, who was prior of the abbey of St. Andrews, and the Earl of Argyle, made an appointment with Knox to meet them on a certain day, in that city. Travelling along the east coast of Fife, he preached at Anstruther and Crail, and on the 9th of June came to St. Andrews. The archbishop, apprised of his design to preach in his cathedral, assembled an armed force, and sent information to him, that if he appeared in the pulpit, he would give orders to the soldiers to fire upon him. The noblemen, having met to consult what ought to be done, were of opinion that Knox should desist from preaching at that time. Their retinue was very slender; they had not yet ascertained the disposition of the town; the queen lay at a small distance with an army, ready to come to the bishop's assistance; and his appearance in the pulpit might lead to the sacrifice of his own life, and the lives of those who were determined to defend him from violence.

There are occasions on which it is a proof of superior wisdom to disregard the ordinary dictates of prudence;

on which, to face danger is to evite it, to flee from it is to incur it. Had the reformers, after announcing their intentions, suffered themselves to be intimidated by the bravading attitude and threats of the archbishop, their cause would, at the very outset, have received a blow, from which it would not easily have recovered. This was prevented by the firmness and intrepidity of Knox. Fired with the recollection of the part which he had formerly acted on that spot, and with the near prospect of realizing the sanguine hopes which he had cherished in his breast for many years, he replied to the solicitations of his brethren,—That he could take God to witness, that he never preached in contempt of any man, nor with the design of hurting an earthly creature; but to delay to preach next day (unless forcibly hindered), he could not in conscience agree: In that town, and in that church, had God first raised him to the dignity of a preacher, and from it he had been reft by French tyranny, at the instigation of the Scots bishops: The length of his imprisonment, and the tortures which he had endured, he would not at present recite; but one thing he could not conceal, that, in the hearing of many yet alive, he had expressed his confident hope of again preaching in St. Andrews: Now, therefore, when providence, beyond all men's expectation, had brought him to that place, he besought them not to hinder him. "As for the fear of danger that may come to me," continued he, "let no man be solicitous; for my life is in the custody of Him whose glory I seek. I desire the hand nor weapon of no man to defend me. I only crave audience; which, if it be denied here unto me at this time, I must seek where I may have it."

Knox's intrepid reply.

This intrepid reply silenced all further remonstrances; and next day Knox appeared in the pulpit, and preached to a numerous assembly, without meeting with the slightest opposition or interruption. He discoursed on the subject of our Saviour's ejecting the profane traffickers from the temple of Jerusalem; from which he took occasion to expose the enormous corruptions which had been introduced into the church, under the papacy, and to point out what was incumbent upon Christians, in their different spheres, for removing them. On the three following days he preached in the same place; and such was the influence of his doctrine, that the provost, bailies, and inhabitants, harmoniously agreed to set up the reformed worship in the town: the church was stripped of images and pictures, and the monasteries pulled down.

The example of St. Andrews was quickly followed in other parts of the kingdom; and, in the course of a few weeks, at Crail, at Cupar, at Lindores, at Stirling, at Linlithgow, and at Edinburgh, the houses of the monks were overthrown, and all the instruments which had been employed to foster idolatry and image-worship were destroyed.

These proceedings were celebrated in the singular lays which were at that time circulated among the reformers.

His cardinalles hes cause to mourne,
His bishops are borne a backe;
His abbots gat an uncouth turne,
When shavellinges went to sacke.
With burges wifes they led their lives,
And fare better than wee.
Hay trix, trim goe trix, under the greene wod-tre

His Carmelites and Jacobinis,
His Dominikes had great adoe;
His Cordelier and Augustines,
Sanct Francis's ordour to;
The sillie friers, mony yeiris
With babling bleerit our ee.
Hay trix, &c.

Had not your self began the weiris,
Your stepillis had bene standand yit,
It was the flattering of your friers
That ever gart Sanct Francis flit:
Ye grew sa superstitious
            In wickednesse.
It gart us grow malicious
            Contrair your messe.

Scarcely any thing in the progress of the Scottish Reformation has been more frequently or more loudly condemned than the demolition of those edifices, upon which
superstition had lavished all the ornaments of the chisel
and pencil. To the Roman Catholics, who anathemat-
ised all who were engaged in this work of inexpiable sa-
crilege, and represented it as involving the overthrow of
all religion, have succeeded another race of writers, who,
although they do not, in general, make high pretensions
to devotion, have not scrupled at times to borrow the
language of their predecessors, and have bewailed the
wreck of so many precious monuments, in as bitter
strains as ever idolater did the loss of his gods. These
are the warm admirers of Gothic architecture, and other
reliques of ancient art; some of whom, if we may judge
from their language, would welcome back the reign of
superstition, with all its ignorance and bigotry, if they
could recover the objects of their adoration. Writers of
this stamp depict the devastation and ravages which
marked the progress of the Reformation, in colours as
dark as ever were employed by the historian in de-
scribing the overthrow of ancient learning, by the irrup-
tions of the barbarous Huns and Vandals. Our Reformer cannot be mentioned by them without symptoms of
horror, and in terms of detestation, as a barbarian, a savage, a ringleader of mobs, for overthrowing whatever was
venerable in respect of antiquity, or sacred in respect of
religion. It is unnecessary to produce instances.

Expectes eadem a summo minimoque poeta.

To remind such persons of the divine mandate to destroy all monuments of idolatry in the land of Canaan,
would be altogether insufferable, and might provoke,
from some of them, a profane attack upon the authority
from which it proceeded. To plead the example of the
early Christians, in demolishing the temples and statues
dedicated to pagan polytheism, would only awaken the
keen regrets which are felt for the irreparable loss. It

would be still worse to refer to the apocalyptic predictions, which some have been so fanatical as to think were
fulfilled in the miserable spoliation of that " Great City,"
which, under all her revolutions, has so eminently proved the nurse of the arts, and given encouragement to
painters, statuaries, and sculptors, to " harpers, and musi-
cians, and pipers, and trumpeters, and craftsmen of whatsoever craft ;" who, to this day, have not forgotten their
obligations to her, nor ceased to bewail her destruction.
In any apology which I make for the reformers, I would
rather alleviate than aggravate the distress which is felt
for the wreck of so many valuable memorials of antiquity.   It has been observed by high authority, that
there are certain commodities which derive their principal value from their great rarity, and which, if found in
great quantities, would cease to be sought after or prized.
A nobleman of great literary reputation has, indeed, questioned the justness of this observation, as far as respects
precious stones and metals.   But I flatter myself, that
the noble author and the learned critic, however much
they differ as to public wealth, will agree that the observation is perfectly just, as applied to those commodities which constitute the wealth of the antiquary.   With
him rarity is always an essential requisite.   His property,
like that of the possessor of the famous Sibylline books,
does not decrease in value by the reduction of its quan-
tity, but, after the greater part has been destroyed, becomes still more precious.   If the matter be viewed in
this light, antiquarians have no reason to complain of
the ravages of the reformers, who have left them such
valuable remains, and placed them in that very state which
awakens in their minds the most lively sentiments of the
sublime and beautiful, by reducing them to—*Ruins*.

But to speak seriously, I would not be thought such
an enemy to any of the fine arts, as to rejoice at the
wanton destruction of their models, ancient or modern,
or to vindicate those who, from ignorance or fanatical
rage, may have excited the mob to this work.   At the

same time, I must reprobate that spirit which disposes
persons to magnify irregularities, and dwell with unceas-
ing lamentations upon losses, which, in the view of an
enlightened and liberal mind, will sink and disappear,
in the magnitude of the incalculable good which rose
from the wreck of the revolution. What! do we celebrate, with public rejoicings, victories over the enemies
of our country, in the gaining of which, the lives of thou-
sands of our fellow-creatures have been sacrificed? and
shall solemn masses and sad dirges, accompanied with
direful execrations, be everlastingly sung, for the man-
gled members of statues, torn pictures, and ruined tow-
ers? I will go farther, and say, that I look upon the
destruction of these monuments as a piece of good policy, which contributed materially to the overthrow of
the Roman Catholic religion, and the prevention of its
re-establishment. It was chiefly by the magnificence of
temples and the splendid apparatus of its worship, that
the popish church fascinated the senses and imaginations
of the people. There could not, therefore, be a more
successful method of attacking it than the demolition of
these. There is more wisdom, than many seem to perceive, in the maxim, which Knox is said to have inculcated, " that the best way to keep the *rooks* from returning, was to pull down their *nests*." In demolishing, or
rendering uninhabitable all those buildings which had
served for the maintenance of the ancient superstition
(except what were requisite for the protestant worship),
the reformers only acted upon the principles of a prudent general, who razes the castles and fortifications
which he is unable to keep, and which might afterwards
be seized, and employed against him by the enemy. Had
they been allowed to remain, the popish clergy would
not have ceased to indulge hopes, and to make efforts to
be restored to them; occasions would have been taken
to tamper with the credulous, and inflame the minds of
the superstitious; and the reformers might soon have
found reason to repent their ill-judged forbearance.

Reasons
for razing
popish
edifices.

PERIOD
V.
1557–1560
A.D.

—————When we had quelled
The strength of Aztlan, we should have thrown down
Her altars, cast her idols to the fire.

—————The priests combined to save their craft;
And soon the rumour ran of evil signs
And tokens; in the temple had been heard
Wailings and loud lament; the eternal fire
Gave dismally a dim and doubtful flame;
And from the censer, which at morn should steam
Sweet odours to the sun, a fœtid cloud,
Black and portentous, rose.—————

SOUTHEY'S MADOC, part i. b. ii.

Our Reformer continued at St. Andrews till the end
of June, when he came to Edinburgh, from which the
regent and her forces had retired. The Protestants in
this city fixed their eyes upon him, and chose him
immediately for their minister. He accordingly entered
upon that charge; but the Lords of the Congregation
having soon after concluded a treaty with the regent, by
which they delivered up Edinburgh to her, they judged
it unsafe for him to remain there, on account of the extreme personal hostility with which the Papists were
inflamed against him. Willock, as being less obnoxious
to them, was therefore substituted in his place, while he
undertook a tour of preaching through the kingdom.
This itinerancy had great influence in extending the
reformed interest. The wide field which was before
him, the interesting situation in which he was placed,
the dangers by which he was surrounded, and the hopes
which he cherished, increased the ardour of his zeal,
and stimulated him to extraordinary exertions both of
body and mind. Within less than two months, he
travelled over the greater part of Scotland. He visited
Kelso, and Jedburgh, and Dumfries, and Ayr, and Stirling, and Perth, and Brechin, and Montrose, and Dundee, and returned again to St. Andrews. The attention
of the nation was aroused; their eyes were opened to the
errors by which they had been deluded; and they panted
for the word of life which they had once tasted. I cannot
better describe the emotions which he felt at his success,
than by quoting from the familiar letters which he

Knox on
a preach-
ing tour
through
Scotland.

wrote on the occasion, at intervals snatched from his constant employment.

"Thus far," says he, in a letter from St. Andrews, June 23, "hath God advanced the glory of his dear Son among us. O that my heart could be thankful for the super-excellent benefit of my God. The long thirst of my wretched heart is satisfied in abundance, that is above my expectation; for now forty days and more hath my God used my tongue, in my native country, to the manifestation of his glory. Whatsoever now shall follow, as touching my own carcase, his holy name be praised. The thirst of the poor people, as well as of the nobility here is wondrous great; which putteth me in comfort, that Christ Jesus shall triumph here in the north and extreme parts of the earth for a space." In another letter, dated September 2d, he says, "Time to me is so precious, that with great difficulty can I steal one hour in eight days, either to satisfy myself, or to gratify my friends. I have been in continual travel since the day of appointment; and, notwithstanding the fevers have vexed me, yet have I travelled through the most part of this realm, where, all praise to his blessed majesty! men of all sorts and conditions embrace the truth. Enemies we have many, by reason of the Frenchmen who lately arrived, of whom our Papists hope golden hills. As we be not able to resist, we do nothing but go about Jericho, blowing with trumpets, as God giveth strength, hoping victory by his power alone."

Immediately after his arrival in Scotland, he wrote to Geneva for his wife and family. On the 13th of June, Mrs. Knox and her mother were at Paris, and applied to Sir Nicolas Throkmorton, the English ambassador, for a safe conduct to pass into England. Throkmorton, who by this time had begun to penetrate the counsels of the French court, not only granted this, but wrote a letter to the queen, in which he urged the propriety of over-looking the offence which Knox had given by his publi-

Knox writes to Geneva for his family.

cation, and of conciliating him by the kind treatment of his wife; seeing he was in great credit with the lords of the Congregation, had been the principal instrument in producing the late change in that kingdom, and was capable of doing essential service to her majesty. Accordingly, Mrs. Knox came into England, and being conveyed to the borders, by the directions of the court, reached her husband in safety, on the 20th of September. Her mother, after remaining a short time in her native country, followed her into Scotland, where she remained until her death.

Christopher Goodman.

The arrival of his family was the more gratifying to our Reformer, that they were accompanied by Christopher Goodman. He had repeatedly written, in the most pressing manner, for his late colleague to come to his assistance, and expressed much uneasiness at the delay of his arrival. Goodman became minister of St. Andrews. The settlement of Protestant ministers took place at an earlier period than is mentioned in our common histories. Previous to September 1559, eight towns were provided with pastors; other places remained unprovided, owing to the scarcity of preachers, which was severely felt.

In the mean time, it became daily more apparent that the lords of the Congregation would be unable, without foreign aid, to maintain the struggle in which they were involved. Had the contest been merely between them and the domestic party of the regent, they would soon have brought it to a successful termination; but they could not withstand the veteran troops which France had sent to her assistance, and was preparing to send, in still more formidable numbers. As far back as the middle of June, our Reformer renewed his exertions

Kircaldy of Grange

for obtaining assistance from England; and persuaded William Kircaldy of Grange, first to write, and afterwards to pay a visit to Sir Henry Percy, who held a public situation on the English marches. Percy immedi-

ately transmitted his representations to London, and an
answer was returned from secretary Cecil, encouraging the correspondence.

Knox himself wrote to Cecil, requesting permission to visit England, and enclosed a letter to queen Elizabeth, in which he attempted to apologise for his rude attack upon female government. There was nothing at which he was more awkward than making apologies. The letter contains professions of strong attachment to Elizabeth's government; but the strain in which it is written is such as, if it was ever read by that high-minded princess, must have aggravated, instead of extenuating his offence. But the sagacious secretary, I have little doubt, suppressed it. He was himself friendly to the measure of assisting the Scottish Congregation, and exerted all his influence to bring over the queen and her council to his opinion. A message was, accordingly, sent to Knox, desiring him to meet with Sir Henry Percy at Alnwick, on the 2d of August, upon business which required the utmost secrecy and dispatch; and Cecil came down to Stamford to hold an interview with him.

The confusion produced by the advance of the regent's army upon Edinburgh, retarded his journey; but no sooner was this settled, than he sailed from Pittenweem to Holy Island. Finding that Percy was recalled from the borders, he applied to Sir James Croft, governor of Berwick. Croft, who was not unapprised of the design upon which he came, dissuaded him from proceeding farther into England, and undertook to dispatch his communications to London, and to procure a speedy return. While he remained at Berwick, Whitlaw came from the English court with answers to the letters formerly sent; and he immediately returned to lay these before a meeting of the protestant lords at Stirling. The irresolution or the caution of Elizabeth's cabinet had led them to express themselves in such general and unsatisfactory terms, that the assembly were both disappointed and displeased; and it was with some difficulty that our Reformer obtained permission from them to write again to London in his own name. The representation which he gave of the urgency of the case, and the danger of further hesitation or delay, produced a speedy reply, desiring them to send a confidential messenger to Berwick, who would receive a sum of money, to assist them in carrying on the war. About the same time, Sir Ralph Saddler was sent down to Berwick, to act as an accredited, but secret agent; and the correspondence between the court of London and the lords of the Congregation continued afterwards to be carried on through him and Sir James Croft, until the English auxiliary army entered Scotland.

If we reflect upon the connection which the religious and civil liberties of the nation had with the contest in which the protestants were engaged, and upon our Reformer's zeal in that cause, we will not be greatly surprised to find him at this time acting in the character of a politician. Extraordinary cases cannot be measured by ordinary rules. In a great emergency, like that under consideration, when all that is valuable and dear to a people is at stake, it becomes the duty of every individual to step forward, and exert the talents with which he is endowed for the public good. Learning was at this time rare among the nobility; and though there were men of distinguished abilities among the protestant leaders, few of them had been accustomed to transact public business. Accordingly, the management of the correspondence with England was for a time devolved chiefly on Balnaves and our Reformer. But he submitted to this merely from a sense of duty and regard to the common cause; and, when the younger Maitland acceded to their party, he expressed the greatest satisfaction at the prospect which this gave him of being relieved from the burden.

It was not without reason that he longed for this deliverance. He now felt that it was almost as difficult to preserve Christian integrity and simplicity amidst the crooked wiles of political intrigue, as he had formerly found it to pursue truth through the perplexing mazes of scholastic sophistry. In performing a task foreign to his habits and repugnant to his disposition, he met with a good deal of vexation and several unpleasant rubs. These were owing partly to his own impetuosity, partly to the grudge entertained against him by the English court, but chiefly to the line of policy which the latter had prescribed to themselves. They were convinced of the danger of suffering the Scottish protestants to be suppressed: but they wished to confine themselves to pecuniary aid, secretly conveyed, by which, they thought, the lords of the Congregation would be enabled to expel the French, and bring the contest to a successful termination, while England would avoid an open breach with France. This plan, which originated in the personal disinclination of Elizabeth to the Scottish war, rather than in the judgment of her wisest counsellors, protracted the contest, and produced several jars between the English agents and those of the Congregation. The former were continually urging the associated lords to attack the regent, before she received fresh succours from France, and blaming their slow operations; they complained of the want of secrecy in their correspondence with England; and even insinuated, that the money, intended for the common cause, was partially applied to private purposes. The latter were offended at this charge, and urged the necessity of military as well as pecuniary aid.

In a letter to Sir James Croft, Knox represented the great importance of their being speedily assisted with troops, without which they would be in much hazard of miscarrying in an attack upon the fortifications of Leith. The court of England, he said, ought not to hesitate at offending France, of whose hostile intentions against them they had the most satisfactory evidence. But " if ye list to craft with thame," continued he, " the sending of a thousand or mo men to us can breake no league nor point of peace contracted betwixt you and

Leith fortified by foreign troops.

France: For it is free for your subjects to serve in warr anie prince or nation for their wages; and if yee fear that such excuses will not prevail, ye may declare thame rebelles to your realme, when ye shall be assured that thei be in our companye." No doubt such things have been often done; and such *political casuistry* (as Keith not improperly styles it) is not unknown at courts. But it must be confessed, that the measure recommended by Knox (the morality of which must stand on the same grounds with the assistance which the English were at that time affording) was too glaring to be concealed by the excuses which he suggested. Croft laid hold of this opportunity to check the impetuosity of his correspondent, and wrote him, that he wondered how he, " being a wise man," would require from them such aid as they could not give " without breach of treaty, and dishonour;" and that the world was not so blind as not to see through the devices by which he proposed to colour the matter. Knox, in his reply, apologised for his " unreasonable request;" but, at the same time, reminded Croft of the common practice of courts in such matters, and of the French court toward themselves in a recent instance; he was not ignorant, he said, of the inconveniences which might attend an open declaration in their favour, but feared that they would have cause to " repent the drift of time, when the remedy shall not be so easy."

This is the only instance in which I have found our Reformer recommending any thing like dissimulation, which was very foreign to the openness of his natural temper, and the blunt and rigid honesty which marked all his actions. His own opinion was, that the English court ought from the first to have done what they found themselves obliged at last to do, to declare openly their resolution to support the Congregation. Keith praises Croft's " just reprimand on Mr. Knox's double-fac'd proposition," and Cecil says, that his " audacite was well tamed." We must not, however, imagine that either of these statesmen had any scruple of conscience or honour on the point. For, on the very day on which Croft answered Knox's letter, he wrote to Cecil that he thought the queen ought openly to take part with the Congregation. And in the same letter in which Cecil speaks of Knox's audacity, he advises Croft to a material adoption of the measure which he had recommended, though in a more plausible shape, by sending five or six officers, who should "steal from thence with appearance of displeasure for lack of interteynment;" and in a subsequent letter, he gives directions to send three or four fit for being captains, who should give out that they left Berwick, "as men desyrous to be exercised in the warres, rather than to lye idely in that towne."

Notwithstanding the prejudice which existed in the English court against our Reformer, on account of his "audacity" in attacking female prerogative, they were too well acquainted with his integrity and influence to decline his services. Cecil kept up a correspondence with him; and in the directions sent from London for the management of the subsidy, it was expressly provided, that he should be one of the council for examining the receipts and payments, to see that it was applied to the common action, and not to any private use.

In the mean time, his zeal and activity in the cause of the Congregation, exposed him to the deadly resentment of the queen regent and the papists. A reward was publicly offered to the person who should seize or kill him, and numbers, actuated by hatred or avarice, lay in wait for his apprehension. But he was not deterred by this from appearing in public, nor from travelling through the country, in the discharge of his duty. His exertions at this period were incredibly great. By day he was employed in preaching, by night in writing letters on public business. He was the soul of the Congregation; was always present at the post of danger; and by his presence, his public discourses, and private advices, ani-

A reward offered to any who should seize or kill him.

mated the whole body, and defeated the schemes employ-ed to corrupt and disunite them.

Our Reformer was now called to take a share in a very delicate and important measure. When they first had recourse to arms in their own defence, the lords of the Congregation had no intention of making any altera-tion in the government, nor of assuming the exercise of the supreme authority. Even after they had adopted a more regular and permanent system of resistance to the measures of the regent, they continued to recognise the station which she held, presented petitions to her, and listened respectfully to the proposals which she made, for removing the grounds of variance. But finding that she was fully bent upon the execution of her plan for subverting the national liberties, and that the title which she held gave her great advantages in carrying on this design, they began to deliberate upon the propriety of adopting a different line of conduct. Their sovereigns were minors, in a foreign country, and under the man-agement of persons who had been the principal instru-ments in producing all the evils of which they complain-ed. The queen dowager held the regency by the au-thority of Parliament; and might she not be deprived of it by the same authority? In the present state of the country, it was impossible for a free and regular Parlia-ment to meet; but the greater and better part of the nation had declared their dissatisfaction with her admi-nistration; and was it not competent for them to provide for the public safety, which was exposed to such immi-nent danger? These were questions which formed the topic of frequent conversation at this time.

Knox called to an assem-bly of nobles, etc., at Edin-burgh.

After much deliberation on this important point, a numerous assembly of nobles, barons, and representatives of boroughs met at Edinburgh on the 21st of October, to bring it to a solemn issue. To this assembly Knox and Willock were called; and the question being stated to them, they were required to deliver their opinions as to the lawfulness of the measure. Willock, who officiated

as minister of Edinburgh, being first asked, declared it
to be his judgment, founded upon reason and Scripture,
that the power of rulers was limited ; that they might
be deprived of it upon valid grounds ; and that the queen
regent having, by the fortification of Leith, and the introduction of foreign troops, evinced a fixed determination to oppress and enslave the kingdom, might justly
be deprived of her authority, by the nobles and barons
the native counsellors of the realm, whose petitions and
remonstrances she had repeatedly rejected. Knox as-
sented to the opinion delivered by his brother, and added, that the assembly might, with safe consciences, act
upon it, provided they attended to the three following
things, first, that they did not suffer the misconduct of
the queen regent to alienate their affections from due
allegiance to their sovereigns, Francis and Mary ; second,
that they were not actuated in the measure by private
hatred or envy of the queen dowager, but by regard to
the safety of the commonwealth ; and, third, that any
sentence which they might pronounce at this time should
not preclude her re-admission to the office, if she afterwards discovered sorrow for her conduct, and a disposi
tion to submit to the advice of the counsellors of the
realm. After this, the whole assembly, having several
ly delivered their opinions, did, by a solemn deed, suspend the queen dowager from her authority as regent of
the kingdom, until the meeting of a free parliament ;
and, in the interval, elected a council for the management
of public affairs.

The preachers have been blamed for interposing their
advice on this question, as incompetent to persons of
their character, and exposing them to unnecessary
odium. But it is not easy to see how they could have
been excused in refusing to deliver their opinion, when
required by those who had submitted to their ministry,
upon a measure which involved a case of conscience, as
well as a question of law and political right. The
advice which was actually given and followed is a matter

of greater consequence than the quarter from which it came. As this proceeded upon principles very different from those which produced resistance to princes, and the limitation of their authority, under feudal governments, and as our Reformer has been the object of much animadversion for inculcating these principles, the reader will pardon another digression from the narrative.

Among the various causes which affected the general state of society and government in Europe, during the middle ages, we are particularly led to notice the influence of religion. Debased by ignorance and fettered by superstition, the minds of men were prepared to acquiesce without examination in the claims of authority, and to submit tamely to every yoke. The genius of Popery is in every view friendly to slavery. The Romish court, while it aimed directly at the establishment of a spiritual despotism in the hands of the ecclesiastics, contributed to rivet the chains of political servitude upon the people. In return for the support which princes yielded to its arrogant claims, it was content to invest them with an absolute authority over the bodies of their subjects. By the priestly unction performed at the coronation of kings, in the name of the Holy See, a sacred character was understood to be communicated, which raised them to a superiority over their nobility which they did not formerly possess, rendered their persons inviolable, and their office divine. Although the sovereign pontiffs claimed, and, on different occasions, exercised the power of dethroning kings, and absolving subjects from their allegiance, yet any attempt of this kind, when it proceeded from the people themselves, was denounced as a crime deserving the severest punishment in this world, and damnation in the next. Hence sprung the divine right of kings to rule independently of their people, and of passive obedience and nonresistance to their will; under the sanction of which they were encouraged to sport with the lives and happiness of their subjects, and to indulge in the most tyrannical

and wanton acts of oppression, without the dread of resistance, or of being called to an account.   Even in
countries where the people were understood to enjoy
certain political privileges, transmitted from remote
ages, or wrested from their princes on some favourable
occasions (as in England), these principles were generally
prevalent; and it was easy for an ambitious and powerful monarch to avail himself of them, to violate the
rights of the people with impunity, and upon a constitution, the forms of which were friendly to popular
liberty, to establish an administration completely de-
spotic and arbitrary.

PERIOD
v.
1557–1560
A. D.

The contest between Papal sovereignty and the authority of General Councils, which was carried on during the
fifteenth century, struck out some of the radical principles of liberty, which were afterwards applied to political
government.   The revival of learning, by unfolding the
principles of legislation and modes of government in the
republics of ancient Greece and Rome, gradually led to
more liberal notions on this subject.   But these were
confined to a few, and had no influence upon the general
state of society.   The spirit infused by philosophy and
literature is too feeble and contracted to produce a radical reform of established abuses; and learned men, satisfied with their own superior illumination, and the liberty
of indulging their speculations, have generally been too
indifferent or too timid to attempt the improvement of
the multitude.   It is to the religious spirit excited
during the sixteenth century, which spread rapidly
through Europe, and diffused itself among all classes of
men, that we are chiefly indebted for the propagation of
the genuine principles of rational liberty, and the consequent amelioration of government.

The Re-
formation
conducive
to liberty.

Civil and ecclesiastical tyranny were so closely combined, that it was impossible for men to emancipate
themselves from the latter without throwing off the
former; and from arguments which established their
religious rights, the transition was easy, and almost

The old
system
and the
new.

unavoidable, to disquisitions about their civil privileges.
In those kingdoms in which the rulers threw off the
Romish yoke, and introduced the Reformation by their
authority, the influence was more imperceptible and
slow; and in some of them, as in England, the power
taken from the ecclesiastical was thrown into the regal
scale, which proved in so far prejudicial to popular liberty.   But where the Reformation was embraced by
the body of a nation, while the ruling powers continued
to oppose it, the effect was visible and immediate.   The
interested and obstinate support which rulers gave to the
old system of error and ecclesiastical tyranny, and their
cruel persecution of all who favoured the new opinions,
drove their subjects to inquire into the just limits of
authority and obedience.   Their judgments once informed as to the rights to which they were entitled, and
their consciences satisfied respecting the means which
they might employ to acquire them, the immense importance of the immediate object in view, their emancipation from religious bondage, and the salvation of themselves and their posterity, impelled them to make the
attempt with an enthusiasm and perseverance which the
mere love of civil liberty could not have inspired.

In effecting that memorable revolution which termi-
nated in favour of religious and political liberty in so
many nations of Europe, the public teachers of the protestant doctrine had a principal influence.   By their instructions and exhortations, they roused the people to
consider their rights and exert their power; they stimulated timid and wary politicians; they encouraged and
animated princes, nobles, and confederated states, with
their armies, against the most formidable opposition, and
under the most overwhelming difficulties, until their exertions were crowned with the most signal success.   These
facts are now admitted, and this honour at last, through
the force of truth, conceded to the religious leaders of the
protestant Reformation, by philosophical writers, who
had too long branded them as ignorant and fanatical.

Our national Reformer had caught a large portion of the spirit of civil liberty. We have already adverted to the circumstance in his education which directed his attention, at an early period, to some of its principles. His subsequent studies introduced him to acquaintance with the maxims and modes of government in the free states of antiquity; and it is reasonable to suppose that his intercourse with the republics of Switzerland and Geneva had some influence on his political creed. Having formed his sentiments independent of the prejudices arising from established laws, long usage, and commonly received opinions, his zeal and intrepidity prompted him to avow and propagate them, when others, less sanguine and resolute, would have been restrained by fear, or despair of success. Extensive observation had convinced him of the glaring perversion of government in the most of the European kingdoms. But his principles led him to desire their reform, not their subversion. His admiration of the policy of republics, ancient or modern, was not so great or indiscriminate as to prevent him from separating the essential principles of equity and freedom which they contained, from others which were incompatible with monarchy. He was perfectly sensible of the necessity of regular government to the maintenance of justice and order among mankind, and aware of the danger of setting men loose from its salutary restraints. He uniformly inculcated a conscientious obedience to the lawful commands of rulers, and respect to their persons as well as to their authority, even when they were chargeable with various mismanagements; as long as they did not break through all the restraints of law and justice, and cease to perform the essential duties of their office.

But, he held that rulers, supreme as well as subordinate, were invested with authority for the public good; that obedience was not due to them in any thing contrary to the divine law; that, in every free and well constituted government, the law of the land was superior to the will of the prince, and that inferior magistrates and subjects might restrain the supreme magistrate from particular illegal acts, without throwing off their allegiance, or being guilty of rebellion; that no class of men have an original, inherent, and indefeasible right to rule over a people independently of their will and consent; that a nation have a right to provide and require that they be ruled by laws, agreeing with the divine, and calculated to promote their welfare; that there is a mutual compact, tacit and implied, if not formal and explicit, between rulers and their subjects; and if the former shall flagrantly violate this, employ that power for the destruction of a commonwealth, which was committed to them for its preservation and benefit; in one word, if they shall become habitual tyrants and notorious oppressors, that the people are absolved from allegiance, have a right to resist them, formally to depose them from their place, and to elect others in their room.

The real power of the Scottish kings was, indeed, always limited, and there are in our history, previous to the æra of the Reformation, many instances of resistance to their authority. But, though these were pleaded as precedents on this occasion, it must be confessed that we cannot trace them to the principles of genuine liberty. They were the effect, either of sudden resentment on account of some flagrant act of maladministration, of the ambition of some powerful baron, or of the jealousy with which the feudal aristocracy watched over the prerogatives of their order. The people who followed the standards of their chiefs had little interest in the struggle, and derived no benefit from the limitations which were imposed upon their sovereign. But, at this time, more just and enlarged sentiments were diffused through the nation, and the idea of a commonwealth, including the mass of the people as well as the privileged orders, began to be entertained. Our Reformer, whose notions of hereditary right, whether in kings or nobles, were not exalted, studied to repress the insolence and oppression of the nobles; he reminded them of the

original equality of men, and the ends for which some
were raised above others; and he taught the people
that they had rights to preserve, as well as duties to perform. Such, in substance, were the political sentiments
of our Reformer. With respect to female government,
he never moved any question among his countrymen,
nor attempted to gain proselytes to his opinion. But
the principles just stated were strenuously inculcated by
him, and acted upon in Scotland in more than one instance during his life. That they should, at that period,
have exposed those who held them to the charge of treason from despotical rulers and their numerous satellites;
that they should have been regarded with a suspicious
eye by some of the learned, who had not altogether
thrown off common prejudices, in an age when the principles of political liberty were only beginning to be understood,—is not much to be wondered at. But it
must excite both surprise and indignation, to find writers,
in the present enlightened age, and under the sunshine
of British liberty (if our sun is not fast going down), expressing their abhorrence of these sentiments, and ex-
hausting upon their authors all the invective and viru-
lence of the former *Anti-monarcho-machi*, and advocates
of passive obedience. They are *essentially* the principles
upon which the free constitution of Britain rests; the
most obnoxious of them was reduced to practice at the
memorable æra of the Revolution, when the necessity of
employing them was not more urgent or unquestionable,
than it was at the suspension of the queen regent of Scotland, and the subsequent sequestration of her daughter.

I have said *essentially ;* for I would not be understood
as meaning, that every proposition advanced by Knox,
on this subject, is expressed in the most guarded and
unexceptionable manner, or that all the cases, in which
he was led to vindicate forcible resistance to rulers, were
such as rendered it necessary, and may be pleaded as
precedents in modern times. The political doctrines
maintained at that time received a tincture from the

PERIOD
V.
1557–1560
A. D.

Dawn of
political
liberty.

spirit of the age, and were accommodated to a rude and unsettled state of society and government. The checks which have since been introduced into the constitution, and the influence which public opinion, expressed by the organ of a free press, has upon the conduct of rulers, are sufficient, in ordinary cases, to restrain dangerous encroachments, or afford the means of correcting them in a peaceable way; and have thus happily superseded the necessity of having recourse to those desperate but decisive remedies which were formerly applied by an oppressed and indignant people. But if ever the time come when these principles shall be generally renounced and abjured, the extinction of the boasted liberty of Britain will not be far off.

Those who judge of the propriety of any measure from the success with which it is accompanied, will be disposed to condemn the suspension of the queen regent. Soon after this step was taken, the affairs of the Congregation began to wear a gloomy appearance. The messenger whom they had sent to Berwick to receive a remittance from the English court, was intercepted on his return, and rifled of the treasure; their soldiers mutinied for want of pay; they were repulsed in a premature assault upon the fortifications of Leith, and worsted in a skirmish with the French troops; the secret emissaries of the regent were too successful among them; their numbers daily decreased; and the remainder disunited, dispirited, and dismayed, came to the resolution of abandoning Edinburgh on the evening of the 5th of November, and retreated with precipitation and disgrace to Stirling.

The Congregation at Stirling. Amidst the universal dejection produced by these disasters, the spirit of Knox remained unsubdued. On the day after their arrival at Stirling, he mounted the pulpit, and delivered a discourse, which had a wonderful effect in rekindling the zeal and courage of the Congregation. Their faces, he said, were confounded, their enemies triumphed, their hearts had quaked for fear, and still remained oppressed with sorrow and shame. What was the cause for which God had thus dejected them! The situation of their affairs required plain language, and he would use it. In the present distressed state of their minds, they were in danger of fixing upon an erroneous cause of their misfortunes, and of imagining that they had offended in taking the sword of self-defence into their hands; just as the tribes of Israel did when twice discomfited in the war which they undertook, by divine direction, against their brethren the Benjamites. Having divided the Congregation into two classes, those who had been embarked in this cause from the beginning, and those who had lately acceded to it, he proceeded to point out what he considered as blameable in the conduct of each; and after exhorting all to amendment of life, prayers, and works of charity, he concluded with an animating address. God, he said, often suffered the wicked to triumph for a while, and exposed his chosen congregation to mockery, dangers, and apparent destruction, in order to abase their self-confidence, and induce them to look to him for deliverance and victory. If they turned unfeignedly to the Eternal, he no more doubted that their present distress would be converted into joy, and followed by success, than he doubted that Israel was finally victorious over the Benjamites, after being twice repulsed with ignominy. The cause in which they were engaged would, in spite of all opposition, prevail in Scotland. It was the eternal truth of the eternal God which they maintained; it might be oppressed for a time, but would ultimately triumph.

Knox's exhortation at Stirling.

The audience, who had entered the church in deep despondency, left it with renovated courage. In the afternoon the council met, and after prayer by the Reformer, unanimously agreed to dispatch Maitland to London to supplicate more effectual assistance from Elizabeth. In the meantime, as they were unable to keep the field, they resolved to divide, and that the one half of the Council should remain at Glasgow, and the

PERIOD V. 1557-1560 A.D.

other at St. Andrews. Knox was appointed to attend the
latter. The French having, in the beginnning of the
year 1560, penetrated into Fife, he encouraged that small
band, which, under the Earl of Arran, and the prior of
St. Andrews, bravely resisted their progress, until the
appearance of the English fleet obliged them to make a
precipitate retreat.

The disaster which caused the protestant army to
leave Edinburgh, turned out to the advantage of their
cause. It obliged the English court to abandon the line
of cautious policy which they had hitherto pursued.
On the 27th of February 1560, they concluded a formal
treaty with the lords of the Congregation ; and, in the
beginning of April, the English army entered Scotland.

The French troops retired within the fortifications of
Leith, and were invested by sea and land ; the queen
regent died in the castle of Edinburgh during the siege ;
and the ambassadors of France were forced to agree to
a treaty, by which it was provided, that the French
troops should be removed from Scotland, an amnesty
granted to all who had been engaged in the late resistance to the measures of the regent, their principal grievances redressed, and a free Parliament called to settle the
other affairs of the kingdom.

During the continuance of the civil war, while the
Protestant preachers were assiduous in disseminating
the knowledge of the truth through all parts of the
kingdom, the Popish clergy used no exertions to coun-
teract them. Too corrupt to think of reforming their
manners, too illiterate to be capable of defending their
errors, they placed their forlorn hope upon the success
of the French arms, and looked forward to the issue
of the contest, as involving the establishment or the
ruin of their religion. One attempt they, indeed, made
to recover their lost reputation, and support their sinking cause, by reviving the stale pretence of miracles
wrought at the shrines of their saints. But the detec-
tion of the imposture exposed them to derision, and was

the occasion of their losing a person, who, by his learning and integrity, was the greatest ornament of their
party.

The treaty, which put an end to hostilities, made no
settlement respecting religious differences; but, on that
very account, it was fatal to Popery. The power was
left in the hands of the Protestants. The Roman Catholic worship was almost universally deserted through
the kingdom, except in those places which had been
occupied by the regent and her foreign auxiliaries; and
no provision was made for its restoration. The firm hold
which it once had of the opinions and affections of the
people was completely loosened; it was supported by
force alone; and the moment that the French troops
embarked, that fabric, which had stood for ages in Scotland, fell to the ground. Its feeble and dismayed priests
ceased, of their own accord, from the celebration of its
rites; and the reformed service was peaceably set up,
wherever ministers could be found to perform it. The
parliament, when it met, had little else to do respecting
religion, than to sanction what the nation had previously
adopted.

Thus did the reformed religion advance in Scotland
from small beginnings, and amidst great opposition,
until it attained a legal establishment. Besides the secret benediction which accompanied the labours of the
preachers and confessors of the truth, the serious and
inquisitive reader will trace the hand of Providence, in
that concatenation of events which contributed to its
rise, preservation, and increase; in the over-ruling of the
caprice, the ambition, the avarice, and the interested
policy of princes and cabinets, many of whom had nothing else in view than to favour that cause, which they
were so instrumental in promoting.

Triumph of the Re-formers.

The breach of Henry VIII. of England with the Romish See, awakened the attention of the inhabitants of the
northern part of the island to a controversy, which had
hitherto been carried on at too great a distance to

interest them, and led not a few to desire a reformation more improved than the model which he had held out to them. The premature death of James V. of Scotland was favourable to these views; and during the short period in which they received the countenance of civil authority, at the commencement of Arran's regency, the seeds of the reformed doctrine were so widely spread, and had taken such deep root, as to be able to resist the violent measures which the regent, after his recantation, employed to extirpate them. Those who were driven from the country by persecution found an asylum in England, under the decidedly Protestant government of Edward VI. After his death, the alliance of England with Spain, and of Scotland with France, the two great contending powers on the continent, prevented any concert between the two courts which might have proved fatal to the Protestant religion in Britain. While the cruelties of the English queen drove preachers into Scotland, the political schemes of the queen regent induced her to favour the Protestants, and connive at the propagation of their opinions. At the critical moment when she had accomplished her favourite designs, and was preparing to crush the Reformation, Elizabeth ascended the throne of England, who, from motives of policy no less than religion, was inclined to support the Scottish reformers. The princes of Lorrain, who, by the accession of Francis II., had obtained the sole direction of the French court, were resolutely bent on their suppression, and being at peace with Spain, seemed to have it in their power to turn the whole force of the empire against them; but at this very time, those intestine dissensions, which continued so long to desolate France, broke out, and forced them to accede to that treaty, which put an end to the French influence, and Roman Catholic religion in Scotland.

PERIOD VI.

FROM HIS SETTLEMENT AS MINISTER OF EDINBURGH, AT THE ESTABLISHMENT OF THE REFORMATION, ANNO 1560, TO HIS ACQUITTAL, FROM A CHARGE OF TREASON, BY THE PRIVY COUNCIL, ANNO 1563.

In the assignation of ministers to the different parts of the kingdom, a measure which engaged the attention of the Protestants immediately after the proclamation of peace, the temporary arrangements formerly made were in general confirmed; and our Reformer resumed his station as minister of Edinburgh. During the month of August, he was employed in composing the Protestant Confession of Faith, which was presented to the Parliament, who ratified it, and abolished the Papal jurisdiction and worship.

The organization of the reformed church was not yet completed. Hitherto the Book of Common Order, agreed upon by the English church at Geneva, had been chiefly followed as a directory for worship and government. But this having been compiled for the use of a single congregation, composed, too, for the most part, of men of education, was found inadequate for an extensive church, consisting of a multitude of confederated congregations. Sensible of the great importance of ecclesiastical polity, for the maintenance of order, the preservation of purity of doctrine and morals, and the general flourishing of religion in the kingdom, our Reformer, at an early period, called the attention of the Protestants to this subject, and urged its speedy settlement. In consequence of this, the Lords of the privy council appointed him, and other five ministers, to draw out such a plan as they judged most agreeable to Scripture, and conducive to the advancement of religion. They met accordingly, and with great pains, and much unanimity,

PERIOD VI.

The First Book of Discipline

formed the book, which was afterwards called the First Book of Discipline.

As our Reformer had a chief hand in the compilation of this book, and the subject is interesting, it may not be altogether foreign to the object of the present work, to give a slight sketch of the form and order of the church of Scotland, at the first establishment of the Reformation.

Form and order of the church of Scotland.

The ordinary and permanent office-bearers of the church were of four kinds: the minister or pastor, to whom the preaching of the gospel and administration of the sacraments belonged; the doctor or teacher, whose province it was to interpret scripture, and confute errors (including those who taught theology in schools and universities); the ruling elder, who assisted the minister in exercising ecclesiastical discipline and government; and the deacon, who had the special oversight of the revenues of the church and the poor. But besides these, it was found necessary, at that time, to employ some persons in extraordinary and temporary charges. As there were not a sufficient number of ministers to supply the different parts of the country, that the people might not be altogether destitute of public worship and instruction, serious persons were appointed to read the scriptures and the common prayers. These were called readers. If they advanced in knowledge, they were encouraged to add a few plain exhortations to the reading of the scriptures. In this case they were called exhorters; but they were examined and admitted, before entering upon this employment.

The same cause gave rise to another temporary expedient. Instead of fixing all the ministers in particular charges, it was judged proper, after supplying the principal towns, to assign to the rest the superintendence of a large district, over which they were appointed regularly to itinerate, for the purpose of preaching, planting churches, and inspecting the conduct of ministers, exhorters, and readers. These were called superintendents.

The number originally proposed was ten; but owing to
the scarcity of proper persons, or rather the want of necessary funds, there were never more than six appointed.
The deficiency was supplied by commissioners or visit-
ors, appointed from time to time by the General Assembly.

The mode of admission to all these offices was by the
free election of the people, examination of the candidate,
and public admission, accompanied with prayer and exhortation. The affairs of each congregation were managed by the minister, elders, and deacons, who constituted the session, which met once a-week, or oftener.
There was a meeting called the weekly exercise, or pro-
phesying, held in every considerable town, consisting of
the ministers, exhorters, and learned men in the vicinity,
for expounding the scriptures. This was afterwards converted into the presbytery, or classical assembly. The
superintendent met with the ministers and delegated
elders of his district, twice a-year, in the provincial
synod, which took cognizance of ecclesiastical affairs
within its bounds. And the General Assembly, which
was composed of ministers and elders commissioned from
the different parts of the kingdom, met twice, sometimes
thrice in the year, and attended to the interests of the
whole national church. Public worship was conducted
according to the Book of Common Order, with a few
variations.

The compilers of the First Book of Discipline paid
particular attention to the state of education. They required that a school should be erected in every parish,
for the instruction of youth in the principles of religion,
grammar, and the Latin tongue. They proposed that a
college should be erected in every "notable town," in
which logic and rhetoric should be taught along with
the learned languages. They seem to have had it in
their eye to revive the system adopted in some of the
ancient republics, in which the youth were considered as
the property of the public rather than of their parents,

7

by obliging the nobility and gentry to educate their children, and providing, at the public expense, for the education of the children of the poor who discovered talents for learning. Their regulations for the three national universities discover an enlightened regard to the interests of literature, and may suggest hints which deserve attention in the present age. If they were not carried into effect, the blame cannot be imputed to the reformed ministers, but to those persons who, through avarice, defeated the execution of their plans. But even as matters stood, and notwithstanding the confusions in which the country was involved, learning continued to make great progress in Scotland, from this period to the close of the century.

We are ready to form very false and exaggerated notions of the rudeness of our ancestors. Perhaps some of our literati, who entertain such a diminutive idea of the taste and learning of those times, might be surprised, if they could be set down at the table of one of our Scottish reformers surrounded with a circle of his children and pupils, where the conversation was all carried on in French, and the chapter of the Bible, at family worship, was read by the boys in Hebrew, Greek, Latin, and French. Perhaps they might have blushed, if the book had been put into their hands, and they had been required to perform a part of the exercises. It is certain, however, that John Row this was the common practice in the house of Mr. John Row, minister of Perth, with whom many of the nobility and gentry boarded their children, for their instruction in the Greek and Hebrew languages, the knowledge of which he contributed to spread through the kingdom. Nor was the improvement of our native tongue neglected at this time.

Judicious as its plan was, and well adapted to promote the interests of religion and learning in the nation, the Book of Discipline, when presented to the Privy Council, was coldly received, and its formal ratification evaded. This did not arise from any difference of sentiment be-

tween them and the ministers respecting ecclesiastical
government, but partly from aversion to the strict discipline which it appointed to be exercised against vice,
and partly from reluctance to comply with its requisi-
tion for the appropriation of the revenues of the popish
church to the support of the new religious and literary
establishments. However, it was subscribed by the
greater part of the members of the council; and as the
grounds of prejudice against it were well known, it was
submitted unto by the nation, and carried into effect in
all its principal ecclesiastical regulations.

The first General Assembly of the reformed church of Chapel of
St. Mary
Magda-
lene scene
of first
General
Assembly,
1560 A.D.
Scotland sat down at Edinburgh on the 20th of December 1560. It consisted of forty members, only six of
whom were ministers. Knox was one of these; and he
continued to sit in most of its meetings until the time of
his death. Their deliberations were conducted at first
with great simplicity and unanimity. It is a singular
circumstance, that they had seven different meetings
without a president or moderator. But as the number
of members increased, and business became more com-
plicated, a moderator was appointed to be chosen at every
meeting; he was invested with authority to maintain
order; and regulations were enacted concerning the
constituent members of the court, the causes which
ought to come before them, and the order of procedure.

In the close of this year our Reformer suffered a heavy
domestic loss, by the death of his valuable wife, who,
after sharing in the hardships of her husband's exile
was removed from him when he had obtained a comfortable settlement for his family. He was left with
the charge of two young children, in addition to his
other cares. His mother-in-law was still with him; but
though he took pleasure in her religious company, the
dejection of mind to which she was subject, and which
all his efforts could never completely cure, rather increased than lightened his burden. His acute feelings
were severely wounded by this stroke; but he endea-

voured to moderate his grief by the consolations which he administered to others, and by application to public duties. He had the satisfaction of receiving, on this occasion, a letter from his much respected friend Calvin, in which expressions of great esteem for his deceased partner were mingled with condolence for his loss. I may take this opportunity of mentioning, that Knox, with the consent of his brethren, consulted the Genevan reformer upon several difficult questions which occurred respecting the settlement of the Scottish Reformation, and that a number of letters passed between them on this subject.

Anxieties on a public account were felt by Knox along with his domestic distress. The Reformation had hitherto advanced with a success equal to his most sanguine expectations; and, at this time, no opposition was publicly made to the new establishment. But matters were still in a very critical state. There was a party in the nation, by no means inconsiderable in numbers and power, who remained addicted to Popery; and, though they had given way to the torrent, they anxiously waited for an opportunity to embroil the country in another civil war, for the restoration of the ancient religon. Queen Mary, and her husband the king of France, had refused to ratify the late treaty, and had dismissed the deputy, sent by the Parliament, with marks of the highest displeasure at the innovations which they had presumed to introduce. A new army was preparing in France for the invasion of Scotland against the spring; emissaries were sent, in the mean time, to encourage and unite the Roman Catholics; and it was doubtful if the queen of England would subject herself to new expense and odium, by protecting them against a second attack.

The danger was not unperceived by our Reformer, who exerted himself to prepare his countrymen, by impressing their minds with a due sense of it, and exciting them speedily to complete the settlement of religion throughout the kingdom, which, he was persuaded, would prove the principal bulwark against the assaults of their adversaries. In the state in which the minds of men then were, his admonitions were listened to by many who had formerly treated them with indifference. The threatened storm blew over, in consequence of the death of the French king; but this necessarily led to a measure which involved the Scottish Protestants in a new struggle, and exposed the reformed church to dangers less obvious and striking, but, on that account, not less to be dreaded than open violence and hostility. This was the invitation given by the Protestant nobility to their young queen, who, on the 19th of August 1561, arrived in Scotland, and assumed the reins of government into her own hands.

The education which Mary had received in France, whatever embellishments it added to her beauty, was the very worst which can be conceived, for fitting her to rule her native country in the present juncture. Of a temper naturally violent, the devotion which she had been accustomed to see paid to her personal charms rendered her incapable of bearing contradiction. Habituated to the splendour and gallantry of the most luxurious and dissolute court of Europe, she could not submit to those restraints which the severe manners of her subjects imposed; and while the freedom of her behaviour gave offence to them, she could not conceal the antipathy and disgust which she felt at theirs. Full of high notions of royal prerogative, she regarded the late proceedings of Scotland as a course of rebellion against her authority. Every means was employed, before she left France, to strengthen the blind attachment to the Roman Catholic religion in which she had been nursed from her infancy, and to inspire her with aversion to the religion which had been embraced by her subjects. She was taught that it would be the great glory of her reign to reduce her kingdom to the obedience of the Romish See, and co-operate with the Popish princes on the continent in extirpating heresy. If she forsook the religion in which she had been educated, she would forfeit their powerful friendship ; if she persevered in it, she might depend upon their assistance to enable her to chastise her rebellious subjects, and prosecute her claims to the English crown against a heretical usurper.

With these fixed prepossessions, Mary came into Scotland, and she adhered to them with singular pertinacity to the end of her life. To examine the subjects of controversy between the Papists and Protestants, with the view of ascertaining on what side the truth lay ; to hear the preachers, or admit them to state the grounds of their faith, even in the presence of the clergy whom she had brought along with her ; to do any thing which might lead to a doubt in her mind respecting the religion in which she had been brought up, she had formed an unalterable determination to avoid. As the Protestants were at present in possession of the power, it was necessary for her to temporise ; but she resolved to withhold her ratification of the late proceedings, and to embrace the first favourable opportunity to overturn them, and re-establish the ancient system.

The reception which she met with on her first arrival in Scotland was flattering ; but an occurrence which took place soon after damped the joy which had been expressed, and prognosticated future jealousies and confusion.

Solemn mass at Holyrood-house.

Resolved to give her subjects an early proof of her firm determination to adhere to the Roman Catholic worship, Mary directed preparations to be made for the celebration of a solemn mass in the chapel of Holyroodhouse, on the first Sunday after her arrival. So great was the horror with which the Protestants viewed this service, and the alarm which they felt at finding it countenanced by their queen, that the first rumour of the design excited violent murmurs, which would have burst into an open tumult, had not the leaders interfered, and by their authority repressed the zeal of the multitude. Knox, from regard to public tranquillity, and to avoid giving offence to the queen and her relations, at the present juncture, used his influence in private conversation to allay the fervour of the more zealous, who were ready to prevent the service by force. But he was not less alarmed at the precedent than the rest of his brethren; and having exposed the evil of idolatry in his sermon on the following Sabbath, he said, that "one mess was more fearfull unto him, than if ten thousand armed enemies wer landed in ony parte of the realme, of purpose to suppress the hole religioun."

At this day, we are apt to be struck with surprise at the conduct of our ancestors, to treat their fears as visionary, or at least highly exaggerated, and summarily to pronounce them guilty of the same intolerance of which they complained in their adversaries. Persecution for conscience' sake is so odious, the least approach to it is so dangerous, that we reckon we can never express too great detestation of any measure which involves it. But let us be just as well as liberal. A little reflection upon the circumstances in which our reforming forefathers were placed, may serve to abate our astonishment, and qualify our censures. They were actuated, it is true, by a strong abhorrence of Popish idolatry, and unwilling to suffer the land to be again polluted with it. But they were influenced also by a proper regard for their own preservation; and neither were their fears fanciful, nor their precautions unnecessary.

The warmest friends of toleration and liberty of conscience, some of whom will not readily be charged with Protestant prejudices, have agreed, that persecution of the most sanguinary kind was inseparable from the system and spirit of Popery which was at that time dominant in Europe; and they cannot deny the inference, that the profession and propagation of it were, on this account, justly subjected to penal restraints, as far, at least, as was requisite to prevent it from obtaining the ascendancy, and reacting the bloody scenes which it had already exhibited. The Protestants of Scotland had

these scenes before their eyes, and fresh in their recollection; and criminal indeed would they have been, if,
under a false security, and by listening to the syren
song of toleration, by which their adversaries, with no
less impudence than artifice, now attempted to lull them
asleep, they had suffered themselves to be thrown off
their guard, and neglected to provide against the most
distant approaches of the danger by which they were
threatened. Could they be ignorant of the perfidious,
barbarous, and unrelenting cruelty with which Protestants were treated in every Roman Catholic kingdom!
in France, where so many of their brethren had been
put to death, under the influence of the relations of their
queen; in the Netherlands, where such multitudes had
been tortured, beheaded, hanged, drowned, or buried
alive; in England, where the flames of persecution were
but lately extinguished, and in Spain, where they continued to blaze? Could they have forgot what had
taken place in their own country, or the perils from
which they had themselves narrowly escaped? "God
forbid!" exclaimed the lords of the privy council, in the
presence of queen Mary, at a time when they were not
disposed to offend her; "God forbid! that the lives of
the faithful stood in the power of the Papists: for just
experience has taught us what cruelty is in their hearts."

Nor was this an event so improbable, as to render the
most jealous precautions unnecessary. The rage for
conquest, on the continent, was now converted into a
rage for proselytism; and steps had already been taken
towards forming that league among the Catholic princes,
which had for its object the universal extermination of
the Protestants. The Scots queen was passionately
addicted to the intoxicating cup of which so many of
"the kings of the earth had drunk." There were
numbers in the nation similarly disposed. The liberty
taken by the queen would soon be demanded for all who
declared themselves Catholics. Many of those who had
hitherto ranged under the Protestant standard were

lukewarm in the cause; the zeal of others had already
suffered a sensible abatement; and it was to be feared,
that the favours of the court, and the blandishments of
an artful and engaging princess would make proselytes
of some, and lull others into a dangerous security, while
designs were carried on pregnant with ruin to the religion
and liberties of the nation. It was in this manner that
some of the most wise persons in the country reasoned,
and, had it not been for the uncommon spirit which at
at that time existed among the reformers, there is every
reason to think that their predictions would have been
verified.

To those who compare the conduct of the Scottish
protestants on this occasion, to the intolerance of Roman
Catholics, I would recommend the following statement
of a sensible French author, who had formed a more just
notion of these transactions than many of our own
writers. "Mary," says he, "was brought up in France
accustomed to see protestants burned to death, and instructed in the maxims of her uncles, the Guises, who
maintained that it was necessary to exterminate, without
mercy, the pretended reformed. With these dispositions
she arrived in Scotland, which was wholly reformed,
with the exception of a few lords. The kingdom receive
her, acknowledge her as their queen, and obey her in all
things according to the laws of the country. I maintain
that, in the state of men's spirits at that time, if a Hu-
guenot queen had come to take possession of a Roman
Catholic kingdom, with the equipage with which Mary
came to Scotland, the first thing they would have done
would have been to arrest her; and if she had persevered in her religion, they would have procured her degra-
dation by the Pope, thrown her into the Inquisition, and
burned her as a heretic. There is not an honest man
who dare deny this." After all, it is surely unnecessary
to apologise for the restrictions which our ancestors
were desirous of imposing on queen Mary, to those who
approve of the present constitution of Britain, which

excludes every papist from the throne, and according to which the reigning monarch, by setting up mass in his chapel, would virtually forfeit his crown. Is popery more dangerous now than it was two hundred and fifty years ago?

Besides his fears for the common cause, Knox had grounds for apprehension as to his personal safety. The queen was peculiarly incensed against him on account of the active hand which he had in the late revolution; the popish clergy who left the kingdom represented him as the ringleader of her factious subjects; and she had signified, before she left France, that she was determined he should be punished. His book against female government was most probably the ostensible charge on which he was to be prosecuted; and accordingly we find him making application through the English resident at Edinburgh, to secure the favour of Elizabeth, reasonably fearing that she might be induced to abet the proceedings against him on this head. But whatever perils he apprehended, from the personal presence of the queen, either to the public or to himself, he used not the smallest influence to prevent her being invited home. On the contrary, he concurred with his brethren in this measure and in defeating a scheme which the duke of Chastelherault, under the direction of the archbishop of St. Andrews, had formed to exclude her from the government. But when the prior of St. Andrews was sent to France with the invitation, he urged that her desisting from the celebration of mass should be one of the conditions of her return; and when he found him and the rest of the council disposed to grant her this liberty within her own chapel, he predicted that "her liberty would be their thraldom."

Soon after her arrival, queen Mary, whether of her own accord or by advice is uncertain, sent for Knox to the palace, and held a long conversation with him, in the presence of her brother, the prior of St. Andrews. She seems to have expected to awe him into submission by her authority, if not to confound him by her arguments. But the bold freedom with which he replied to all her charges, and vindicated his own conduct, convinced her that the one expectation was not more vain than the other; and the impression which she wished to make was left on her own mind. She accused him of raising her subjects against her mother and herself; of writing a book against her just authority, which, she said, she would cause the most learned men in Europe to answer; of being the cause of sedition and bloodshed when he was in England; and of accomplishing his purposes by magical arts.

To these heavy charges Knox replied, that, if to teach the truth of God in sincerity, to rebuke idolatry, and exhort a people to worship God according to his word, were to excite subjects to rise against their princes, then he stood convicted of that crime; for it had pleased God to employ him, among others, to disclose unto that realm the vanity of the papistical religion, with the deceit, pride, and tyranny of the Roman Antichrist. But if the true knowledge of God and his right worship were the most powerful inducements to subjects cordially to obey their princes (as they certainly were), he was innocent. Her Grace, he was persuaded, had at present as unfeigned obedience from the protestants of Scotland, as ever her father or any of her ancestors had from those called bishops. With respect to what had been reported to her Majesty, concerning the fruits of his preaching in England, he was glad that his enemies laid nothing to his charge but what the world knew to be false. If any of them could prove, that in any of the places where he had resided there was either sedition or mutiny, he would confess himself to be a malefactor. So far from this being the case, he was not ashamed to say, that in Berwick, where bloodshed among the soldiers had formerly been common, God so blessed his weak labours, that there was as great quietness during the time he resided in it, as there was at present in Edinburgh. The slander of practising magic (an art which he had condemned where-ever he preached) he could more easily bear, when he recollected that his master, the Lord Jesus, had been de-famed as one in league with Beelzebub. As to the book which seemed so highly to offend her majesty, he owned that he wrote it, and was willing that all the learned should judge of it. He understood that an Englishman had written against it, but he had not read him. If he had sufficiently confuted his arguments, and establish-ed the contrary propositions, he would confess his error, but to that hour he continued to think himself alone more able to sustain the things affirmed in that work than any ten in Europe were to confute them.

"You think I have no just authority?" said the queen.

"Please your Majesty," replied he, "learned men in all ages have had their judgments free, and most commonly disagreeing from the common judgment of the world; such also have they published both with pen and tongue; notwithstanding, they themselves have lived in the com-mon society with others, and have borne patiently with the errors and imperfections which they could not amend. Plato the philosopher wrote his book Of the Commonwealth, in which he condemned many things that then were maintained in the world, and required many things to have been reformed; and yet, notwith-standing, he lived under such policies as then were uni-versally received, without further troubling of any state. Even so, madam, am I content to do, in uprightness of heart, and with a testimony of a good conscience." He added, that his sentiments on that subject should be con-fined to his own breast; and that, if she refrained from persecution, her authority would not be hurt, either by him, or his book, "which was written most especially against the wicked Jesabell of England."

"But ye speak of women in general," said the queen. "Most true it is, madam; yet it appeareth to me, that wisdom should persuade your Grace never to raise trou-ble for that which to this day has not troubled your majesty, neither in person nor in authority : for of late years many things, which before were held stable, have been called in doubt ; yea, they have been plainly impugned. But yet, madam, I am assured that neither protestant nor papist shall be able to prove, that any such question was at any time moved either in public or in secret. Now, madam, if I had intended to have troubled your state, because ye are a woman, I would have chosen a time more convenient for that purpose, than I can do now, when your presence is within the realm."

Changing the subject, she charged him with having taught the people to receive a religion different from that allowed by their princes; and asked, if this was not contrary to the divine command, that subjects should obey their rulers? He replied, that true religion derived not its original or authority from princes, but from the eternal God; that princes were often most ignorant of the true religion ; and that subjects were not bound to frame their religion according to the arbitrary will of their rulers, else the Hebrews would have been bound to adopt the religion of Pharaoh, Daniel and his associates that of Nebuchadnezzar and Darius, and the primitive Christians that of the Roman Emperors. "Yea," replied the queen, qualifying her assertion ; "but none of these men raised the sword against their princes." "Yet you cannot deny," said he, "that they resisted ; for those who obey not the commandment given them do in some sort resist." "But they resisted not with the sword," rejoined the queen, pressing home the argument. "God, madam, had not given unto them the power and the means." "Think you," said the queen, "that subjects, having the power, may resist their princes?" "If princes exceed their bounds, madam, no doubt they may be resisted, even by power. For no greater honour, or greater obedience, is to be given to kings and princes, than God has commanded to be given to father and mother. But the father may be struck

A lengthy conversation.

with a phrensy, in which he would slay his children.
Now, madam, if the children arise, join together, apprehend the father, take the sword from him, bind his
hands, and keep him in prison, till the phrensy be over;
think you, madam, that the children do any wrong?
Even so, madam, is it with princes that would murder
the children of God that are subject unto them. Their
blind zeal is nothing but a mad frensy; therefore, to
take the sword from them, to bind their hands, and to
cast them into prison, till they be brought to a more
sober mind, is no disobedience against princes, but just
obedience, because it agreeth with the will of God."

The queen, who had hitherto maintained her courage
in reasoning, was completely overpowered by this bold
answer: her countenance changed, and she continued in
a silent stupor. Her brother spoke to her, and inquired
the cause of her uneasiness; but she made no reply.
At length, recovering herself, she said, " Well then, I
perceive that my subjects shall obey you, and not me,
and will do what they please, and not what I command;
and so must I be subject to them, and not they to me."
" God forbid!" answered Knox, " that ever I take upon
me to command any to obey me, or to set subjects at liberty to do whatever pleases them. But my travel is,
that both princes and subjects may obey God. And
think not, madam, that wrong is done you, when
you are required to be subject unto God; for it is he
who subjects people under princes, and causes obedience
to be given unto them. He craves of kings, that they
be as foster-fathers to his church, and commands queens
to be nurses to his people. And this subjection, madam
unto God and his church, is the greatest dignity that
flesh can get upon the face of the earth; for it shall raise
them to everlasting glory."

" But you are not the church that I will nourish,"
said the queen: " I will defend the church of Rome;
for it is, I think, the true church of God." " Your will,
madam is no reason; neither doth your thought make

the Roman harlot to be the true and immaculate spouse
of Jesus Christ. Wonder not, madam, that I call Rome
an harlot, for that church is altogether polluted with all
kinds of spiritual fornication, both in doctrine and manners." He added, that he was ready to prove that the
Romish church had declined farther from the purity of
religion taught by the apostles, than the Jewish church
had degenerated from the ordinances which God gave
them by Moses and Aaron, at the time when they denied and crucified the Son of God. "My conscience is not
so," said the queen. "Conscience, madam, requires
knowledge; and I fear that right knowledge you have
none." She said, she had both heard and read. "So,
madam, did the Jews who crucified Christ; they read
the law and the prophets, and heard them interpreted
after their manner. Have you heard any teach but such
as the pope and cardinals have allowed? and you may be
assured, that such will speak nothing to offend their own
estate."

"You interpret the Scriptures in one way," said the
queen evasively, "and they in another: whom shall I
believe, and who shall be judge?" "You shall believe
God, who plainly speaketh in his word," replied the
Reformer, "and farther than the word teacheth you,
you shall believe neither the one nor the other. The
word of God is plain in itself; if there is any obscurity
in one place, the Holy Ghost, who is never contrary to
himself, explains it more clearly in other places, so that
there can remain no doubt, but unto such as are obstinately ignorant." As an example, he selected one of the
articles in controversy, that concerning the sacrament of
the Supper, and proceeded to shew, that the popish doctrine of the sacrifice of the mass was destitute of all
foundation in scripture. But the queen, who was determined to avoid all discussion of the articles of her
creed, interrupted him, by saying, that she was unable
to contend with him in argument, but if she had those
present whom she had heard, they would answer him.

"Madam," replied the Reformer fervently, "would to God that the learnedest Papist in Europe, and he whom you would best believe, were present with your Grace to sustain the argument, and that you would wait patiently to hear the matter reasoned to the end! for then, I doubt not, madam, but you would hear the vanity of the Papistical religion, and how little ground it hath in the word of God." "Well," said she, "you may perchance get that sooner than you believe." "Assuredly, if ever I get that in my life, I get it sooner than I believe; for the ignorant Papist cannot patiently reason, and the learned and crafty Papist will never come, in your audience, madam, to have the ground of their religion searched out. When you shall let me see the contrary, I shall grant myself to have been deceived in that point."

The hour after dinner afforded an occasion for breaking off this singular conversation. At taking leave of her majesty, the Reformer said, "I pray God, madam, that you may be as blessed within the commonwealth of Scotland, as ever Deborah was in the commonwealth of Israel."

The Papistry alarmed.

This interview excited great speculation, and different conjectures were formed as to its probable consequences. The Catholics, whose hopes now depended solely on the queen, were alarmed, lest Knox's rhetoric should have shaken her constancy. The Protestants cherished the expectation that she would be induced to attend the Protestant sermons, and that her religious prejudices would gradually abate. Knox indulged no such flattering expectations. He had made it his study during the late conference, to discover the real character of the queen; and he formed, at that time, the opinion, which he never saw reason afterwards to alter, that she was proud, crafty, obstinately wedded to the Popish church, and averse to all means of instruction. He resolved, therefore, vigilantly to watch her proceedings, that he might give timely warning of any danger which might result from them to the reformed

interest; and the more that he perceived the zeal of the
Protestant nobles to cool, and their jealousy to be laid
asleep, by the winning arts of the queen, the more frequently and loudly did he sound the alarm. Vehement
and harsh as his expressions often were; violent, seditious, and insufferable, as his sermons and prayers have
been pronounced, I have little hesitation in saying, that
as the public peace was never disturbed by them, so they
were useful to the public safety, and even a principal
means of warding off those confusions in which the
country was involved, and which brought on the ultimate ruin of the infatuated queen. His uncourtly and
rough manner was not, indeed, calculated to gain upon
her mind, nor is there reason to think that an opposite
manner would have had this effect, and his admonitions
often irritated her; but they obliged her to act with
greater reserve and moderation ; and they operated, to
an indescribable degree, in arousing and keeping awake
the zeal and the fears of the nation, which, at that
period, were the two great safeguards of the Protestant
religion in Scotland. We may form an idea of the effect
produced by his pulpit-orations, from the account of
the English ambassador, who was one of his constant
hearers. "Where your honour," says he, in a letter to
Cecil, "exhorteth us to stoutness, I assure you the voice
of one man is able, in an hour, to put more life in us,
than six hundred trumpets continually blustering in our
ears."

The Reformer was not ignorant that some of his
friends thought him too severe in his language, nor was
he always disposed to vindicate the expressions which
he employed. Still, however, he was persuaded, that
the times required the utmost plainness ; and he was
afraid that snares lurked under the smoothness which
was recommended and practised by courtiers. Cecil,
having given him an advice on this head, in one of his
letters, we find him replying, " Men deliting to swym
betwix two waters have often compleaned upon my

severitie. I do fear that that which men terme lenitie and dulcenes do bring upon thameselves and others mor fearful destruction, than yit hath ensewed the vehemency of any preacher within this realme."

The abatement of zeal which he dreaded from "the holy water of the court," soon began to appear among the Protestant leaders. The General Assemblies of the church were a great eye-sore to the queen, who was very desirous to have them put down. At the first Assembly after her arrival, the courtiers, through her influence, absented themselves, and, when challenged for this, began to dispute the propriety of such conventions without her majesty's pleasure. On this point, there was sharp reasoning between Knox and Maitland, who was now made secretary of state. "Take from us the liberty of assemblies, and take from us the gospel," said the Reformer. "If the liberty of the church must depend upon her allowance or disallowance, we shall want not only assemblies, but also the preaching of the gospel." He was still more indignant at their management in settling the provision for the ministers of the church. Hitherto they had lived mostly on the benevolence of their hearers, and many of them had scarcely the means of subsistence; but repeated complaints having obliged the privy council to take up the affair, they came at last to a determination, that the ecclesiastical revenues should be divided into three parts; that two of these should be given to the ejected Popish clergy; and that the other part should be divided between the court and the Protestant ministry! The persons appointed to modify the stipends were disposed to gratify the queen, and the sums allotted to the ministers were as ill paid as they were paltry and inadequate. "Weall!" exclaimed Knox, when he heard of this disgraceful arrangement, "if the end of this ordour, pretendit to be takin for sustenatioun of the ministers, be happie, my judgement failes me. I sie twa pairtis freelie gevin to the devill, and the thrid mon be devyded betwix God and devill. Quho wald have thocht, that quhen Joseph reulled in Egypt, his brethren sould have travellit for victualles; and have returned with emptie sackes unto thair families? O happie servands of the devill, and miserabill servants of Jesus Christ, if efter this lyf thair wer not hell and heavin!"

He vented his mind more freely on this subject, as his complaints could not be imputed to personal motives; for his own stipend, though moderate, was liberal when compared with those of the most of his brethren. From the time of his last return to Scotland, until the conclusion of the war, he had been indebted to the liberality of individuals for the support of his family. After that period, he lodged for some time in the house of David Forrest, a burgess of Edinburgh, from which he removed to the lodging which had belonged to Durie, abbot of Dunfermline. As soon as he began to preach statedly in the city, the town council assigned him an annual stipend of two hundred pounds, to be paid quarterly; besides discharging his house-rent and re-imbursing some individuals the money which they had expended in maintaining his family. Subsequent to the settlement made by the privy council, it would seem that he received his stipend from the common fund allotted to the ministers of the church; but the good town had still an opportunity of testifying their generosity, by supplying the deficiencies of the legal allowance. Indeed, the uniform attention of the town council to his external accommodation and comfort was honourable to them, and deserves to be recorded to their commendation.

In the beginning of the year 1562, he went to Angus to preside in the election and admission of John Erskine of Dun as superintendent of Angus and Mearns. That respectable baron was one of those whom the first General Assembly declared "apt and able to minister;" and having already contributed in different ways, to the advancement of the Reformation, he now devoted him-

self to the service of the church, in a laborious employment, at a time when she stood eminently in need of the
assistance of all the learned and pious. Knox had formerly presided at the installation of John Spottiswood,
as superintendent of Lothian.

The influence of our Reformer appears from his being
employed on different occasions to compose variances of
a civil nature, which arose among the protestants. He
was applied to frequently to intercede with the town
council in behalf of some of the inhabitants, who had
subjected themselves to punishment by their disorderly
conduct. In March this year, the earl of Bothwell urged him to assist in removing a deadly feud which subsisted between him and the earl of Arran. He was
averse to interfere in this business, which had already
baffled the authority of the privy council; but, at the
desire of some friends, he yielded, and, after considerable
pains, had the satisfaction of bringing the parties to an
amicable interview, at which they mutually promised to
bury all differences. But he was exceedingly mortified
by the information, which Arran, immediately on the
back of this agreement, communicated to him, of a conspiracy which Bothwell had proposed to him; which
produced the imprisonment of both, and, notwithstanding the lunacy of the informer, created great jealousies
in the minds of the principal courtiers.

In the month of May, Knox had another interview
with the queen, on the following occasion. The family
of Guise were at this time making the most vigorous efforts to regain that influence in France which they had
been deprived of since the death of Francis II. and, as
zeal for the Catholic religion was the cloak by which
they covered their ambitious designs, they began by stirring up persecution against the protestants. The massacre of Vassy, in the beginning of March this year, was
a prelude to this, in which the duke of Guise and cardinal of Lorrain attacked, with an armed force, a congregation assembled for worship, killed a number of them,

and wounded and mutilated others, not excepting women
and children. Intelligence of the success which attended
the measures of her uncles was brought to queen Mary,
who immediately after gave a splendid ball to her foreign servants, at which the dancing was prolonged to a
late hour.

Knox was advertised of the festivities in the palace,
and the occasion of them. He always felt a lively interest in the concerns of the French protestants, with
many of whom he was intimately acquainted, and he entertained a very bad opinion of the princes of Lorrain.
In his sermon on the following Sabbath, he introduced
some severe strictures upon the vices to which princes
were addicted, their oppression, ignorance, hatred of virtue, attachment to bad company, and fondness for foolish pleasures. Information of this discourse was quickly conveyed to the queen, with many exaggerations; and
the preacher was next day ordered to attend at the palace. Being conveyed into the royal chamber, where the
queen sat with her maids of honour and principal counsellors, he was accused of having spoken of her majesty
irreverently, and in such a manner as to bring her under
the contempt and hatred of her subjects.

Knox
again
ordered
into the
royal
presence.

After the queen had made a long speech on that theme,
he was allowed to state his defence. He told her majesty, that she had been treated as persons usually were
who refused to attend the preaching of the word of God:
she had been obliged to trust to the false reports of flatterers. For, if she had heard the calumniated discourse,
he did not believe she could have been offended with any
thing that he had said. She would now, therefore, be
pleased to hear him repeat, as exactly as he could, what
he had preached yesterday. Having done this, he added,
"If any man, madam, will say, that I spake more, let
him presently accuse me." Several of the company attested that he had given a just report of the sermon.
The queen, after turning round to the informers, who
were dumb, told him, that his words, though sharp

enough as related by himself, were reported to her in a different way. She added, that she knew that her uncles and he were of a different religion, and therefore did not blame him for having no good opinion of them; but if he heard any thing about her conduct which displeased him, he should come to herself, and she would be willing to hear him. Knox easily saw through the artifice of this fair proposal. He replied, that he was willing to do any thing for her Majesty's contentment, which was consistent with his office; if her Grace chused to attend the public sermons, she would hear what pleased or displeased him in her and in others: or if she pleased to appoint a time when she would hear the substance of the doctrine which he preached in public, he would most gladly wait upon her Grace's pleasure, time, and place: but to come and wait at her chamber-door, and then to have liberty only to whisper in her ear what people thought and said of her, that would neither his conscience nor his office permit him to do. "For," added he, in a strain which he sometimes used even on serious occasions, "albeit at your Grace's commandment, I am heir now, yit can I not tell quhat uther men shall judge of me, that, at this tyme of day, am absent from my buke, and waiting upoun the court." "Ye will not alwayes be at your buke," said the queen pettishly, and turned her back.

"He is not afraid!" As he left the room "with a reasounable merry countenance," some of the popish attendants said in his hearing, "He is not afraid!" "Why sould the plesing face of a gentilwoman afray me?" said he, regarding them with a sarcastic scowl, "I have luiked in the faces of mony angry men, and yit have not bene affrayed above measour."

There was at this time but one place of worship in the city of Edinburgh. The number of inhabitants was indeed small, when compared with its present population; but still they must have formed a very large congregation. The place used for worship in St. Giles's church was capacious: on some occasions, three thousand persons assembled in it to hear sermon. In this church, Knox had, since 1560, performed all the parts of ministerial duty, without any other assistant but John Cairns, who acted as reader. He preached twice every Sabbath, and thrice on other days of the week. He met regularly once every week with the session of the parish, for discipline, and with the assembly of the neighbourhood, for the exercise on the scriptures. He attended, besides, the meetings of the provincial synod, and General Assembly; and at almost every meeting of the last mentioned court, he received an appointment to visit and preach in some distant part of the country. These labours must have been oppressive to a constitution which was already impaired ; especially as he did not indulge in extemporaneous effusions, but devoted a part of every day to study. His parish were sensible of this ; and, in April 1562, the Town Council came to an unanimous resolution to solicit John Craig, the minister of Canongate, or Holyroodhouse, to undertake the half of the charge. The ensuing General Assembly approved of the council's proposal, and appointed Craig to remove to Edinburgh. His translation did not, however, take place before June 1563, owing, as it would seem, to the difficulty of obtaining an additional stipend.

During the autumn of 1562, the Roman Catholics entertained great hopes of a change in their favour. After several unsuccessful attempts to cut off the principal Protestant courtiers, the Earl of Huntly openly took arms in the north, to rescue the queen from their hands; while the archbishop of St. Andrews endeavoured to unite and rouse the Papists of the south. On this occasion, our Reformer acted with his usual zeal and foresight. Being appointed by the General Assembly a commissioner to visit the churches of the west, he persuaded the gentlemen of that quarter to enter into a new bond of defence. Hastening into Galloway and Nithsdale, he, by his sermons and conversation, confirmed the Protestants of these places. He employed the master of

PERIOD
VI.
1560–1563
A.D.

John
Craig

Maxwell to write to the Earl of Bothwell, who had escaped from confinement, and meant, it was feared, to join Huntly. He himself wrote to the Duke of Chastelherault, warning him not to listen to the solicitations of his brother, the archbishop, nor accede to a conspiracy which would infallibly prove the ruin of his house. By these means, the southern parts of the kingdom were preserved in a state of peace, while the vigorous measures of the council crushed the rebellion in the north. The queen expressed little satisfaction at the victory, and there is every reason to think, that if she was not privy to the rising of Huntly, she expected to turn it to the advancement of her projects. She scrupled not to say, at this time, that she "hoped, before a year was expired, to have the mass and Catholic profession restored through the whole kingdom."

While these hopes were indulged, the Popish clergy thought it necessary to gain credit to their cause, by appearing more openly in defence of their tenets than they had lately done. They began to preach publicly, and boasted that they were ready to dispute with the Protestant ministers. The person who stepped forward as their champion was Quintin Kennedy, uncle of the Earl of Cassilis, and abbot of Crossraguel. The abbot appears to have spent the greater part of his life in the same negligence of the duties of his office with the rest of his brethren; but he was roused from his inactivity by the success of the Protestant preachers, who, in the years 1556 and 1557, attacked the Popish faith, and inveighed against the idleness and corruption of the clergy. At an age when others retire from the field, he began to rub up his long neglected theological weapons, and to gird on his armour.

His first appearance was in 1558, when he published a short system of Catholic tactics, under the title of Ane Compendious Tractive, shewing "the nerrest and onlie way" to establish the conscience of a Christian man, in all matters which were in debate concerning faith and re-

Quintin
Kennedy.

ligion. This way was no other than that of implicit faith in the decisions of the church or clergy. The scripture was only a witness, the church was the judge, in every controversy, whose determinations, in general councils canonically assembled, were to be humbly received and submitted to by all the faithful. This was no doubt the most compendious and nearest way of establishing the conscience of every Christian man, and deciding every controversy which might arise, without examination, reasoning, and debate.

But as the stubborn reformers would not submit to this easy and short mode of decision, the abbot was reluctantly obliged to enter the lists of argument with them. Accordingly, when Willock preached in his neighbourhood, in the beginning of 1559, he challenged him to a dispute on the sacrifice of the mass. The challenge was accepted, the time and place were fixed; but the abbot refused to appear, unless his antagonist would previously engage to submit to the interpretations of Scripture which had been given by the ancient doctors of the church. From this time he seems to have made the mass the great subject of his study, and endeavoured to qualify himself for defending this key-stone of the Popish arch.

George Hay having been sent by the General Assembly to preach in Carrick and Cunningham, during the autumn of 1562, Kennedy offered to dispute with him; but no meeting took place between them. On the 30th of August, the abbot read in his chapel of Kirk Oswald, a number of articles respecting the mass, purgatory, praying to saints, the use of images, &c., which he said he would defend against any who should impugn them, and promised to declare his mind more fully respecting them on the following Sunday. Knox, who was in the vicinity, came to Kirk Oswald on that day, with the design of hearing the abbot, and granting him the disputation which he had courted. The abbot not making his appearance, he himself preached in the chapel. When he

Knox at Kirk Oswald.

came down from the pulpit, there was a letter from Kennedy put into his hand, stating, that he understood he had come to that country to seek disputation, and offering to meet with him on the following Sunday in any house in Maybole, provided there were not more than twenty persons on each side admitted. Knox replied, that he had come, not purposely to dispute, but to preach the gospel; he was, however, willing to meet with him; he was under a previous engagement to be in Dumfries on the day mentioned by the abbot, but if he sent him his articles, he would, with all convenient speed, return and fix a time.

Knox accepts the challenge.

A correspondence was carried on between them on this subject, which is fully as curious as the dispute which ensued. Knox wished that his reasoning should be as public as the abbot had made his articles, and proposed that it should take place in St. John's church in Ayr; but the abbot refused to dispute publicly. The earl of Cassilis wrote to Knox, expressing his disapprobation of the proposed disputation, as unlikely to do any good, and calculated to endanger the public peace; to which the Reformer replied, by signifying, that his relation had given the challenge, which he was resolved not to decline, and that his lordship ought to encourage him to keep the appointment, from which no bad effects were to be dreaded. Upon this the abbot, feeling his honour touched, wrote a letter to the Reformer, in which he told him that he would have "rencountered" him the last time he was in the country, had it not been for the interposition of the earl of Cassilis, and charged him with stirring up his nephew to write that letter, in order to bring him into disgrace. "Ye sal be assured," says he, "I sal keip day and place in Mayboill, according to my writing, and I haif my life, and my feit louse;" and in another letter to Knox and the bailies of Ayr, he says, "keip your promes, and pretex na joukrie, be my lorde of Cassilis writing." The abbot being in this state of mind, the conditions of the combat were speedily settled.

The disputants agree to meet in Maybole.

They agreed to meet on the 28th of September, at eight o'clock *ante meridiem*, in the house of the provost of Maybole Forty persons on each side were to be admitted as witnesses of the dispute, with " as many mo as the house might goodly hold, at the sight of my lord of Cassilis." And notaries or scribes were appointed to record the papers which might be given in by the parties, and the arguments which they advanced in the course of reasoning, to prevent unnecessary repetition, or a false report of the proceedings. These conditions were formally subscribed by the abbot and the Reformer, on the day preceding the meeting.

When they met, " John Knox addressed him to make publick prayer, whereat the abbot was soir offended at the first, but whil the said John wold in nowise be stayed, he and his gave audience; which being ended, the abbote said, Be my faith, it is weill said." The reasoning commenced by reading a paper presented by the abbot, in which, after rehearsing the occasion of his present appearance, and protesting that his entering into dispute was not to be understood as implying that the points in question were disputable or dubious, being already determined by lawful general councils, he declared his readiness to defend the articles which he had exhibited, beginning with that concerning the sacrifice of the mass. To this paper Knox gave in a written answer in the course of the disputation : in the meantime, after stating his opinion respecting general councils, he proceeded to the article in dispute. It was requisite, he said, to state clearly and distinctly the subject in controversy; and he thought it contained the four following things, the name, the form and action, the opinion entertained of it, and the actor with the authority which he had to do what he pretended to do : all of which he was prepared to shew were destitute of any foundation in scripture. The abbot was aware of the difficulty of managing the dispute on such broad ground, and he had taken up ground of his own, which he thought he could

maintain against his antagonist. "As to the masse
that he will impung," said he, "or any mannes masse,
yea, and it war the paipes awin masse, I wil mantein na
thing but Jesus Christes masse, conforme to my article,
as it is written, and diffinition contened in my buik,
quhilk he hes tane on hand to impung."

Knox expressed his delight at hearing the abbot say
that he would defend nothing but the mass of Christ, for
if he adhered to this, they were "on the verray point of
an christiane agrement," as he was ready to allow whatever could be shewn to have been instituted by Christ.

As to his lordship's book, he confessed he had not read
it, and (without excusing his negligence,) requested the
definition to be read to him from it.   The abbot qualified his assertion, by saying, that he meant to defend no
other mass, except that which in its "substance, institution, and effect," was appointed by Christ; and he defin-
ed the mass, as concerning the substance and effect, to
be the sacrifice and oblation of the Lord's body and blood,
given and offered by him in the last supper; and for the
first confirmation of this, he rested upon the oblation
of bread and wine by Melchizedeck.   His argument was,
that the scripture declared that Christ was a priest after
the order of Melchizedeck: Melchizedeck offered bread
and wine to God : therefore Christ offered or made oblation of his body and blood in the last supper, which
was the only instance in which the priesthood of Christ
and Melchizedeck could agree.

Knox said that the ceremonies of the mass, and the
opinion entertained of it, as procuring remission of sins
to the quick and the dead, were viewed as important
parts of it, and having a strong hold of the consciences of
the people, ought to be taken into the argument ; but as
the abbot declared himself willing to defend these afterwards, he would proceed to the substance, and proposed,
in the first place, to fix the sense in which the word
sacrifice or oblation was used in the argument.   There
were sacrifices *propitiatoriæ, for expiation,* and *eucharis-*

ticœ, of thanksgiving; in which last sense the mortification of the body, prayer, and alms-giving, were called
sacrifices in Scripture. He wished, therefore, to know
whether the abbot understood the word in the first or
second of these senses in this dispute. The abbot said,
that he would not at present dispute what his opponent
meant by a sacrifice *propitiatorium;* but he held the
sacrifice on the cross to be the only sacrifice of redemption, and that of the mass to be the sacrifice of commemoration of the death and passion of Christ. Knox
replied, that the chief head which he intended to impugn
seemed to be yielded by the abbot ; and he, for his part,
cheerfully granted, that there was a commemoration of
Christ's death in the right use of the ordinance of the
supper.

The abbot insisted that he should proceed to impugn
the warrant which he had taken from Scripture for his
article. " Protesting," said the Reformer, " that this
mekle is win, that the sacrifice of the messe being denied
by me to be a sacrifice *propitiatorie* for the sins of the
quick and the dead, (according to the opinion thereof
before conceaved) hath no patron at the present, I am
content to procede."—" I protest he hes win nothing of
me as yit, and referres it to black and quhite contened
in our writing."—" I have openlie denied the masse to be
an sacrifice propitiatorie for the quick, &c., and the
defence thereof is denied. And, therefore, I referre me
unto the same judges that my lord hath clamed."—" Ye
may denie quhat ye pleis ; for all that ye denie I tak not
presentlie to impung ; but quhair I began thair will I
end, that is, to defend the messe conform to my artickle."
" Your lordship's ground," said Knox, after some altercation, " is, that Melchizedeck is the figure of Christe in
that he did offer unto God bread and wine, and that it
behoved Jesus Christ to offer, in his latter supper, his
body and blude, under the forms of bread and wine. I
answer to your ground yet againe, that Melchizedeck
offered neither bread nor wine *unto God;* and therefore,

it that ye would thereupon conclude hath no assurance of your ground." "Preve that," said the abbot. Knox replied, that, according to the rules of just reasoning, he could not be bound to prove a negative; that it was incumbent on his opponent to bring forward some proof for his affirmation, concerning which the text was altogether silent; and that until the abbot did this, it was sufficient for him simply to deny. But the abbot said, he "stuck to his text," and insisted that his antagonist should shew for what purpose Melchizedeck brought out the bread and wine, if it was not to offer it unto God. After protesting that the abbot's ground remained destitute of any support, and that he was not bound in argument to shew what became of the bread and wine, or what use was made of them, Knox consented to state his opinion, that they were intended by Melchizedeck to refresh Abraham and his company. The abbot had now gained what he wished; and he had a number of objections ready to start against this view of the words, by which he was able at least to protract and involve the dispute. And thus ended the first day's contest.

Second day's contest.

When the company convened on the following day, the abbot proceeded to impugn the view which his opponent had given of the text. He urged first, that Abraham and his company had a sufficiency of provision in the spoils which they had taken from the enemy in their late victory, and did not need Melchizedeck's bread and wine; and, secondly, that the text said that Melchizedeck brought them forth, and it was improbable that one man, and he a king, should carry as much as would refresh three hundred and eighteen men. To these objections Knox made such replies as will occur to any person who thinks on the subject. In this manner did the second day pass. When they met on the third day, the abbot presented a paper, in which he stated another objection to Knox's view of the text. After some more altercation on the subject, Knox desired his opponent to proceed to the promised proof of the argument upon which he had rested his cause. But the abbot, being indisposed, rose up, and put into Knox's hand a book to which he referred him for the proof. By this time, the noblemen and gentlemen present were completely wearied out. For besides the tedious and uninteresting mode in which the disputation had been managed, they could find entertainment neither for themselves nor for their retinue in Maybole; so that if any person had brought in bread and wine among them, it is presumable that they would not have debated long upon the purpose for which it was brought. Knox proposed that they should adjourn to Ayr and finish the dispute, which was refused by the abbot, who said he would come to Edinburgh for that purpose, provided he could obtain the queen's permission. Upon this the company dismissed.

The abbot, or his friends, having circulated the report that he had the advantage in the disputation, Knox afterwards published the account of it from the records of the notaries, and added a prologue and short marginal notes. The prologue and his answer to the abbot's first paper, especially the latter, are pieces of good writing. I have been more minute in the narration of this dispute than its merits deserve, because no account of it has hitherto appeared, the tract itself being so exceedingly rare, as to have been seen by few for a long period.

Another priest who advocated the Roman Catholic cause at this time was Ninian Wingate, who had been schoolmaster of Linlithgow, from which situation he was removed by Spottiswood, superintendent of Lothian, on account of his attachment to Popery. In the month of February 1562, he sent to Knox a writing, consisting of eighty-three questions upon the principal topics of dispute between the Papists and Protestants, which he had drawn up in the name of the inferior clergy and laity of the Catholic persuasion in Scotland. To some of these, particularly the questions which related to the

Ninian
Wingate.

call of the Protestant ministers, the Reformer returned an answer from the pulpit, and Wingate addressed several letters to him, complaining that his answers were not satisfactory. These letters, with addresses to the queen, nobility, bishops, and magistrates of Edinburgh, Wingate committed to the press, but the impression being seized in the printer's house (according to bishop Lesley), the author escaped and went to the continent. Knox intended to publish an answer to Wingate's questions, and to defend the validity of the Protestant ministry; but it does not appear that he carried his intention into execution.

In the beginning of 1563, Knox went to Jedburgh, by appointment of the General Assembly, to investigate a scandal which had broken out against Paul Methven, the minister of that place, who was suspected of adultery. The accused was found guilty, and excommunicated. He fled to England, but having afterwards returned and offered to submit to the discipline of the church, a severe and humiliating course of public repentance was prescribed to him. He went through a part of it, with professions of deep sorrow; but overwhelmed with shame, or despairing to regain his lost reputation, he stopped in the midst of it, and again retired to England. Prudential considerations were not awanting to induce the reformed church of Scotland to stifle this fama, and screen from public ignominy a man who had acted a distinguished part in the late Reformation of religion. But they refused to listen to these; and by instituting a strict scrutiny into the fact, and inflicting an exemplary punishment upon the criminal, they "approved themselves to be clear in this matter," and effectually shut the mouths of their Popish adversaries.

Rigorous
discipline.

The mode of public repentance enjoined on this occasion was appointed to be afterwards used in all cases of aggravated immorality. There was nothing in which the Scottish reformers approached nearer to the primi-

tive church than in the rigorous and impartial exercise
of ecclesiastical discipline, the relaxation of which, under
the Papacy, they justly regarded as one great cause of
the universal corruption of religion. While they rejected many of the ceremonies in worship which were used
by the Christians during the three first centuries after
the time of the apostles, they, from detestation of vice,
and a desire to restrain it, did not scruple to conform to
a number of their penitentiary regulations. In some
instances, they might carry their rigour against offenders
to an extreme; but it was a virtuous extreme, compared
with the dangerous laxity, or rather total disuse of discipline, which has gradually crept into almost all the
churches which retain the name of reformed: even as
the scrupulous delicacy with which our forefathers
shunned the society of those who had transgressed the
rules of morality, is to be preferred to modern manners,
by which the virtuous and vicious are equally admitted
to good company.

> 'Twas heard perhaps on here and there a waif,
> Desirous to return, and not received:
> But was an wholesome rigour in the main,
> And taught the unblemished to preserve with care
> That purity, whose loss was loss of all.
> ———————— But now——yes, now,
> We are become so candid and so fair,
> So liberal in construction, and so rich
> In Christian charity, (good-natured age!)
> That they are safe, sinners of either sex,
> Transgress what laws they may.
>
> COWPER, Task, B. iii.

PERIOD
VI.
1560 – 1563
A.D.

In the month of May, the queen sent for Knox to
Lochlevin. The Popish priests, presuming upon her
avowed partiality to them, and secret promises of protection, had of late become more bold, and during the
late Easter, masses had been openly celebrated in the
different parts of the kingdom. The queen in council
had issued various proclamations against this, but as the
execution had hitherto been left to her, nothing had followed upon them. The Protestants of the west, who

Knox sum-
moned to
Loch-
levin.

8

were the most zealous, perceiving that the laws were eluded, resolved to execute them, without making any application to the court, and apprehended some of the offenders by way of example. These decided proceedings highly offended the queen, as they were calculated to defeat the scheme of policy which she had formed; but finding that the signification of her displeasure had not the effect of stopping them, she wished to avail herself of the Reformer's influence for accomplishing her purpose.

She dealt with him very earnestly, for two hours before, supper to persuade the western gentlemen to desist from all interruption of the Catholic worship. He told her majesty, that if she would exercise her authority in executing the laws of the land, he could promise for the peaceable behaviour of the Protestants; but if her majesty thought to elude them, he feared there were some who would let the Papists understand that they should not offend with impunity. "Will ye allow, that they shall take my sword in their hands?" said the queen. "The sword of justice is God's," replied the Reformer with equal firmness, "and is given to princes and rulers for one end, which if they transgress, sparing the wicked and oppressing the innocent, they who, in the fear of God, execute judgment where God has commanded, offend not God, although kings do it not." He added, that the gentlemen of the west were acting strictly according to law; for the act of parliament gave power to all judges within their bounds, to search for and punish those who should transgress its enactments. He concluded with advising her majesty to consider the terms of the mutual contract between her and her subjects, and that she could not expect to receive obedience from them, if she did not grant unto them protection, and the execution of justice. The queen broke off the conversation with evident marks of displeasure.

The queen displeased

Having communicated what had passed between them to the earl of Murray, (which was the title now conferred on the prior of St. Andrews), Knox meant to return to

Edinburgh next day, without waiting for any further communication with the queen. But a message was delivered him early in the morning, desiring him not to depart until he had again spoken to her majesty. He accordingly met with her west from Kinross, where she took the amusement of hawking. This interview was very different from that of the preceding evening. Waving entirely the subject on which they had differed, she introduced a variety of topics, upon which she conversed with the greatest familiarity and apparent confidence. Lord Ruthven, she said, had offered her a ring; but she could not love him. She knew that he used enchantment; and yet he was made one of her privy council. Lethington, she said, was the sole cause of that appointment. "I understand," said she, introducing another subject of discourse, "that ye are appointed to go to Dumfries, for the election of a superintendent to be established in these countries." He answered in the affirmative. "But I understand the bishop of Athens would be superintendent." "He is one, madam, that is put in election." "If you knew him as well as I do, you would not promote him to that office, nor yet to any other within your kirk." Knox said that he deceived many more than him, if he did not fear God. "Well, do as you will; but that man is a dangerous man."

When Knox was about to take his leave of her majesty, she pressed him to stay. "I have one of the greatest matters that have touched me since I came into this realm to open to you, and I must have your help in it," said she, with an air of condescension and confidence as enchanting as if she had put a ring on his finger. She then entered into a long discourse concerning a domestic difference between the earl of Argyle and his lady. Her ladyship had not, she said, been so circumspect in every thing as she could have wished, but still she was of opinion that his lordship had not treated her in an honest and godly manner. Knox said that he was not unacquainted with the disagreeable variance which had subsisted between that honourable couple, and, before her majesty's arrival in this country, he had effected a reconciliation. On that occasion, the countess had promised not to complain to any creature before acquainting him; and as he had never heard from her, he concluded that there was nothing but concord. "Well," said the queen, "it is worse than ye believe. But do this much, for my sake, as once again to put them at unity, and if she behave not herself as she ought to do, she shall find no favour of me; but in any wise let not my lord know that I have requested you in this matter." Then introducing the subject of their reasoning on the preceding evening, she said, "I promise to do as ye required: I shall cause summon all offenders; and ye shall know that I shall minister justice." "I am assured then," said he, "that ye shall please God, and enjoy rest and tranquillity within your realm, which to your majesty is more profitable than all the pope's power can be." Upon this he took his leave of the queen.

This interview strikingly exhibits one part of queen Mary's character. It shews how far she was capable of dissembling, what artifice she could employ, and what condescensions she could make, in order to accomplish the schemes upon which she was bent. She had formerly attacked the Reformer on another quarter without success; she now resolved to try if she could soothe his stern temper by flattering his vanity, and disarm his jealousy by strong marks of confidence. There is some reason to think that she partly succeeded in her design. For though he was not very susceptible of flattery, and must have been struck with the sudden change in the queen's views and behaviour, there are few minds that can altogether resist the impression made by the condescending familiarity of persons of superior rank; and our feelings, on such occasions, chide as uncharitable the cold suspicions suggested by our judgment. In obedience to her majesty's request, he wrote a letter to the earl of Argyle, which was not very pleasing to that nobleman.

From deference to the opinion which she had expressed of the bishop of Galloway, he inquired more narrowly into his conduct, and postponed the election. And the report which he gave of the queen's gracious answer operated in her favour on the public mind.

But if his zeal suffered a temporary intermission, it soon re-kindled with fresh ardour. On the 19th of May, the archbishop of St. Andrews and a number of the principal Papists were arraigned, by the queen's orders, before the lord Justice-General, for transgressing the laws; and having come in her Majesty's will, were committed to ward. But this was merely a stroke of policy, to enable her more easily to carry her measures in the parliament which met on the following day.

This was the first parliament which had met since the queen's arrival in Scotland; and it was natural to expect that they would proceed to ratify the treaty of peace made in July 1560, and the establishment of the protestant religion. If the acts of the former parliament were invalid, as the queen had repeatedly declared, the protestants had no law on their side; they held their religion at the mercy of their sovereign, and might be required, at her pleasure, to submit to popery, as the religion which still possessed the legal establishment. But so well had she laid her plans, such was the effect of her insinuating address, and, above all, so powerful was the temptation of self-interest on the minds of the protestant leaders, that, by general consent, they passed from this demand, and lost the only favourable opportunity, during the reign of Mary, for giving a legal security to the reformed religion, and thereby r moving one principal source of jealousies. An act of oblivion, securing indemnity to those who had been engaged in the late civil war, was indeed passed; but the mode of its enactment virtually implied the invalidity of the treaty in which it had been originally embodied; and the protestants, on their bended knees, supplicated, as a boon from their sovereign, what they had formerly won with their swords, and repeatedly demanded as their right. The other acts made to please the more zealous reformers were expressed with such studied and glaring ambiguity, as to offer an insult to their understandings.

Our Reformer was thunderstruck when first informed of the measures which were in agitation, and could scarcely believe them serious. He immediately procured an interview with some of the principal members of parliament, to whom he represented the danger of allowing that meeting to dissolve without obtaining the ratification of the acts of the preceding parliament, or at least those acts which established the Reformation. They alleged that the queen would never have agreed to call this meeting, if they had persisted in these demands; but there was a prospect of her speedy marriage, and on that occasion they would obtain all their wishes. In vain he reminded them that poets and painters had represented *Occasion* with a bald hind-head; in vain he urged, that the event to which they looked forward would be accompanied with difficulties of its own, which would require all their skill and circumspection. Their determination was fixed. He now perceived the full extent of the queen's dissimulation; and the selfishness and servility of the protestant leaders affected him deeply.

Rupture between Knox and Murray.

So hot was the altercation between the Earl of Murray and him on this subject, that an open rupture ensued. He had long looked upon that nobleman as one of the most steady and sincere adherents to the reformed cause; and therefore felt the greater disappointment at his conduct. Under his first irritation he wrote a letter to the earl, in which, after reminding him of his condition at the time when they first became acquainted in London, and the honours to which providence had now raised him, he solemnly renounced friendship with him as one who preferred his own interest and the pleasure of his sister to the advancement of religion, left him to the guidance of the new counsellors which he had chosen, and exonerated him from all future concern in his affairs. This variance, which continued nearly two years, was very gratifying to the queen and others, who disliked their former familiarity, and failed not, as Knox informs us, to "cast oil into the flame, until God did quench it by the water of affliction."

Before the dissolution of the parliament, the Reformer embraced an opportunity of disburdening his mind in the presence of the greater part of the members assembled in his church. After discoursing of the great mercy of God shewn to Scotland, in marvellously delivering them from bondage of soul and body, and of the deep ingratitude which he perceived in all ranks of persons, he addressed himself particularly to the nobility. He praised God that he had an opportunity of pouring out the sorrows of his heart in their presence, who could attest the truth of all that he had spoken. He appealed to their consciences if he had not, in their greatest extremities, exhorted them to depend upon God, and assured them of preservation and victory, if they preferred his glory to their own lives and secular interests. " I have been with you in your most desperate temptations," continued he, in a strain of impassioned eloquence : " in your most extreme dangers I have been with you. St. Johnston, Cupar-moor, and the Craggs of Edinburgh, are yet recent in my heart ; yea, that dark and dolorous night wherein all ye, my lords, with shame and fear, left this town, is yet in my mind, and God forbid that ever I forget it ! What was, I say, my exhortation to you, and what has fallen in vain of all that ever God promised unto you by my mouth, ye yourselves yet live to testify. There is not one of you against whom was death and destruction threatened perished ; and how many of your enemies has God plagued before your eyes ? Shall this be the thankfulness that ye shall render unto your God ? To betray his cause, when ye have it in your hands to establish it as you please ?" He saw nothing, he said, " but a cowardly desertion of Christ's standard.

Knox unburdens his mind.

Some had even the effrontery to say that they had neither law nor parliament for their religion. They had the authority of God for their religion, the truth of which was independent of human laws; but it was also accepted within this realm in public parliament; and that parliament he would maintain to have been as lawful as any ever held in the kingdom.

In the conclusion of his discourse, he adverted to the reports of her majesty's marriage, and the princes who courted this alliance; and, desiring the audience to mark his words, predicted the consequences which were to be dreaded, if ever the nobility consented that their sovereign should marry a Papist.

Protestants as well as Papists were offended with the freedom of this sermon, and some who had been most familiar with the preacher now shunned his company. Flatterers were not wanting to run to the queen, and inform her that John Knox had preached against her marriage. After surmounting the opposition to her measures, and managing so successfully the haughty and independent barons of her kingdom, Mary was incensed that there should yet be one man of obscure condition, who ventured to condemn her proceedings; and as she could not tame his stubbornness, she determined to punish his temerity. Knox was ordered instantly to appear before her. Lord Ochiltree, with several gentlemen, accompanied him to the palace; but the superintendent of Angus alone was allowed to go with him into the royal presence.

Knox
again or-
dered to
the pres-
ence of
the queen.

Her majesty received him in a very different manner from what she had done at Lochlevin. Never had prince been handled, she passionately exclaimed, as she was: she had borne with him in all his rigorous speeches against herself and her uncles; she had sought his favour by all means; she had offered unto him audience whenever he pleased to admonish her. "And yet," said she, "I cannot be quit of you. I vow to God I shall be once revenged."—On pronouncing these words with great violence, she burst into a flood of tears which interrupted her speech. When the queen had composed herself, he proceeded calmly to make his defence. Her grace and he had, he said, at different times been engaged in controversy, and he never before perceived her offended with him. When it should please God to deliver her from the bondage of error in which she had been trained through want of instruction in the truth, he trusted that her majesty would not find the liberty of his tongue offensive. Out of the pulpit he thought few had occasion to be offended with him; but there he was not master of himself, but bound to obey Him who commanded him to speak plainly, and to flatter no flesh on the face of the earth.

"But what have you to do with my marriage?" said the queen. He was proceeding to state the extent of his commission as a preacher, and the reasons which led him to touch on that delicate subject; but she interrupted him by repeating her question; "What have ye to do with my marriage? Or what are you in this commonwealth?"—"A subject born within the same, madam," replied the Reformer, piqued by the last question, and the contemptuous tone in which it was proposed. "And albeit I be neither earl, lord, nor baron in it, yet has God made me (how abject that ever I be in your eyes) a profitable member within the same. Yea, madam, to me it appertains no less to forewarn of such things as may hurt it, if I foresee them, than it doth to any of the nobility; for both my vocation and conscience requires plainness of me. And therefore, madam, to yourself I say that which I spake in public place: "Whensoever the nobility of this realm shall consent that ye be subject to an unfaithful husband, they do as much as in them lieth to renounce Christ, to banish his truth from them, to betray the freedom of this realm, and perchance shall in the end do small comfort to yourself." At these words, the queen began again to weep and sob with great bitterness. The superintendent, who was a man of mild and gentle spirit, tried to mitigate her grief and resentment: he praised her beauty and her accomplishments; and told her, that there was not a prince in Europe who would not reckon himself happy in gaining her hand. During this scene, the severe and inflexible mind of the Reformer displayed itself. He continued silent, and with unaltered countenance, until the queen had given vent to her feelings. He then protested, that he never took delight in the distress of any creature; it was with great difficulty that he could see his own boys weep when he corrected them for their faults, far less could he rejoice in her majesty's tears: but seeing he had given her no just reason of offence, and had only discharged his duty, he was constrained, though unwillingly, to sustain her tears, rather than hurt his conscience, and betray the commonwealth through his silence.

This apology inflamed the queen still more: she ordered him immediately to leave her presence, and wait the signification of her pleasure in the adjoining room. There he stood as "one whom men had never seen;" all his friends (lord Ochiltree excepted) being afraid to shew him the smallest countenance. In this situation he addressed himself to the court-ladies, who sat in their richest dress in the chamber. "O fair ladies, how plesing war this lyfe of yours, if it sould ever abyde, and then, in the end, that we might pas to hevin with all this gay gear!" Having engaged them in a conversation, he passed the time till Erskine came and informed him, that he was allowed to go home until her majesty had taken further advice. The queen insisted to have the judgment of the lords of Articles, whether the words he had used in the pulpit were not actionable; but she was persuaded to desist from a prosecution. "And so that storme quietit in appearance, bot nevir in the hart."

No expressions are sufficiently strong to describe the horror which many feel at the monstrous insensibility and inhumanity of Knox, in remaining unmoved, while "youth, beauty, and royal dignity" were dissolved in

tears before him. Enchanting, surely, must the charms
of the queen of Scots have been, and iron-hearted the
Reformer who could resist their impression, when they
continue to this day to exercise such a sway over the
hearts of men, that even grave and serious authors, not
addicted to the language of gallantry and romance, can
protest that they cannot read of the tears which she shed
on this occasion, without feeling an inclination to weep
along with her. There may be some, however, who,
knowing how much real misery there is in the world,
are not disposed to waste their feelings unnecessarily,
and who are of opinion, that there was not much to com-
miserate in the condition of the queen, nor to reprobate
in the conduct of the Reformer. Considering that she
had been so fortunate in her measures, and found her
nobility so ready to gratify her wishes, the passion by
which she suffered herself to be transported was extravagant, and her tears must have been those of anger and
not of grief. On the other hand, when we consider that
Knox was at this time deserted by his friends, and stood
almost alone in resisting the will of a princess, who accomplished her measures chiefly by caresses and tears,
we may be disposed to form a more favourable idea of
his conduct and motives. We behold not, indeed, the
enthusiastic lover, mingling his tears with those of his
mistress, and vowing to revenge her wrongs; nor the
man of nice sensibility, who loses every other consideration in the gratification of his feelings; but we behold
what is more rare, the stern patriot, the rigid reformer,
who, in the discharge of his duty, and in a public cause,
can withstand the tide of tenderness as well as the storm
of passion. There have been times when such conduct
was regarded as the proof of a superior mind ; and the
man who, from such motives, " hearkened not to the wife
of his bosom, nor knew his own children," has been the
object not of censure, but admiration, in sacred as well
as pagan story.

Fertur pudicæ conjugis osculum,
Parvosque natos, ut capitis minor,
Ab se removisse, et virilem
Torvus humi posuisse vultum.   HOR. lib. iii. Od. v.

When Knox lay under the displeasure of the court,
and had lost the confidence of his principal friends, his
enemies judged it a favourable opportunity for attacking
him in (what was universally allowed to be irreproachable) his moral conduct.   At the very time that he was
engaged in scrutinizing the scandal against Methven, and
inflicting upon him the highest censure of the church, it
was alleged that he himself was guilty of a similar
crime.   Euphemia Dundas, an inhabitant of Edinburgh,
inveighing one day, in the presence of a circle of her acquaintances, against the protestant doctrine and ministers, said, among other things, that John Knox had been
a common whoremonger all his days, and that, within a
few days past, he "was apprehendit and tane furth of
ane killogye with ane commoun hure."   This might perhaps have been passed over by Knox and the church as
an effusion of popish spleen, and female scandal; but the
recent occurrence at Jedburgh, the situation in which
the Reformer at present stood, the public manner in
which the charge had been brought, and the specification
of a particular instance, seemed to them to justify and
call for a legal prosecution.   Accordingly, the clerk of
the General Assembly, on the 18th of June, gave in a
formal representation and petition to the Town Council,
praying that the woman might be called before them,
and the matter examined; that if the accusation was
found true, the accused might be punished with all rigour without partiality; and that, if false, the accuser
might be dealt with according to the demerit of her offence.   She was called, and, appearing before the Council,
Convicted flatly refused that she had ever used any such words;
calumny. although Knox's procurator afterwards produced respectable witnesses to prove that she had spoken them.
   This convicted calumny, which never gained the

smallest credit at the time, would scarcely have deserved notice, had it not been revived, after the Reformer's death, by the Popish writers, who, having caught hold of the report, and dressed it out in all the horrid colours which malice, or credulity could suggest, circulated it industriously, by their publications, through the continent. Though I had not been able to trace these slanders to their source, the atrocity of the imputed crimes, the unspotted reputation which the accused uniformly maintained among all his contemporaries, the glaring self-contradictions of the accusers, and, above all, the notour spirit of slander and wanton defamation for which they have long been stigmatized in the learned world, would have been grounds sufficient for rejecting such charges with detestation. Those who are acquainted with the writings of that period will not think that I speak too strongly.

PERIOD VI. 1560-1563 A.D.

The queen flattered herself that she had at last caught the Reformer in an offence, which would infallibly subject him to exemplary punishment. During her residence at Stirling, in the month of August, the domestics whom she had left behind her in Holyroodhouse celebrated the Popish worship with greater publicity than had been usual when she herself was present; and at the time when the sacrament of the Supper was dispensed in Edinburgh, they revived certain superstitious practices which had been laid aside by the Roman Catholics, since the establishment of the Reformation. This boldness offended the Protestants, and some of them went down to the palace to mark the inhabitants who repaired to the service. Perceiving numbers entering, they burst into the chapel, and presenting themselves at the altar, which was prepared for mass, asked the priest, how he durst be so *malapert* as to proceed in that manner, when the queen was absent? Alarmed at this intrusion, the mistress of the household dispatched a messenger to the comptroller, who was attending sermon in St. Giles's church, desiring him to come instantly to

Holyroodhouse invaded.

PERIOD
VI.
1560-1563
A.D.

save her life and the palace. Having hurried down, accompanied with the magistrates, and a guard, the comptroller found every thing quiet and no appearance of tumult, except what was occasioned by the company which he brought along with him. When the report of this affair was conveyed to the queen, she declared her resolution not to return to Edinburgh unless this riot was punished, and indicted two of the Protestants, who had been most active, to stand trial "for forethought felony, hamesuckin, and invasion of the palace." Fearing that she intended to proceed to extremities against these men, and that their condemnation was a preparative to some hostile attempts against their religion, the Protestants in Edinburgh resolved that Knox, agreeably to a commission, should write a circular letter to the principal gentlemen of their persuasion, informing them of the circumstances, and requesting their presence on the day of trial. He wrote the letter according to their request. A copy of it having come into the hands of Sinclair, bishop of Ross, and president of the Court of Session, who was a great personal enemy to Knox, he conveyed it immediately to the queen at Stirling. She communicated it to the privy council, who, to her great satisfaction, pronounced it *treasonable;* but to give the greater solemnity to the proceedings, it was resolved that an extraordinary convention of the counsellors and other

Knox
cited to
appear before the
convention.

noblemen should be called to meet at Edinburgh, in the end of December, to try the cause. The Reformer was summoned to appear before this convention.

Previous to the day of trial, great influence was used in private to persuade or intimidate him to acknowledge a fault, and throw himself on the queen's mercy. This he peremptorily refused to do. The master of Maxwell (afterwards Lord Herries), with whom he had long been very intimate, threatened him with the loss of his friendship, and told him that he would repent, if he did not submit to the queen, for men would not bear with him as they had hitherto done. He replied, that he did not understand such language; he had never opposed her majesty except in the article of religion, and surely it was not meant that he should bow to her in that matter; if God stood by him, which he would do as long as he confided in him, and preferred His glory to his own life, he regarded little how men should behave towards him; nor did he know wherein they had borne with him, unless in hearing the word of God from his mouth, which, if they should reject, he would mourn for them, but the danger would be their own.

The Earl of Murray, and secretary Maitland, sent for him to the clerk register's house, and had a long conversation with him to the same purpose. They represented the pains which they had taken to mitigate the queen's resentment, and that nothing could save him but a timely submission. He gave them the same answer, that he never would confess a fault when he was conscious of none, and had not learned to cry treason at every thing which the multitude called treason, nor to fear what they feared. The wily secretary endeavoured to bring on a dispute on the subject, and to draw from him the defence which he meant to make for himself; but Knox, aware of his craft, declined the conversation, and told him that it would be foolish to intrust with his defences one who had already prejudged his cause.

On the day appointed for the trial, the public anxiety was greatly raised, and the palace-yard, with all the avenues, was crowded with people, who waited to learn the result. The pannel was conducted to the chamber in which the lords were already assembled, and engaged in consultation. When the queen had taken her seat and perceived Knox standing uncovered at the foot of the table, she burst into a loud fit of laughter. "That man," she said, "had made her weep, and shed never a tear himself: she would now see if she could make him weep." The secretary opened the proceedings, by stating in a speech addressed to the Reformer, the reasons why the queen had convened him before her nobility. "Let him acknowledge his own hand-writing," said the queen, " and then we shall judge of the contents of the letter." A copy of the circular letter being handed to him, he looked at the subscription, and said that it was his; and though he had subscribed a number of blanks, he had such confidence in the fidelity of the scribe, that he was ready to acknowledge both the subscription and the contents. " You have done more than I would have done," said Maitland. " Charity is not suspicious," replied the other. " Well, well," said the queen, " read your own letter, and then answer to such things as shall be demanded of you." " I will do the best I can," said he; and having read the letter with an audible voice, returned it to the queen's advocate, who was commanded to accuse him.

And examined in the royal presence.

" Heard you ever, my lords, a more despiteful and treasonable letter?" said the queen, looking round the table. " Mr. Knox, are you not sorry from your heart, and do you not repent that such a letter has passed your pen, and from you has come to the knowledge of others?" said Maitland. " My lord secretary, before I repent I must be taught my offence."—" Offence! if there were no more but the convocation of the queen's lieges, the offence cannot be denied."—" Remember yourself, my lord, there is a difference between a lawful convocation and an unlawful. If I have been guilty in this, I offended oft since I came last into Scotland; for what convocation of the brethren has ever been to this hour, unto which my pen served not?"—" Then was then, and now is now," said the secretary; " we have no need of such convocations as sometimes we have had."—" The time that has been is even now before my eyes," rejoined the Reformer; " for I see the poor flock in no less danger than it has been at any time before, except that the devil has got a vizor upon his face. Before he came in with his own face, discovered by open tyranny, seeking the destruction of all that refused idolatry; and then, I think, you will confess the breth-

ren lawfully assembled themselves for defence of their
lives: and now the devil comes under the cloak of justice, to do that which God would not suffer him to do
by strength"—

"What is this?" interrupted her majesty, who was
offended that the pannel should be allowed such liberty
of speech, and thought that she could bring him more
closely to the question. "What is this? Methinks
you trifle with him. Who gave him authority to make
convocation of my lieges? Is not that treason?" "No,
madam," replied Lord Ruthven, displeased at the active keenness which the queen shewed in the cause ; "for
he makes convocation of the people to hear prayer and
sermon almost daily; and whatever your Grace or others
will think thereof, we think it no treason."—"Hold
your peace," said the queen; "and let him make answer for himself."—"I began, madam," resumed Knox,
"to reason with the secretary (whom I take to be a better dialectician than your Grace) that all convocations
are not unlawful; and now my Lord Ruthven has given
the instance."—"I will say nothing against your religion, nor against your convening to your sermons; but
what authority have you to convocate my subjects
when you will, without my commandment?" He answered, that at his own will he had never convened four
persons in Scotland, but at the orders of his brethren he
had given many advertisements, and great multitudes
had assembled; and if her Grace complained that this
had been done without her command, he would answer,
that so was all that had been done as to the Reformation
of religion in this kingdom. He must, therefore, be
convicted by a just law, before he would profess sorrow for what he had done: he thought he had done no
wrong.

"You shall not escape so," said the queen. "Is it
not treason, my lords, to accuse a prince of cruelty? I
think there be acts of Parliament against such whisper-
ers." Several of their lordships said that there were

Trial con-
tinued.

such laws. "But wherein can I be accused of this?"—— "Read this part of your own bill," said the queen, who shewed herself an acute prosecutor. She then caused the following sentence to be read from his letter: "This fearful summons is directed against them, [the two persons who were indicated] to make no doubt a preparative on a few, that a door may be opened to execute cruelty upon a greater multitude."—"Lo!" exclaimed the queen exultingly; "what say you to that?" The eyes of the assembly were fixed on the pannel, anxious to know what answer he would make to this charge.

"Is it lawful for me, madam, to answer for myself? or, shall I be condemned unheard?"—"Say what you can; for I think you have enough to do."—"I will first then desire of your Grace, madam, and of this most honourable audience, Whether your Grace knows not, that the obstinate Papists are deadly enemies to all such as profess the gospel of Jesus Christ, and that they most earnestly desire the extermination of them, and of the true doctrine that is taught within this realm?"—The queen was silent: but the lords, with one voice, exclaimed, "God forbid, that ever the lives of the faithful, or yet the staying of the doctrine, stood in the power of the Papists! for just experience has taught us what cruelty lies in their hearts."—"I must proceed then," said the Reformer. "Seeing that I perceive that all will grant, that it were a barbarous thing to destroy such a multitude as profess the gospel of Christ within this realm, which oftener than once or twice they have attempted to do by force,—they, by God and by his providence being disappointed, have invented more crafty and dangerous practices, to wit, to make the prince a party under colour of law; and so what they could not do by open force, they shall perform by crafty deceit. For who thinks, my lords, that the insatiable cruelty of the Papists (within this realm I mean) shall end in the murdering of these two brethren, now unjustly summoned, and more unjustly to be accused?—And therefore, madam, cast up, when you list, the acts of your Parliament; I have offended nothing against them; for I accuse not, in my letter, your Grace, nor yet your nature, of cruelty. But I affirm yet again, that the pestilent Papists, who have inflamed your Grace against those poor men at this present, are the sons of the devil, and therefore must obey the desires of their father, who has been a liar and manslayer from the beginning."—" You forget yourself! you are not now in the pulpit," said one of the lords. " I am in the place where I am demanded of conscience to speak the truth; and therefore the truth I speak, impugn it whoso list." He added, again addressing the queen, that persons who appeared to be of honest, gentle, and meek natures, had often been corrupted by wicked counsel; that the Papists who had her ear were dangerous counsellors, and such her mother had found them to be.

Mary perceiving that nothing was to be gained by reasoning, began to upbraid him with his harsh behaviour to her, at their last interview. He spake "fair enough" at present before the lords, she said, but on that occasion he caused her to shed many salt tears, and said, " he set not by her weeping." This drew from him a vindication of his conduct, in which he gave a narration of that conference. After this, the secretary having spoken with the queen, told Knox that he was at liberty to return home for that night. " I thank God and the queen's majesty," said he.

When Knox had withdrawn, the judgment of the nobility was taken respecting his conduct. All of them, with the exception of the immediate dependents of the court, voted, that he was not guilty of any breach of the laws. The secretary, who had assured the queen of his condemnation, was enraged at this decision. He brought her majesty, who had retired before the vote, again into the room, and proceeded to call the votes a second time in her presence. This attempt to overawe them incensed the nobility. " What!" said they, " shall the laird of Lethington have power to controul us? or, shall the presence of a woman cause us to offend God, and to condemn an innocent man, against our consciences?" With this they repeated their votes, absolving him from all offence, and praising his modest appearance and judicious defences.

Mary was unable to conceal her mortification and displeasure, at this unexpected acquittal. When the bishop of Ross, who had been the informer, gave his vote on the same side with the rest, she taunted him openly in the presence of the court. "Trouble not the child! I pray you trouble him not! for he is newly awakened out of his sleep. Why should not the old fool follow the footsteps of those that passed before him?" The bishop replied coldly, that her majesty might easily know, that his vote was not influenced by partiality to the accus

Mary's disappointment.

ed. "That nicht was nyther dancing nor fiddeling in the court; the madam was disappoynted of hir purpose, quhilk was to have had Johne Knox in hir will, be vote of hir nobility."

PERIOD VII.

FROM HIS ACQUITTAL, FROM A CHARGE OF TREASON, BY THE PRIVY COUNCIL, ANNO 1563, TO HIS BEING STRUCK WITH APOPLEXY, ANNO 1570.

THE indignation of the queen at the Reformer's escape from punishment did not soon abate, and the effects of it fell both upon the courtiers who had voted for his exculpation, and upon those who had opposed it. The Earl of Murray was among the former; Maitland among the latter. In order to appease her, they again attempted to persuade him to condescend to some voluntary submission to her; and they engaged that all the punishment which should be inflicted on him would merely be to go

Plan to appease the royal indignation.

within the walls of the castle, and return again to his own house. But he refused to make any such compliances, by which he would throw discredit on the judgment of the nobility who had acquitted him, and confess himself to have been a mover of sedition. Disappointed in this, they endeavoured to injure him by whispers and detraction, circulating that he had no authority from his brethren for what he had done; and that he arrogated a Papal and arbitrary power over the Scottish church, issuing his letters, and exacting obedience to them. These charges were very groundless and injurious; for there never was perhaps any one who had as much influence, that was so careful in avoiding all appearance of assuming superiority over his brethren, or acting by his own authority, in matters of public and common concern.

In the General Assembly which met in the close of this year, he declined taking any share in the debates. When their principal business was settled, he requested liberty to speak on an affair which concerned himself. He stated what he had done in writing the late circular letter, the proceedings to which it had given rise, and the surmises which were still circulated to his prejudice; and insisted that the church should now examine his conduct in that matter, and particularly that they should declare whether or not they had given him a commission to advertise the brethren, when he foresaw any danger threatening their religion, or any difficult case which required their advice. The courtiers strenuously opposed the decision of this question; but it was taken up, and the Assembly, by a great majority, found that he had been burthened with such a commission, and, in the advertisement which he had lately given, had not gone beyond the bounds of his commission.

Knox had remained a widower upwards of three years. But in March 1564, he contracted a second marriage with Margaret Stewart, daughter of Lord Ochiltree, a nobleman of amiable dispositions, who had been long familiar with our Reformer, and steadily adhered to him when he was deserted by his other friends. She continued to discharge the duties of a wife to him, with pious and affectionate assiduity, until the time of his death. The Popish writers, who envied the honours of the Scottish Reformer, have represented this marriage as a proof of his great ambition; and, in the excess of their spleen, have ridiculously imputed to him the project of aiming to raise his progeny to the throne of Scotland; because the family of Ochiltree were of the blood royal! They are quite clear, too, that he gained the heart of the young lady by means of sorcery, and the assistance of the devil. But it seems, that powerful as his black-footed second was, he could not succeed in another attempt which he had previously made; for the same writers inform us, that he had paid his addresses to the lady Fleming, eldest daughter to the Duke of Chastelherault, and was repulsed.

The country continued in a state of quietness during the year 1564; but the same jealousies still subsisted between the court and the church. Her majesty's prejudices against the reformed religion were unabated, and she maintained a correspondence with its sworn enemies on the continent, which could not altogether escape the vigilance of her Protestant subjects. The preachers, on their side, did not relax in their zealous warnings against Popery, and concerning the dangers which they apprehended; they complained of the beggary unto which the greater part of their own number was reduced, and of the growing lukewarmness of the Protestant courtiers. The latter were uneasy under these reproaches, and, in concert with the queen, were anxious to restrain the license of the pulpit. They began by addressing themselves in private to some of the most moderate and complying of the ministers, whom they gained over, by their persuasions, to a partial approbation of their measures. Having in so far succeeded, they ventured to propose the matter more publicly, and to request the sanction of the leading members of the General Assembly.

Without designing to vindicate the latitude which might be taken by particular preachers at this time, I may say, in general, that a systematic attempt to restrain the liberty of speech in the pulpit (farther than the correction of any occurring excess might require) would have been a measure fraught with danger to the Protestant interest. The ministers were the most vigilant and incorrupt guardians of the public safety. Better it is to be awaked with rudeness, or even by a false alarm, than to be allowed to sleep on in the midst of dangers. Who would muzzle the mouth of the wakeful animal, who guards the house against thieves, because the inhabitants are frequently disturbed by his nocturnal vociferation? or substitute in his place, a "dumb dog, that cannot bark, sleeping, lying down, loving to slumber?"

Knox, the freedom and sharpness of whose censures the courtiers felt most deeply, was the person whom they chiefly wished to restrain; but it was no easy matter either to overawe or reason him into silence. In a conference which they demanded with the leading members of the General Assembly, in the month of June, this subject was discussed; and a long debate ensued between Maitland and Knox, on the principal points of his doctrine which gave offence to the court. This debate "admirably displays the talents and character of both the disputants; the acuteness of the former, embellished with learning, but prone to subtility; the vigorous understanding of the latter, delighting in bold sentiments, and superior to all fear." The dispute has been recorded at large by Knox in his history of the Reformation. After giving so full a view of some former disputes in which he was engaged, I must content myself with a brief account of the leading heads of the present.

There were two things which Maitland found fault with in the Reformer's public services; the mode in which he prayed for her majesty, and the doctrine which he taught as to the authority of princes and duty of subjects. Knox repeated his usual prayer for the queen, and desired to know what was faulty in it. Maitland said, that he prayed for her conversion conditionally, thereby infusing doubts into the minds of the people as to the probability of that event; and he spake of her as under the bondage of Satan, which was an irreverend expression, not fit to be applied to princes. The Reformer replied, that the conduct of her majesty gave just grounds to doubt of any change, and that his strongest expressions were warranted by the plain language of Scripture. "Prayers and tears," we have sometimes been reminded, are the only arms which Christians ought to employ against violence. But those who have deprived them of other weapons, have usually envied them of these also; and if their prayers have not been smoothed down to the temper of their adversaries, so as to become mere compliments to princes, under colour of an address to the Almighty, they have often been pronounced seditious and treasonable.

On the limited authority of princes.
The second part of the debate related to Knox's doctrine respecting the limited authority of princes, and the right of the people to controul them in the abuse of their power. Under this head, the lawfulness of suppressing the queen's mass was discussed. Even here, Maitland was hardly pushed by his antagonist, and found it difficult to maintain his ground, after the resistance which he himself had made to the supreme powers, and the principles which he held in common with the Reformer. For it is to be observed, that both parties held that idolatry might justly be punished by death. Into this sentiment they were led in consequence of their having adopted the untenable opinion, that the judicial laws given to the Jewish nation were binding upon Christian nations, as to all offences against the moral law.

In the course of the debate, Knox's colleague, Craig, gave an account of an interesting dispute on the same question, which he had heard in the university of Bologna, in Italy; in which the judgments of the learned men, and the decision of the question, were strongly in favour of popular liberty, and the limited power of princes.

After long conference, Maitland insisted that the votes should be called, and that some order should be established for preventing the recurrence of the evils of which he had complained. But Knox protested against any decision of the question, which belonged to the whole General Assembly; and the sentiments of the members being divided, the conference broke up without coming to any determinate resolution.

In the month of August, Knox went, by appointment of the General Assembly, as visitor of the churches in Aberdeen and the north, where he remained six or seven weeks. The subsequent Assembly gave him a similar appointment to Fife and Perthshire.

Our Reformer's predictions at the last meeting of parliament were now fully realised. Another parliament was held in the end of 1564, but nothing was done for securing the protestant religion. The queen's marriage approached, and the lords demanded this as the condition of their consent; but she artfully evaded the demand, and accomplished her object. While she was arranging her plans for the marriage, she sent for the superintendents of Lothian, Glasgow, and Fife (for Knox was now inadmissible to her presence), and amused them with fair words. She was not yet persuaded, she said, of the truth of their religion, but she was willing to hear conference and reasoning on the subject: she was even content to attend the public sermons of some of them; and, "above all others, she would gladly hear the superintendent of Angus, for he was a mild and sweet-natured man, with true honesty and uprightness, Sir John Erskine of Dun." But as soon as her marriage with lord Darnly was over, she told them in very plain and determined language, "her majesty neither will, nor may leave the religion wherein she has been nourished, and brought up." And there was no more word of hearing either sermon or conference.

The friendship between the Earl of Murray and the Reformer was renewed in the beginning of 1565. The latter was placed in a very delicate predicament, by the insurrection under Murray, and the other lords who opposed the queen's marriage. His father-in-law was one of the number. They professed that the security of the protestant religion was the principal ground of their taking arms; and they came to Edinburgh, to collect men to their standard. But whatever favour he might have for them, he kept himself clear from any engagement. If he had taken part in this unsuccessful revolt, we need not doubt that her majesty would have embraced the opportunity of punishing him for it, when his principal friends had fled the kingdom.

We find, in fact, that she immediately proceeded against him on a different, but far more slender pretext. The young king, who could be either papist, or protestant as it suited, went sometimes to mass with the queen, and sometimes attended the reformed sermons. To silence the suspicions of his alienation from the reformed religion, circulated by the insurgent lords, he, on the 19th of August, made a solemn appearance in St. Giles's church, sitting on a throne, which had been prepared for his reception. Knox preached that day on Isaiah xxvi. 13, &c. and happened to prolong the service beyond his usual time. In one part of the sermon, he quoted these words of scripture : "I will give children to be their princes, and babes shall rule over them : children are their oppressors, and women rule over them ;" and in another part of it, he mentioned that God punished Ahab, because he did not correct his idolatrous wife Jesabel. Though no particular application was made by the preacher, the king applied these passages to himself and the queen, and, returning to the palace in great wrath, refused to taste dinner. The papists, who had accompanied him to the church, inflamed his resentment and that of the queen, by their representations.

That very afternoon Knox was taken from bed, and carried before the Privy Council. Some respectable inhabitants of the city, understanding his situation, accompanied him to the palace. He was told that he had offended the king, and must desist from preaching as long as their majesties were in Edinburgh. He replied, that "he had spoken nothing but according to his text; and if the church would command him to speak or abstain, he would obey, so far as the word of God would permit him." Spottiswood says, that he not only stood to what he had said in the pulpit, but added, "That as the king, for" the queen's "pleasure, had gone to mass, and dishonoured the Lord God, so should he in his justice make her the instrument of his overthrow. This speech," continues the archbishop's manuscript, "esteemed too bold at the time, came afterwards to be remembered, and was reckoned among other his prophetical sayings, which certainly were marvellous. The queen, enraged at this answer, burst forth into tears."

The report of the inhibition laid upon the Reformer created great agitation in the city. His colleague, who was appointed to supply his place during the suspension, threatened to desist entirely from preaching. The Town Council met, and appointed a deputation to wait on their majesties, and request the removal of the inhibition; and in a second meeting, on the same day, they came to an unanimous resolution, that they would "in no manner of way consent or grant that his mouth be closed," but that he should be desired, "at his pleasure, and as God should move his heart, to proceed forward to true doctrine as before, which doctrine they would approve and abide at to their life's end."

It does not appear that he continued any time suspended from preaching. For the king and queen left Edinburgh before the next Sabbath, and the prohibition extended only to the time of their residence in the city. Upon their return, it is probable that the court judged it unadvisable to enforce an order which had already created much discontent, and might alienate the minds of the people still farther from the present administration. Accordingly, we find him exercising his ministry in Edinburgh with the same boldness as formerly. Complaints were made to the Council of the manner in which he prayed for the exiled noblemen; but secretary Maitland, who had formerly found so much fault with his prayers, defended them on the present occasion, saying that he had heard them, and they were such as no body could blame.

Christopher Goodman had officiated with much acceptance as minister of St. Andrews, since the year 1560; but he was prevailed on, by the solicitations of his friends in England, to return, about this time, to his native country. The commissioners from St. Andrews were instructed to petition the General Assembly, which met in December this year, that Knox should be translated from Edinburgh to their city. They claimed a right to him, as he had commenced his ministry among them; and they might think that the dissensions between the court and him would induce him to prefer a more retired situation. But the petition was refused.

Import-
ant ser-
vices im-
posed
upon
Knox.

This Assembly imposed on him several important services. He was commissioned to visit the churches in the south of Scotland, and appointed to write " a comfortable letter," exhorting the ministers, exhorters, and readers, throughout the kingdom, to persevere in the discharge of their functions, which many of them were threatening to throw up, on account of the non-payment of their stipends, and exciting the people among whom they laboured to relieve their necessities. He had formerly received an appointment to draw up the Form of Excommunication and Public Repentance. At this time he was required to compose a Treatise of Fasting. The Assembly, having taken into consideration the troubles of the country, and the dangers which threatened the whole Protestant interest, appointed a general fast to be kept through the kingdom. The form and order to be observed on that occasion they left to be drawn out by Knox and his colleague. As nothing had been hitherto published expressly on this subject, they were authorised to explain the duty, as well as state the reasons which at this time called for that solemn exercise. The whole was appointed to be ready before the time of the fast, to serve as a directory to ministers and people. The treatise does credit to the compilers, both as to matter and form. It is written in a perspicuous and nervous style. In the grounds assigned for fasting, the critical state of all the Reformed churches, the late decree of the Council of Trent for the extirpation of the Protestant name, the combination of the Popish princes for carrying this into execution, and the barbarities exercised towards their brethren in different countries, are all held forth as a warning to the Protestants of Scotland, and urged as calls to repentance and prayer.

In fact, strong as their apprehensions were, the danger was nearer to themselves than they imagined. The most zealous and powerful Protestants being exiled, the queen determined to carry into execution the design of which she had never lost sight; and while she amused the nation with proclamations against altering the received religion, and tantalized the ministers with offers of more adequate support, was preparing for the immediate restoration of the Roman Catholic worship. No means were left unattempted for gaining over the nobility to that religion. The king openly professed himself a Papist, and officiated in some of their most superstitious rites. The Earls of Lennox, Cassilis, and Caithness, with Lords Montgomery and Seton, did the same. The friars were employed to preach at Holyroodhouse, and, to gain the favour of the people, endeavoured to imitate the popular method of the Protestant preachers. In

the beginning of February 1566, a message arrived from
the cardinal of Lorrain, with a copy of the league for
the general extirpation of the Protestants, and instructions to obtain her subscription to it, and her consent to
proceed to extremities against the exiled nobility. Mary
scrupled not to set her hand to this league. The exiled
noblemen were summoned to appear before the parliament on the 12th of March. The lords of the Articles
were chosen according to the queen's pleasure; the
Popish ecclesiastics were restored to their place in parliament; the altars to be erected in St. Giles's church
for the Roman Catholic worship were prepared.

But these measures, when ripe for execution, were
blasted, in consequence of a secret engagement which
the king had entered into with some of the Protestant
nobles. The first effect produced by this engagement
was the well known assassination of Rizio, an unworthy
favourite of the queen, who was the principal instigator
of the measures against the Protestant religion and the
banished lords, and had incurred the jealousy of the
king, the contempt of the nobility, and the hatred of the
people. The removal of this minion from her majesty's
counsels and presence would have been a meritorious
act; but the manner in which it was accomplished was
marked with the barbarous manners of the age.

A complete change in the state of the court followed
upon this: the Popish counsellors fled from the palace;
the banished lords returned out of England; and the
parliament was prorogued, without accomplishing any
of the objects for which it had been assembled. But
the queen soon persuaded the weak and uxorious king
to desert the noblemen, retire with her to Dunbar, and
emit a proclamation, disowning his consent to the late
attempt, by which he exposed himself to the contempt
of the nation, without regaining her affection. Having
collected an army, she returned to Edinburgh, threatening to inflict the most exemplary vengeance on all who
had been accessory to the murder of her secretary, and

Mary's
threaten-
ing.

the indignity shewn to her person. She round herself, however, unable to resume her plan for altering the received religion; and the Earl of Murray, with the other lords who had opposed her marriage, were soon after pardoned.

When the queen came to Edinburgh, Knox left it, and retired to Kyle. There is no reason to think that he was privy to the conspiracy which proved fatal to Rizio. But it is probable that he had expressed his satisfaction at an event, which contributed to the safety of religion and the commonwealth, if not also his approbation of the conduct of the conspirators. At any rate, he was, on other grounds, sufficiently obnoxious to the queen; and as her resentment, on the present occasion, was exceedingly inflamed, it was deemed prudent for him to withdraw.

Having, at last, "got quit" of one who had long been troublesome to her, the queen was determined to prevent his return to the capital. We need not doubt that the Town Council and inhabitants, who had formerly refused to agree to his suspension from preaching for a short time, would exert themselves to obtain his restoration. But she resisted the importunities of all his friends. She was even unwilling that he should find a refuge Mary wills that Knox should be banished the kingdom. within the kingdom, and wrote to a nobleman in the west country, with whom he resided, to banish him from his house. It does not appear that he returned to Edinburgh, or, at least, that he resumed his ministry in it, until the queen was deprived of the government.

Being banished from his flock, he judged this a favourable opportunity for paying a visit to England. Parental affection, on the present occasion, increased the desire which he had long felt to accomplish this journey. His two sons had some time ago been sent by him into that kingdom, probably at the desire of their mother's relations, to obtain their education in some of the English seminaries. Having obtained the queen's safe-conduct, he applied to the General Assembly, which met in December 1566, for their liberty to remove. They readily granted it, upon condition of his returning against the time of their next meeting in June ; and, at the same time, gave him a most ample and honourable testimonial, in which they describe him as " a true and faithful minister, in doctrine pure and sincere, in life and conversation in our sight inculpable," and one who

Testi-
mony of
the Gen-
eral As-
sembly.

" has so fruitfully used that talent granted to him by the Eternal, to the advancement of the glory of his godly name, to the propagation of the kingdom of Jesus Christ, and edifying of them who heard his preaching, that of duty we most heartily praise his godly name, for that so great a benefit granted unto him for our utility and profit."

The Reformer was charged with a letter from the Assembly, to the bishops and ministers of England, interceding for lenity to such of their brethren as scrupled to use the sacerdotal dress, enjoined by the laws. The controversy on that subject was at this time carried on with great warmth among the English clergy. It is not improbable, that the Assembly interfered in this business at the desire of Knox, to whom the composition of the letter was committed. He could not have forgotten the trouble which he himself had suffered on a similar ground, and he had a high regard for many of the scruplers. This interposition did not procure for them any relief. Even though the superior clergy had been more zealous to obtain it than they were, Elizabeth was inflexible, and would listen neither to the supplications of her bishops, nor the advice of her counsellors. Knox's good opinion of the English queen does not seem to have been improved by this visit.

Attempt
to restore
Popery.

There was one piece of public service which he performed, before undertaking his journey to England. On the 23d of December, the queen granted a commission to the archbishop of St. Andrews, under the privy seal, restoring him to his ancient jurisdiction, which had been abolished, in 1560, by act of parliament. This step was

A Dickinson Robinson Group Product

John Knox's House, Edinburgh
Situated in the High Street, this 16th century house
was built by the goldsmith to Mary, Queen of Scots,
and is reputed to have been at one time the property
of John Knox

PED/22301

Printed in Scotland by J. ARTHUR DIXON

taken, partly to prepare for the restoration of the popish religion, and partly to facilitate another dark design which was soon after disclosed. The protestants could not fail to be both alarmed and enraged at this daring measure. The Reformer, moved both by his own zeal, and the advice of his brethren, addressed a circular letter to the principal protestants in the kingdom, requesting their immediate advice on the measures most proper to be adopted on this occasion, and inclosing a copy of a proposed supplication to the queen. This letter discovers all the ardour of the writer's spirit, called forth by such an alarming occurrence. After mentioning the late acts for the provision of the ministry, by which the queen attempted to blind them, he says: "How that any such assignation, or any promise made thereof, can stand in any stable assurance, when that Roman Antichrist, by just laws once banished from this realm, shall be intrusted above us, we can no ways understand. Yea, farther, we cannot see what assurance can any within this realm, that hath professed the Lord Jesus, have of life, or inheritance, if the head of that odious beast be cured among us." Having enforced his request, he adds: "As from the beginning we have neither spared substance nor life, so mind we not to faint unto the end, to maintain the same, so long as we can find the concurrence of brethren; of whom (as God forbid), if we be destitute, yet are we determined never to be subject to the Roman Antichrist, neither yet to his usurped tyranny; but when we can do no farther to suppress that odious Beast, we mind to seal it with our blood to our posterity, that the bright knowledge of Jesus Christ hath banished that Man of Sin, and his venomous doctrine, from our hearts and consciences. Let this our letter and request bear witness before God, before his church, before the world, and before your own consciences." The supplication of the General Assembly to the lords of the Privy Council, on the same subject, also bears marks of the Reformer's pen.

PERIOD
VII.
1563–1570
A.D.

The circular letter.

During the time that Knox was in England, that tra-
gedy, so well known in Scottish history, was acted,
which led to a complete revolution in the government
of the kingdom, and, contrary to the designs of the actors, threw the power solely into the hands of the protestants. Mary's affection for her husband, which had
cooled soon after their marriage, was, from the time of
Rizio's assassination, converted into a fixed hatred,
which she was at little pains to conceal. In proportion
as her mind was alienated from the king, the unprincipled Earl of Bothwell grew in her favour. He engrossed the whole management of public affairs, and was treated by her majesty with every mark of regard and affection. In these circumstances, the neglected, unhappy

king was decoyed to Edinburgh, lodged in a solitary
dwelling at the extremity of the city, and murdered on
the night of February 9, 1567; the house in which he
lay being blown up with gunpowder.

It would be impertinent to enter here into the controversy respecting the authors of this murder, which has
been agitated with uncommon keenness, from that day
to the present time. The accusation of the Earl of Murray as a party to the deed, which was at first circulated
with the evident design of turning away the public mind
from the real perpetrators, insinuated, and afterwards
brought forward directly in the conference at York, by
way of retortion of the charge exhibited by him against
the queen, and still kept up by some of the zealous par-
tizans of Mary, is destitute of all proof, and utterly incredible. That Bothwell was the prime contriver and
agent in the murder cannot admit of a doubt with any
impartial and reasonable inquirer. And that Mary was
privy, and accessory to it, by permission and approbation, there is, I think, all the evidence, moral and legal,
which could reasonably be expected in a case of the kind.
The whole of her behaviour towards the king, from the
time that she brought him from Glasgow till she left
him on the fatal night; the remissness which she disco-

vered in inquiring into the murder; the shameful manner in which the farce of Bothwell's trial was conducted; and the glaring act (which struck with horror the whole of Europe, and even her own friends) of taking to her bed, with indecent haste, the man who was stigmatised as the murderer of her husband, afford the strongest presumption of her guilt; and when taken in connexion with the direct evidence arising from letters and depositions, would have been sufficient long ago to shut the mouths of any but the defenders of Mary queen of Scots.

Knox was absent from Edinburgh at the time of the queen's marriage with Bothwell; but his colleague ably supported the honour of his place and order on that occasion, when the whole nobility of Scotland observed a passive and disgraceful silence. Being required by both the parties to publish the banns, he, after considerable reluctance, agreed, by the advice of his session, to make known the purpose; but he at the same time protested from the pulpit, on three several days, and took heaven and earth to witness, that he abhorred and detested the intended marriage as unlawful and scandalous, and solemnly charged the nobility to use their influence to prevent the queen from taking a step, which would cover her with infamy. Being called before the Council, and accused of having exceeded the bounds of his commission, he boldly replied, that the bounds of his commission were the word of God, good laws, and natural reason, to all of which the proposed marriage was contrary. And Bothwell being present, he charged him with the crime of adultery, the precipitancy with which the process of divorce had been carried through, the suspicions entertained of collusion between him and his wife, of his having murdered the king, and ravished the queen, all of which would be confirmed, if they carried their purpose into execution.

The events which followed in rapid succession upon this infamous marriage; the confederation of the nobility for revenging the king's death, and preserving the person of the infant prince ; the flight of Bothwell ; the surrender and imprisonment of Mary ; her resignation of the government ; the coronation of her son ; and the appointment of the Earl of Murray as regent during his minority, are all well known to the readers of Scottish history.

Knox seems to have returned to his charge at the time that the queen fled with Bothwell to Dunbar. He was present in the General Assembly which met at Edinburgh on the 25th of June, and was delegated by them to go to the west country, and endeavoured to persuade the Hamiltons, and others who still stood aloof from the confederated lords, to join with them in settling the distracted affairs of the country, and to attend a general convention of the delegates of the churches, to be held on the 20th of July following. He was unsuccessful in this negociation. But the convention was held, and the nobles, barons, and other commissioners, who were present, subscribed a number of articles, with reference to religion and the state of the nation.

On the 29th of July, the Reformer preached the sermon at the coronation of king James VI. in the parish church of Stirling. He objected to the ceremony of unction, as a Jewish rite, abused under the papacy; but it was deemed inexpedient to depart from the accustomed ceremonial on the present occasion. It was therefore performed by the bishop of Orkney, the superintendents of Lothian and Angus assisting him to place the crown on the king's head. After the coronation, Knox, along with some others, took instruments, and craved extracts of the proceedings.

The disposal of Mary.

When the queen was confined by the lords in the castle of Lochlevin, they had not resolved in what manner they should dispose of her person for the future. Some proposed that she should be allowed to leave the kingdom ; some that she should be imprisoned during life ; while others insisted that she ought to suffer capital punishment. Of this last opinion was Knox, with almost all the ministers, and the great body of the people. The chief ground upon which they insisted for this, was not her maladministration in the government, or the mere safety and peace of the commonwealth; which were the reasons upon which the parliament of England, in the following century, proceeded to the execution of her grandson. But they grounded their opinion upon the personal crimes with which Mary was charged. Murder and adultery, they reasoned, were crimes to which the punishment of death was allotted by the law of God, and of nations. From this penalty persons of no rank could plead exemption. The ordinary forms of judicial procedure, indeed, made no provision for the trial of a supreme magistrate for these crimes; because the laws did not suppose that such enormous offences would be committed by them. But extraordinary cases required extraordinary remedies; and new offences gave birth to new laws. There were examples in Scripture of the capital punishment of princes, and precedents for it in the history of their own country.

PERIOD
VII.
1563–1570
A.D.

Upon these grounds, Knox scrupled not publicly to maintain, that the estates of the kingdom ought to bring Mary to a trial, and if she was found guilty of the murder of her husband, and an adulterous connection with Bothwell, that she ought to be put to death. Throkmorton, the English ambassador, had a conference with him, with the view of mitigating the rigour of this judgment; but though he acquiesced in the resolution adopted by the lords to detain her in prison, he retained his sentiment, and, after the civil war was kindled by her escape, repeatedly said, that he considered the nation as suffering for their criminal lenity.

The Earl of Murray, being established in the regency, directed his attention, at an early period, to the settlement of religion, and the redressing of the principal grievances of which the church had long complained. A parliament being summoned to meet in the middle of

The Earl
of Murray
regent.

December, he, with the advice of the Privy Council, previously nominated certain barons, and commissioners of boroughs, to consult upon and digest such overtures as were proper to be laid before that assembly. With these he joined Knox, and other four ministers, to assist in matters which related to the church. This committee met in the beginning of December, and sat until the opening of the parliament. The record of their proceedings, both as to civil and ecclesiastical affairs, is preserved ; and, as many of their propositions were not adopted by the parliament, it is valuable as a declaration of the sentiments of a number of the most able men in the kingdom.

Opening
of Parliament.
On the 15th December, Knox preached at the opening of the Parliament, and exhorted them to begin with the affairs of religion, in which case they would find better success in their other business. The Parliament ratified all the acts which had been passed, in 1560, in favour of the Protestant religion, and against Popery. New statutes of a similar kind were added. It was provided, that no prince should afterwards be admitted to the exercise of authority in the kingdom, without taking an oath to maintain the Protestant religion ; and that none but Protestants should be admitted to any office, not hereditary nor held for life. The ecclesiastical jurisdiction, exercised by the different assemblies of the church, was formally ratified, and commissioners appointed to define more exactly the causes which properly came within the sphere of their judgment. The thirds of benefices were appointed to be paid immediately to collectors appointed by the church, who were to account to the exchequer for the overplus after paying the stipends of the ministers. And the funds of provostries, prebendaries, and chaplainries were appropriated to maintain bursars in colleges.

Knox
appointed
a commissioner.
In the act ratifying the jurisdiction of the church, Knox was appointed one of the commissioners for drawing out the particular points which pertained to eccle-

siastical jurisdiction, to be presented to next meeting of Parliament. The General Assembly, which met about the same time, gave him a commission, along with some others, to act for them in this matter, and, in general, to consult with the regent and council on such ecclesiastical questions as occurred after the dissolution of that Assembly. He was also appointed to assist the superintendent of Lothian in his visitation, and afterwards to visit the churches in Kyle, Carrick, and Cunningham.

During the regency of Murray, there were no jars between the church and the court, nor any of those unpleasant complaints which had been made at every meeting of the General Assembly before that time, and which were afterwards renewed. All the grievances of which they complained were not, indeed, redressed; and the provision made by law was still inadequate for the support of such an ecclesiastical establishment as the nation required, including the seminaries of education. But the regent not only received the addresses of the General Assemblies in a "manner very different from that to which they had been accustomed;" but shewed a disposition to grant their petitions, as far as was in his power. It was chiefly through his influence that the favourable arrangement concerning the thirds of benefices was made; and he endeavoured, though unsuccessfully, to obtain the consent of Parliament to the dissolution of the prelacies, and the appropriation of their revenues to the common fund of the church.

Our Reformer had now reached that point from which A retrospect. he could take a calm and deliberate view of the dangerous and bustling scene through which he had passed, and the termination to which the arduous struggle in which he had been so long engaged, was now happily brought. Superstition and ignorance were overthrown and dispelled; true religion was established; the supreme government of the nation was in the hands of one in whose wisdom and integrity he had the greatest confidence;

the church was freed from many of those grievances under which she had hitherto groaned, and enjoyed the prospect of obtaining the redress of such as still remained. The work on which his heart had been so ardently set for such a long period, and for the success of which he had so often trembled, had prospered beyond his utmost expectation. He now congratulated himself on being released from all burden of public affairs, and spending the remainder of his days in religious meditation, and preparation for that event of which his increasing infirmities admonished him. He even secretly cherished the wish of resigning his charge in Edinburgh, and retiring to that privacy, from which he had been drawn at the commencement of the Scottish Reformation.

But "the way of man is not in himself." Providence had allotted to him further trials of a public nature: he was yet to see the security of the reformed religion endangered, and the country involved in another civil war, even more distressing than the former, in as much as the principal persons on each side were professed protestants. From the time that the government was transferred from Mary to her infant son, and the Earl of Murray appointed to the regency, a number of the nobility, with the house of Hamilton at their head, had stood aloof, and, from other motives as much as attachment to the queen, had refused to acknowledge the authority of the regent. Upon the escape of the queen from imprisonment, they collected to her standard, and avowed their design to restore her to the full exercise of the

royal authority. In consequence of the defeat at Langside, Mary was driven from the kingdom, and her party broken; and the regent, by his vigorous measures, reduced the whole kingdom to a state of obedience to the king's authority. Despairing to accomplish their object during his life, the partisans of Mary resolved to cut him off by private means.

During the year 1568, two persons were employed to assassinate him; but the design was discovered. This did not hinder new machinations. Hamilton of Both-wellhaugh, a nephew of the archbishop of St. Andrews, undertook to perpetrate the deed. He was one of the prisoners taken at the battle of Langside, and after being arraigned, condemned, and brought out to execution, had his life given him by the regent. Sometime after he was set at liberty along with the other prisoners. It is said that he was actuated by revenge, on account of an injury which he had received, by detaining one of his forfeited estates, or by the cruel manner in which his wife had been dispossessed of it. Whether this was really the case, or whether it was afterwards circulated to diminish the odium of his crime, and turn it away from his party, cannot perhaps be certainly determined. But it does not appear, that he ever suffered any thing rom the regent which can be pleaded as an excuse for his bursting the ties of gratitude by which he was bound to him. Having concerted the design with some of the leading persons of his faction, who incited him to carry it into execution, he followed the regent in his progress to Glasgow, Stirling, and Linlithgow; and finding an opportunity in the last of these places, shot him through the body with a musket-ball. The wound proved mortal, and the regent died on the same evening. While some of his friends, who stood round his bed, lamented the excessive lenity which he had shewn to his enemies, and, in particular, to his murderer, he replied, with a truly noble and Christian spirit, that nothing would make him repent an act of clemency.

The consternation which is usually produced by the fall of a distinguished leader was absorbed in the deep distress which the tidings of the regent's murder spread through the nation. The common people, who had experienced the beneficial effects of his short administration, to a degree altogether unprecedented in the country, felt as if each had lost a father, and loudly demanded vengeance against the authors of the parricide. Many who had envied or hated him during his life were now forward to do justice to his virtues. Those who had not been able to conceal their satisfaction on the first intelligence of his death, became ashamed of the indecent exultation which they had imprudently expressed. The Hamiltons were anxious to clear themselves from the imputation of a crime which they saw to be universally detested. The murderer was dismissed by them, and was glad to conceal his ignominy, by condemning himself to perpetual banishment. The only one of his crimes for which the archbishop of St. Andrews afterwards expressed contrition, before his execution, was his accession to the murder of the regent. Nor were these feelings confined to Scotland; the sensation was general through England, and the expressions of grief and condolence from that country evinced the uncommon esteem in which he was held by all ranks.

Early principles of the regent.

It was the happiness of the regent, that, in his early years, he fell into the company of men who cultivated his vigorous understanding, gave a proper direction to his activity, and instilled into his mind the principles of religion and virtue. His early adoption of the reformed sentiments, the steadiness with which he adhered to them, the uniform correctness of his morals, his integrity, sagacity, and enterprising but cool courage, soon placed him in the first rank among those who embarked in the struggle for the reformation of religion, and maintenance of national liberties, and secured to him their cordial and unbounded confidence. The honours which queen Mary conferred on him were not too great for the services which he rendered to her; and had she continued to trust him with the direction of her counsels, those measures would have been avoided which precipitated her ruin. He was repeatedly placed in a situation which would have tempted the ambition of others, less qualified, to aspire to the supreme authority; yet he shewed no disposition to grasp at this. When he accepted the regency, it was in compliance with the decided and uncorrupted voice of the acting majority in the nation, pointing him out as the fittest person for occupying that high station. His conduct, in one of the most delicate and embarrassing situations in which a governor was ever placed, shewed that his countrymen were not mistaken in their choice. He united, in no ordinary degree, those qualities which are rarely combined in the same individual, and which make up the character of an accomplished prince. Excelling equally in the arts of war and peace, he reduced the country to universal obedience to the king's authority by his military skill and valour, and preserved it in a state of tranquillity and order by the wise and impartial administration of justice. Successful in all his warlike enterprizes, he never once tarnished the laurels of victory by cruelty, or unnecessary rigour to the vanquished. He knew how to maintain the authority of the laws, and bridle the licentious, by salutary severity, and at the same time to temper the rigour of justice by the interposition of mercy. He used to sit personally in the courts of judicature, and exerted himself to obtain for all the subjects an easy and expeditious decision of litigated causes. His uncommon liberality to his friends, to the learned, and to his servants, and his unostentatious charity to the poor, have been celebrated by one who had the best opportunities of becoming acquainted with them. Nor has the breath of calumny, which has laboured in many ways to blast his reputation, ever insinuated that he oppressed or burdened the public during his regency, in order to enrich himself or his family. Add to all, his exemplary piety, the only source of genuine virtue. His family was so regulated as to resemble a church rather than a court. Not a profane nor lewd word was to be heard from any of his domestics. Besides the ordinary exercise of devotion, a chapter of the Bible was always read at dinner and supper; and it was his custom, on such occasions, to require his chaplain, or some other learned men (of whom he had always a number about him) to give their opinion upon the pas-

PERIOD
VII.
1563–1570
A.D.

Character
of Regent
Murray.

sage, for his own instruction and that of his family. "A man truly good," says archbishop Spottiswood, "and worthy to be ranked amongst the best governors that this kingdom hath enjoyed, and, therefore, to this day honoured with the title of the Good Regent."

This may be deemed, by some readers, an improper digression from the subject of this work. But even though it had been still less connected with it than it is, though there had not subsisted that intimate familiarity and co-operation between the regent and the Reformer, I could scarcely have denied myself the satisfaction of paying a small tribute to the memory of one of the greatest men of his age, who has been traduced and vilified in a most unjustifiable and wanton manner in modern times, and whose character has been drawn with unfavourable, and, in my opinion, with unfair colours, by the most moderate of our historians. All that I have attempted is to sketch the most prominent features of his character. That he was faultless, I am far from wishing to insinuate; but the principal charges which have been brought against him, I consider as either irrelevant, or unproved, or greatly exaggerated. That his exaltation to the highest dignity in the state which a subject could enjoy, produced no unfavourable change on his behaviour, is what none can be prepared to affirm; but I have not seen the contrary established. The confidence which he reposed in his friends was great, and he was inclined to be biassed by their advice; but that he became the dupe of worthless favourites, and fell by listening to their flattery, and refusing to hearken to wholesome advice, and not by the treachery of his friends, and the malice of his implacable enemies, are assertions which have been repeated upon the authority of a single witness, are unsupported by facts, and capable of being disproved.

Assertions capable of being disproved.

The regent died on the evening of Saturday; and the intelligence of his murder was conveyed early next morning to Edinburgh. It is impossible to describe the anguish which the Reformer felt on this occasion. A cordial and intimate friendship had long subsisted between them. Of all the Scottish nobility, he placed the greatest confidence in Murray's attachment to religion; and his conduct after his elevation to the regency had served to heighten the good opinion which he formerly entertained of him. He looked upon his death as the greatest calamity which could befal the nation, and the forerunner of other evils. When the shock produced by the melancholy tidings had subsided, the first thought that rushed into his mind was, that he had himself been the instrument of obtaining, from his clemency, a pardon to the man who had become his murderer: a thought which naturally produced a very different impression on him from what it did on the dying regent.

In his sermon that day, he introduced the subject; and after saying, that God in his great mercy raised up godly rulers, and took them away in his displeasure on account of the sins of a nation, he thus poured out the sorrows of his heart in an address to God. "O Lord, in what misery and confusion found he this realm! To what rest and quietness now by his labours suddenly he brought the same, all estates, but especially the poor commons, can witness. Thy image, O Lord, did so clearly shine in that personage, that the devil, and the wicked to whom he is prince, could not abide it; and so to punish our sins and our ingratitude (who did not rightly esteem so precious a gift), thou hast permitted him to fall, to our great grief, in the hands of cruel and traitorous murderers. He is at rest, O Lord: we are left in extreme misery."

Only a few days before this, when the murder was fully concerted, the abbot of Kilwinning applied to Knox to intercede with the regent in behalf of his kinsmen, who were confined for practising against the government. He signified his readiness to do all in his power for the relief of any of that family who were

willing to own the authority of the king and regent;
but he intreated him not to abuse him, by employing his
services, if any mischief were intended against the regent:
for " I protest, said he, before God, who is the only witness now betwixt us, that if there be any thing attempted, by any of that surname, against the person of that
man, in that case, I discharge myself to you and them
for ever.'" After the assassination, the abbot sent to desire another interview; but Knox refused to see him, and
desired the messenger to say to him, " I have not now
the regent to make suit unto for the Hamiltons."

At this time there was handed about a fabricated account of a pretended conference held by the late regent
with Lord Lindsay, Wishart of Pittarrow, the tutor of
Pitcur, James Macgill, and Knox, in which they were
represented as advising him to set aside the young king,
and place the crown on his own head. The modes of
expression peculiar to each of the persons were carefully
imitated in the speeches put into their mouths, to give
it the greater air of credibility. The design of it evi-
dently was to lessen the odium of the murder, and the
veneration of the people for the memory of Murray; but
it was universally regarded as an impudent and gross
forgery. Its fabricator was Thomas Maitland, a young
man of talents, but corrupted by his brother the secretary, who before this had engaged himself to the queen's
party, and was suspected of having a deep hand in the
plot for cutting off the regent.

An omin-
ous paper.
On the day on which the weekly conference was held
in Edinburgh, the same person slipped into the pulpit a
schedule, containing words to this effect, " Take up
now the man whom you accounted another God, and
consider the end to which his ambition hath brought
him." Knox, whose turn it was to preach that day,
took up the paper on entering the pulpit, supposing it
to be a note requesting the prayers of the congregation
for a sick person, and, having read it, laid it aside without any apparent emotion. But towards the conclusion

of his sermon, having deplored the loss which the church and commonwealth had recently sustained, and declared the account of the conference, which had been circulated, to be false and calumnious, he said that there were persons who rejoiced at the treasonable murder, and scrupled not to make it the subject of their merriment; particularly there was one present who had thrown in a writing insulting over an event which was the cause of grief to all good men. "That wicked man, whosoever he be, shall not go unpunished, and shall die where there shall be none to lament him." Maitland, when he went home, said to his sister, that the preacher was raving, when he spake in such a manner of a person who was unknown to him; but she understanding that her brother had written the line, reproved him, saying with tears, that none of that man's denunciations were wont to prove idle. Spottiswood (who had his information personally from the mouth of that lady) says, that Maitland died in Italy, "having no known person to attend him."

Upon Tuesday the 14th of February, the regent's corpse was brought from the palace of Holyroodhouse, and interred in the south aisle of the collegiate church of St. Giles. Before the funeral, Knox preached a sermon on these words, "Blessed are the dead which die in the Lord." Three thousand persons were dissolved in tears before him, while he described the regent's virtues, and bewailed his loss. Buchanan paid his tribute to the memory of the deceased, by writing the inscription placed on his monument, with that expressive simplicity and brevity which are dictated by genuine grief. A convention of the nobility was held after the funeral, at which it was resolved to avenge his death; but different opinions were entertained as to the mode of doing this, and the commons complained loudly of the remissness with which it was carried into execution. The General Assembly, at their first meeting, testified their detestation of the crime, by ordering the assassin to be publicly excommunicated in all the chief towns of the kingdom, and appointed the same process to be used against all who should afterwards be convicted of accession to the conspiracy.

During the sitting of the convention, Knox received a number of letters from his acquaintances in England, expressive of their high regard for the character of the regent, and their sorrow at so grievous a loss. One of his correspondents, Dr. Laurence Humphrey, urged him to write a memoir of the deceased. Had he done this, he would no doubt, from his intimate acquaintance with him, have communicated a number of particulars of which we must now be content to remain ignorant. But though he had been disposed to undertake this task, the state of his health must have prevented its execution.

The grief which he indulged, in consequence of this mournful event, and the confusions which followed it, preyed upon his spirits, and injured his health. In the month of October, he had a stroke of apoplexy, which affected his speech to a considerable degree. Upon this occasion, his enemies exulted, and circulated the most exaggerated tales. The report ran through England as well as Scotland, that John Knox would never preach nor speak more ; that his face was turned into his neck ; that he was become the most deformed creature ever seen ; that he was actually dead ;—a most unequivocal expression of the high consideration in which he was held, which our Reformer received in common with some other great men of his age.

PERIOD VIII.

THOSE who flattered themselves that the Reformer's disorder was mortal were disappointed ; for he convalesced, recovered the use of his speech, and was able, in the course of a few days, to resume preaching, at least on Sabbath days. He never recovered, however, from the debility which was produced by the stroke.

PERIOD VIII.

The confusions which he had augured from the death of the good regent soon broke out, and again spread the flames of civil discord through the nation. The Hamiltons openly raised the queen's standard. Kircaldy of Grange, governor of the castle of Edinburgh, who had been corrupted by Maitland, after concealing his defection for a time under the flag of neutrality, declared himself on the same side, and became the principal agent in attempting to overturn the government which he had been so zealous in erecting. The defection of Grange was a source of great injury to the inhabitants of Edinburgh, and of distress to Knox. He had a warm affection for the governor, on account of the important services which he had rendered to the Reformation ; and he continued always to think that he was at bottom a sincere friend to religion. Under this conviction, he spared no pains in endeavouring to prevent him from renouncing his fidelity to the king, and afterwards to reclaim him from his apostasy. But in both he was unsuccessful.

In the end of the year 1570, he was personally involved in a disagreeable quarrel with Grange. A servant of the latter having been imprisoned on a charge of murder, he sent a company of soldiers from the castle, who forced the prison, and carried off the criminal. Knox, in his sermon on the following Sabbath, condemned this riot, and violation of the house of justice. Had it been done by the authority of a blood-thirsty man, and one who had no fear of God, he would not, he said, have been so much moved at it; but he was affected to think that one of whom all good men had formed so great expectations, should have fallen so far as to act such a part; one who, when formerly in prison, had refused to purchase his own liberty by the shedding of blood. An exaggerated report of this censure being conveyed to the castle, the governor, in great rage, made his complaint, first to Knox's colleague, and afterwards formally to the kirk-session, that he had been traduced as a murderer, and required that his character should be vindicated as publicly as it had been calumniated. Knox explained and vindicated what he had said. On a subsequent Sabbath, Grange, who had been absent from the church nearly a whole year, came down to it, accompanied with a number of the persons who had been active in the murder and riot. Knox, looking upon this as an attempt to out-brave the scandal which his conduct had given, took occasion to discourse particularly of the sin of forgetting benefits received from God, and warned his hearers against confiding in the divine mercy while they were knowingly transgressing any of the commandments, or proudly defending their transgression.

Grange
incensed
at Knox.
Grange was much incensed at these warnings, which he considered as levelled at him, and in speaking of the preacher, made use of very threatening language. The report having spread that the governor of the castle was become a sworn enemy to Knox, and intended to kill him, several of the noblemen and gentlemen of Kyle and Cunningham sent a letter to Grange, in which, after mentioning his former appearances for religion, and the reports which had reached their ears, they warned him

against doing any thing to the prejudice of the man whom "God had made the first planter and chief waterer of his church among them," and protested that "his death and life were as dear to them as their own deaths and lives."

Knox was not to be deterred, by threatenings, from doing what he considered to be his duty. He persisted in warning his hearers to avoid all participation with those, who, by supporting the pretensions of the queen, prevented the punishment of notorious crimes, and sought the overthrow of the king's authority, and the reformed religion. When the General Assembly met in March 1571, anonymous libels were thrown into the assembly-house, and placards fixed on the church-door, accusing him of seditious railing against their sovereign the queen, refusing to pray for her welfare and conversion, representing her as a reprobate, whose repentance was hopeless, and uttering imprecations against her. The Assembly having, by public intimation, required the accusers to come forward and substantiate their charges, another anonymous bill appeared, promising that the writer would do so against next Assembly, if the accused continued his offensive speeches, and was "then law-byding, and not fugitive according to his accustomed manner."

Several of his friends dealt with him to pass over these anonymous libels in silence, but he refused to comply with this advice, considering that the credit of his ministry was implicated. Accordingly, he produced them in the pulpit, and returned a particular answer to the accusations which they contained. That he had charged the late queen with the crimes of which she had notoriously been guilty, he granted, but that he had railed against her, they would not, he said, be able to prove, without proving Isaiah, Jeremiah, and other inspired writers, to be railers. "He had learned plainly and boldly to call wickedness by its own terms, a fig a fig, and a spade a spade." He had never called her reprobate, nor said that her repentance was impossible; but he had affirmed that pride and repentance could not remain long together in one heart. He had prayed that God, for the comfort of his church, would oppose his power to her pride, and confound her, and her assistants, in their impiety: this prayer, let them call it imprecation or execration, as they pleased, had stricken, and would yet strike, whoever supported her. To the charge of not praying for her, he answered, " I am not bound to pray for her in this place, for sovereign to me she is not; and I let them understand that I am not a man of law that has my tongue to sell for silver, or favour of the world." What title she now had, or ever had to the government, he would not dispute: the estates had deprived her of it, and it belonged to them to answer for this: as for him, he had hitherto lived in obedience to all lawful authority within this kingdom. To the insinuation that he might not be " law-byding" against next Assembly, he replied, that his life was in the custody of Him who had preserved him to that age at which he was not apt to flee, nor could any yet accuse him of leaving the people of his charge, except at their own command.

Knox
fights
against
"shadows
and houl-
ets."

After these defences, his enemies fled, as their dernier-resort, to an attack upon his Blast of the Trumpet, and accused him of inconsistency in writing against female government, and yet praying for queen Elizabeth, and seeking her aid against his native country. This accusation he also met in the pulpit, and refuted with great spirit. After vindicating his consistency, he concludes in the following manner: " One thing, in the end, I may not pretermit, that is, to give him a lie in his throat, that either dare, or will say, that ever I sought support against my native country. What I have been to my country, albeit this unthankful age will not know, yet the ages to come will be compelled to bear witness to the truth. And thus I cease, requiring of all men that has to oppose any thing against me, that he will do it so plainly as I make myself and all my doings manifest to the world ; for to me it seems a thing most unreasonable, that, in my decrepid age, I shall be compelled to fight against shadows and houlets, that dare not abide the light."

The conduct of our Reformer at this time affords a striking display of the unextinguishable ardour of his mind. He was so debilitated in body, that he never went abroad except on Sabbath days, to preach in the forenoon. He had given up with attendance upon church courts. He had, previous to the breaking out of the last disturbances, weaned his heart from public affairs. But whenever he saw the welfare of the church and commonwealth threatened, he forgot his resolutions and his infirmities, and entered into the cause with all the keenness of his more vigorous days. Whether the public proceedings of the nation, or his own conduct, were arraigned and condemned, whether the attacks upon them were open or clandestine, he stood prepared to repel them, and convinced the adversaries, that they could not accomplish their designs without opposition, as long as he was able to move a tongue.

His situation in Edinburgh became very critical in April 1571, when Grange received the Hamiltons, with their forces, into the castle. Their inveteracy against him was so great, that his friends were obliged to watch his house during the night. They wished to form a guard for his protection when he went abroad ; but the governor of the castle forbade this, as implying a suspicion of him, and offered to send Melvill, one of his officers, to conduct him to and from church. " He wold gif the woulf the wedder to keip," says Bannatyne. The Duke and his friends refused to pledge their word for his safety, because " there were many rascals among them who loved him not." Intimations were often given him of threatenings against his life ; and one evening, as he sat in his house, a musket ball was fired in at the window, and lodged in the roof of the room. It happened that he sat at the time in a different part of the

PERIOD
VIII.
1570–1572
A.D.

room from his usual, otherwise the ball, from the direction which it took, must have struck him.   Upon this a number of the inhabitants, along with his colleague, repaired to him, and renewed a request which they had formerly made, that he would remove from Edinburgh, to a place where his life would be in greater safety, until such time as the queen's party should evacuate the town.   But he refused to yield to them, apprehending that his enemies wished to intimidate him into flight, that they might carry on their designs more quietly, and then accuse him of cowardice.   Being unable to persuade him by any other means, they at last had recourse to an argument which prevailed.   They told him that they were determined to defend him, if attacked, at the peril of their lives, and if blood was shed in the quarrel, which was highly probable, they would leave it on his head. Upon this, he consented, "sore against his will," to leave that city.

Knox
takes
refuge in
St. An-
drews.

On the fifth of May he left Edinburgh, and crossing the firth at Leith, travelled by short stages to St. Andrews, which he had chosen as the place of his retreat.   Alexander Gordon, bishop of Galloway, occupied his pulpit.   He preached and prayed in a manner more acceptable to the queen's party than his predecessor, but little to the satisfaction of the people, who despised him on account of his weakness, and disliked him for supplanting their favourite pastor. The church of Edinburgh was for a time dissolved.   A great number of its most respectable members either were driven from the city, or left it through dissatisfaction.   The celebration of the Lord's Supper was suspended.   During a whole week "there was neither preaching nor prayer, neither was there any sound of bell heard in all the town, except the ringing of the cannon."

Amidst the extreme hostility by which both parties were inflamed, and which produced several disgraceful acts of mutual retaliation, many proofs were exhibited

of the personal antipathy which the queen's adherents
bore to the Reformer. An inhabitant of Leith was
assaulted, and his body mutilated, because he was of the
same name with him. A servant of John Craig being
met one day by a reconnoitring party, and asked who
was his master, answered in his trepidation, Mr. Knox,
upon which he was seized; and, although he immediately
corrected his mistake, they desired him to "hold at his
first master," and haled him to prison. Having fortified
St. Giles's steeple, to overawe the town, the soldiers
baptized one of the cannons by the name of *Knox*,
which they were so fond of firing, that it burst, killed
two of the party, and wounded others. They circulated
the most ridiculous tales respecting his conduct at St.
Andrews. John Law, the letter-carrier of St. Andrews,
being in the castle of Edinburgh, "the ladie Home and
utheris wald neidis thraip in his face, that" John Knox
"was banist the said toune, becaus that in the yarde he
had reasit *sum sanctis*, amongis whome thair came up *the
devill with hornis*, which when his servant Richart sawe,
[he] ran woode, and so died."

Although he was free from personal danger, Knox did
not find St. Andrews that peaceful retreat which he had
expected. The Kircaldies and Balfours were a considerable party in that quarter, and the Hamiltons had
their friends both in the university and among the
ministry. These were thorns in the Reformer's side,
and made his situation uneasy, as long as he resided
among them. Having left Edinburgh, because he could
not be permitted to discharge his conscience, in testifying
against the designs of persons whom he regarded as conspirators against the legal government of the country,
and the security of the reformed religion, it was not to
be expected that he would preserve silence on this subject at St. Andrews. In the discourses which he
preached on the eleventh chapter of Daniel's prophecy,
he frequently took occasion to advert to the transactions
of his own time, and to inveigh against the murder of

the late king, and the regent.   This was very grating to the ears of the opposite faction, particularly to Robert and Archibald Hamilton, the former a minister of the city, and the latter a professor in one of the colleges. Displeased with his censures of his relations, and aware of his popularity in the pulpit, Robert Hamilton circulated in private, that it did not become Knox to exclaim so loudly against murderers, for he had seen his subscription, along with that of the Earl of Murray, to a bond for assassinating Darnly.   But when the Reformer applied to him, Hamilton denied that he had ever spoken such words.

Archibald Hamilton being complained of for withdrawing from Knox's sermons, and accusing him of intolerable railing, endeavoured to bring the matter under the cognition of the masters of the university, among whom his influence was great.   Knox did not scruple to give an account of his conduct before the professors, for their satisfaction ; but he judged it necessary to enter a protestation, that his appearance should not prejudge the liberty of the pulpit, nor the authority of the regular church-courts, to whom, and not to any university, the judgment of religious doctrine belonged.   This incident accounts for the zeal with which he expresses himself on this subject, in his letter to the General Assembly which met in August 1572 ; in which he exhorts them, above all things, to preserve the church from the bondage of the universities, and not to exempt them from ecclesiastical jurisdiction.

A scheme concerted under the regency of Lennox.   Another source of distress to the Reformer, at this time, was a scheme which the courtiers had formed for altering the policy of the church, and securing to themselves the principal part of the ecclesiastical revenues. This plan seems to have been concerted under the regency of Lennox ; it began to be put into execution during that of Mar, and was afterwards completed by Morton.   We have already had occasion to notice the aversion of many of the nobility to the Book of Discipline, and the principal source from which this aversion sprung. While the Earl of Murray administered the government, he prevented any new encroachments upon the rights of the church; but the succeeding regents were either less friendly to them, or less able to bridle the avarice of the more powerful nobles. Several of the richest benefices becoming vacant by the decease, or by the sequestration of the Popish incumbents, who had been permitted to retain them, it was necessary to determine in what manner they should be disposed of for the future. The church had uniformly required that their revenues should be divided, and applied to the support of the religious and literary establishments; but with this demand the courtiers were by no means disposed to comply. At the same time, the total secularization of them was deemed too bold a step; nor could laymen, with any shadow of consistency, or by a valid title, hold benefices which the law declared to be ecclesiastical. The expedient resolved on was, that the bishoprics and other livings should be presented to certain ministers, who, previous to their admission, should make over the principal part of their revenues to such noblemen as had obtained the patronage of them from the court.

Accordingly, in a convention of certain ministers and courtiers, held at Leith in January 1572, it was agreed that the name and office of archbishop, bishop, &c. should be continued during the king's minority, and that qualified persons from among the ministers should be advanced to these dignities. No greater power, however, was allotted to them than to superintendents, with whom they were equally subject to the assemblies of the church. Such was the origin and nature of that species of episcopacy which was introduced into the reformed church of Scotland, in the minority of James VI. It does not appear to have proceeded in any degree from predilection to hierarchical government, but from the desire which the courtiers had to secure to themselves

A convention held at Leith.

the revenues of the church. This was emphatically expressed by the name of tulchan bishops,* which was commonly applied to those who were at this time admitted to the office.

Encroachments were, however, made upon the jurisdiction of the church in different ways, particularly by the presentation of unqualified persons, who were sometimes continued in the enjoyment of livings, without the admission of the church; by the granting of pluralities, and even by civil courts assuming the cognizance of causes of an ecclesiastical nature. Of all these we find the ministers complaining about this time.

It has been insinuated, that Knox approved of the resolutions of the convention at Leith to restore the episcopal office; and the articles sent by him to the General Assembly, August 1572, have been appealed to as a proof

Knox's
share in
the con-
vention.

of this. But all that can be deduced from these articles is, that he desired the conditions and limitations agreed upon by that convention to be strictly observed, in the election of bishops, in opposition to the granting of bishoprics to laymen (of which one glaring instance had just taken place), and also to the simoniacal pactions which the ministers made with the nobles on receiving presentations. Provided one of the propositions made by him to the Assembly had been enforced, and the bishops had been bound to give an account of the whole of their rents, and either to support ministers in the particular places from which they derived these, or else to pay into the funds of the church the sums requisite for this purpose, it is evident that the mercenary views both of the patrons and presentees would have been defeated, and the church would have gained her object, the use of the episcopal revenues. It was the prospect of this that induced some honest ministers to agree to the proposed regulations, at the convention held in Leith. But it required a greater portion of disinter-

---

* A *tulchan* is a calf's skin stuffed with straw, set up to make the cow give her milk freely.

ested firmness than falls to the most of men to act upon this principle, and the nobles were able to find, even at this period, a sufficient number of pliant, needy, or covetous ministers, to be the partners or the dupes of their avarice.

There is no reason, however, to think that our Reformer departed, on this occasion, from his principles, which, as we have already seen, were hostile to episcopacy. At this very time he received a letter from his friend Beza, expressing his satisfaction that they had banished the order of bishops from the Scottish church, and admonishing him and his colleagues to beware of suffering it to re-enter under the deceitful pretext of preserving unity. In the General Assembly which met at St. Andrews in March 1572, the " making of bishops" was introduced, and he " opponit himself directlie" unto it.

He had an opportunity of declaring his mind more publicly on this head. The Earl of Morton, who had obtained from the crown a gift of the archbishopric of St. Andrews, bargained for it with John Douglas, rector of the university, and provost of the new college, "a good upright hearted man, but ambitious and simple," and now superanuated. Knox was offended with this appointment in every point of view. Having preached on the day appointed for the inauguration of the new archbishop, Morton desired him to preside in the service; but he positively refused, and pronounced an anathema against both the donor and the receiver. The provost of St. Salvador having said that his conduct proceeded from disappointment, because the bishopric had not been conferred on himself, he, on the following Sabbath, repelled the invidious charge. He had refused, he said, a greater bishopric than that of St. Andrews, which he might have had by the favour of greater men than Douglas had his; what he had spoken was for the exoneration of his conscience, that the church of Scotland might not be subject to that order, especially after a

very different one had been established in the Book of
Discipline, had been subscribed by the nobility, and ratified by Parliament. He lamented also that a burden
should be laid upon one old man, which twenty men of
the best gifts could not sustain. At the meeting of the
General Assembly, he entered a formal protest against
this procedure. In a private letter written by him
about this time to Wishart of Pittarrow, as well as in
his public letter to the Assembly which met at Stirling,
in 1571, he expressed his strong disapprobation of the
new plans for defrauding the church of her patrimony,
and encroaching upon her free jurisdiction.

While he was engaged in these contests, his bodily
strength was every day sensibly decaying. Yet he continued to preach, although unable to walk to the pulpit
without assistance; and, when warmed with his subject,
he forgot his weakness, and electrified the audience with
his eloquence. James Melville, afterwards minister of
Anstruther, was then a student at the college, and one
of his constant hearers. The account which he has given
of his appearance is exceedingly striking; and as any
translation would enfeeble it, I shall give it in his own
words.

Melville's
testimony.
"Of all the benefits I haid that year [1571], was the
coming of that maist notable profet and apostle of our
nation, Mr. Jhone Knox, to St. Andrews, who, be the
faction of the queen occupeing the castell and town of
Edinbrugh, was compellit to remove therefra, with a
number of the best, and chusit to come to St. Andrews.
I heard him teache there the prophecies of Daniel, that
simmer, and the wintar following. I haid my pen and
my litle buike, and tuk away sic things as I could
comprehend. In the opening up of his text, he was
moderat the space of an half houre; but when he en-
terit to application, he made me so to grew, and tremble
that I could not hald a pen to wryt.—He was very
weik. I saw him, everie day of his doctrine, go hulie
and fear, with a furring of marticks about his neck, a

staffe in the an hand, and gud godlie Richart Ballanden, his servand, haldin up the uther oxter, from the abbey to the parish kirk, and, be the said Richart, and another servant, lifted up to the pulpit, whar he behovit to lean, at his first entrie; bot, er he haid done with his sermone, he was sa active and vigorous, that he was lyk to ding the pulpit in blads, and flie out of it."

During his stay at St. Andrews, he published a vindication of the reformed religion, in answer to a letter written by a Scots Jesuit, called Tyrie. The argumentative part of the work was finished by him in 1568; but he sent it abroad at this time, with additions, as a farewell address to the world, and a dying testimony to the truth which he had so long taught and defended. Along with it he published one of the religious letters which he had formerly written to his mother-in-law, Mrs. Bowes; and, in an advertisement, prefixed to this, he informs us that she had lately departed this life, and that he could not allow the opportunity to slip of acquainting the public, by means of this letter, with the principal cause of that intimate Christian friendship which had so long subsisted between them.

The ardent desire which he felt to be released, by death, from the troubles of the present life, appears in all that he wrote about this time. "Wearie of the world," and "thristing to depart," are expressions frequently used by him. The dedication of the above work is thus inscribed: "John Knox, the servant of Jesus Christ, now wearie of the world, and daylie luiking for the resolution of this my earthly tabernacle, to the faithful that God of his mercie shall appoint to fight after me." In the conclusion of it he says, "Call for me, deir brethren, that God, in his mercy, will pleis to put end to my long and paneful battell. For now being unable to fight, as God sumtymes gave strength, I thrist an end, befoir I be moir troublesum to the faithfull. And yet, Lord, let my desyre be moderat be thy Holy Spirit." In a prayer subjoined to the dedication are these words. "To thee,

O Lord, I commend my spirit. For I thrist to be resolved from this body of sin, and am assured that I sall
rise agane in glorie; howsoever it be that the wicked for
a tyme sall trode me and others thy servandes under
their feit. Be merciful, O Lord, unto the kirk within
this realme; continew with it the light of thy evangell;
augment the number of true preicheris. And let thy
mercyfull providence luke upon my desolate bedfellow,
the fruit of hir bosome, and my two deir children, Na-
thaneal and Eleazer. Now, Lord, put end to my mise-
rie." The advertisement "to the Faithful Reader,"
dated from St. Andrews, 12th July 1572, concludes in
the following manner: "I hartly salute and take my
good night of all the faithful in both realmes, earnestly
desyring the assistance of their prayers, that, without
any notable slander to the evangel of Jesus Christ, I
may end my battel. For as the world is wearie of me
so am I of it."

The General Assembly being appointed to meet at
Perth on the 6th August, he took his leave of them in a
letter, along with which he transmitted certain articles
and questions which he recommended to their consideration. The Assembly returned him an answer, declaring
their approbation of his propositions, and their earnest
desires for his preservation and comfort. The last piece
of public service which he performed at their request,
was examining and approving a sermon which had been
lately preached by David Ferguson, minister of Dunfermline. His subscription to this sermon, like every
thing which proceeded from his mouth or pen, about
this time, is uncommonly striking. "John Knox, with
my dead hand, but glaid heart, praising God, that of his
mercy he levis such light to his kirk in this desolatioun."

Declining
health.

From the rapid decline of our Reformer's health, in
spring 1572, there was every appearance of his ending
his days in St. Andrews; but it pleased God that he
should be restored once more to his flock, and allowed to
die peaceably in his own bed. In consequence of a ces-

sation of arms agreed to, in the end of July, between the regent and the adherents of the queen, the city of Edinburgh was abandoned by the forces of the latter, and secured from the annoyance of the garrison in the castle. As soon as the banished citizens returned to their houses, they sent a deputation to St. Andrews, with a letter to their minister, expressive of their earnest desire "that once again his voice might be heard among them," and entreating him immediately to come to Edinburgh, if his health would at all permit him. After reading the letter, and conversing with the commissioners, he agreed to return, but under the express condition, that he should not be urged to observe silence respecting the conduct of those who held the castle against the regent; "whose treasonable and tyrannical deeds," he said, "he would cry out against, as long as he was able to speak." He, therefore, desired them to acquaint their constituents with this, lest they should afterwards repent of his austerity, and be apprehensive of ill-treatment on his account. This he repeated upon his return to Edinburgh, before he entered the pulpit. Both the commissioners and the rest of their brethren assured him, that they did not mean to put a bridle in his mouth; but wished him to discharge his duty as he had been accustomed to do.

On the 17th of August, to the great joy of the queen's faction, whom he had overawed during his residence among them, the Reformer left St. Andrews, along with his family, and was accompanied on his journey by a number of his brethren and acquaintances. Being obliged by his weakness to travel slowly, it was the 23d of the month before he reached Leith, from which, after resting a day or two, he came to Edinburgh. The inhabitants enjoyed the satisfaction of seeing him again in his own pulpit, on the first Sabbath after he arrived; but his voice was now so enfeebled that he could not be heard by the half of the congregation. Nobody was more sensible of this than himself. He therefore requested his session to provide a smaller house in which he could be heard, if it were only by a hundred persons; for his voice, even in his best time, was not able to extend over the multitude which assembled in the large church, much less now when he was so debilitated. This was done accordingly.

During his absence, a coolness had taken place between his colleague and the parish, who found fault with him for temporizing during the time that the queen's faction retained possession of the city. In consequence of this, they had separated, and Craig was gone to another part of the country. Knox, perceiving that he would not long be able to preach, and that he was already incapacitated for all other ministerial duties, was extremely solicitous to have one settled as his colleague, that the congregation might not be left "as sheep without a shepherd," when he was called away. The last General Assembly having

granted to the church of Edinburgh liberty to choose any minister within the kingdom, those of Dundee and Perth excepted, they now unanimously fixed upon James Lawson, sub-principal of the college of Aberdeen. This choice was very agreeable to the Reformer, who, in a letter sent along with those of the superintendent and session, urged him to comply with the call without delay. Though this letter has already appeared in print, yet as it is not long, and is very descriptive of his frame of mind at this interesting period, I shall lay it before the reader.

"All worldie strenth, yea ewin in thingis spirituall, decayes; and yit sall never the work of God decay. Belovit brother, seing that God of his mercie, far above my expectatione, has callit me ones agane to Edinburgh, and yet that I feill nature so decayed, and daylie to decay, that I luke not for a long continewance of my battell, I wald gladlie anes discharge my conscience into your bosome, and into the bosome of vtheris, in whome I think the feare of God remanes. Gif I hath had the habilitie of bodie, I suld not have put you to the pane to the whilk I now requyre you, that is, anes to visit me, that we may conferre to-

gether of heawinlie things; for into earth there is no sta-
bilite, except the kirk of Jesus Christ, ever fightand
vnder the crosse, to whose myghtie protectione I hartlie
comit yeu. Of Edinburgh the vii of September, 1572.
JHONE KNOX."

In a postscript these expressive words were added,
" Haste, brother, lest you come too late."

In the beginning of September, intelligence came to
Edinburgh, that the Admiral of France, the brave, the
generous, the pious Coligni was murdered in the city of
Paris, by the orders of Charles IX. Immediately on the
back of this, tidings arrived of that most detestable and
unparalleled scene of barbarity and treachery, the general massacre of the Protestants throughout that kingdom. Post after post brought fresh accounts of the most
shocking and unheard-of cruelties. Hired cut-throats,
and fanatical cannibals marched from city to city, par-
aded the streets, and entered into the houses of those that
were marked out for destruction. No reverence was
shewn to the hoary head, no respect to rank or talents,
no pity to tender age or sex. Aged matrons, women upon the point of their delivery, and children, were trodden
under the feet of the assassins, or dragged with hooks into
the rivers; others, after being thrown into prison, were
instantly brought out, and butchered in cold blood.
Seventy thousand persons were murdered in one week.
For several days the streets of Paris literally ran with
blood. The savage monarch, standing at the windows
of the palace, with his courtiers, glutted his eyes with
the inhuman spectacle, and amused himself with firing
upon the miserable fugitives who sought shelter at his
merciless gates.

The intelligence of this massacre (for which a solemn
thanksgiving was offered up at Rome by order of the
Pope) produced the same horror and consternation in
Scotland as in every other protestant country. It in-
flicted a deep wound on the exhausted spirit of Knox.
Besides the blow struck at the whole reformed body.

10

he had to lament the loss of many individuals eminent for piety, learning, and rank, whom he numbered among his acquaintances. Being conveyed to the pulpit, and summoning up the remainder of his strength, he thundered the vengeance of Heaven against that cruel murderer and false traitor, the King of France, and desired Le Croc, the French ambassador, to tell his master, that sentence was pronounced against him in Scotland, that the divine vengeance would never depart from him, nor from his house, if repentance did not ensue; but his name would remain an execration to posterity, and none proceeding from his loins would enjoy that kingdom in peace. The ambassador complained of the indignity offered to his master, and required the regent to silence the preacher; but this was refused, upon which he left Scotland.

Anathema
pronounced
against
Charles
IX. of
France.

Lawson, having received the letters of invitation, hastened to Edinburgh, and had the satisfaction to find that Knox was still able to receive him. Having preached to the people, he gave universal satisfaction. On the following Sabbath, 21st September, Knox began to preach in the Tolbooth church, which was now fitted up for him. He chose for the subject of his discourses, the account of our Saviour's crucifixion, as recorded in the 27th chapter of the gospel according to Matthew, a theme upon which he often expressed a wish to close his ministry. On Sabbath the 9th of November, he presided in the installation of Lawson as his colleague and successor. The sermon was preached by him in the Tolbooth church; after it was ended, he removed, with the audience, to the large church, where he went through the accustomed form of admission, by proposing the questions to the minister and people, addressing an exhortation to both, and praying for the divine blessing upon the connection. Upon no former occasion did he deliver himself more to the satisfaction of those who were able to hear him. After declaring the mutual duties of pastor and congregation, he protested, in the pre-

sence of Him before whom he expected soon to appear,
that he had walked among them with a good conscience,
preaching the gospel of Jesus Christ in all sincerity, not
studying to please men nor to gratify his own affections;
he praised God, that he had been pleased to give them a
pastor in his room, when he was now unable to teach;
he fervently prayed, that any gifts which had been conferred on himself might be augmented a thousand fold
in his successor; and, in a most serious and impressive
manner, he exhorted and charged all present to adhere
stedfastly to the faith which they had professed. Having finished the service, and pronounced the blessing with
a cheerful but exhausted voice, he came down from the
pulpit, and, leaning upon his staff, crept down the street,
which was lined with the audience, who, as if anxious to
take the last sight of their beloved pastor, followed him
until he entered his house, from which he never again
came out alive.

On the Tuesday following, (Nov. 11.) he was seized
with a severe cough, which together with the defluxion,
greatly affected his breathing. When his friends, anxious to prolong his life, proposed to call in the assistance of
physicians, he readily acquiesced, saying, that he would
not neglect the ordinary means of health, although he
was persuaded that the Lord would soon put an end to
all his troubles. It was his ordinary practice to read
every day some chapters of the Old and New Testa-
ments; to which he added a certain number of the
Psalms of David, the whole of which he perused regularly once a month. On Thursday the 13th, he sickened, and was obliged to desist from his course of reading;
but he gave directions to his wife, and to his secretary
Richard Bannatyne, that one of them should every day
read to him, with a distinct voice, the 17th chapter of
the Gospel according to John, the 53d of Isaiah, and a
chapter of the Epistle to the Ephesians. This was punctually complied with during the whole time of his sickness; so that scarcely an hour passed in which some

part of Scripture was not read. Besides the above passages, he, at different times fixed on certain Psalms, and some of Calvin's French sermons on the Ephesians. Sometimes as they were reading these sermons, thinking him to be asleep, they asked him if he heard, to which he answered, " I hear (I praise God), and understand far better," which words he uttered for the last time, about four hours before his death.

The same day on which he sickened, he desired his wife to discharge the servants' wages; and next day wishing to pay one of his men servants himself, he gave him twenty shillings above his fee, adding, " Thou wilt never receive more of me in this life." To all his servants he gave suitable exhortations to walk in the fear of God, and as became Christians who had been educated in his family.

His weakness increasing.

On Friday the 14th, he rose from bed sooner than his usual hour; and, thinking that it was the Sabbath, said that he meant to go to church, and preach on the resurrection of Christ, upon which he had meditated through the whole night. This was the subject upon which he should have preached in his ordinary course. But he was so weak, that he needed to be supported from his bed-side by two men, and it was with great difficulty that he could sit on a chair.

Next day at noon, John Durie, and Archibald Steward, two of his intimate acquaintances, came into his room, not knowing that he was so sick. He rose, however, on their account; and having prevailed on them to stay dinner, he came to the table, which was the last time that he ever sat at it. He ordered a hogshead of wine which was in his cellar to be pierced; and, with a hilarity which he delighted to indulge among his friends, desired Archibald Steward to send for some of it as long as it lasted, for he would not tarry until it was all drunk.

On Sabbath he kept his bed, and mistaking it for the first day of the fast appointed on account of the French massacre, refused to take any dinner. Fairley of Braid, who was present, informed him that the fast did not commence until the following Sabbath, and sitting down, and dining before his bed, prevailed on him to take a little food.

He was very anxious to meet once more with the session of his church, to leave them his dying charge, and bid them a last farewell. In compliance with his wish, his colleague, the elders, and deacons, with David Lindsay, one of the ministers of Leith, assembled in his room on Monday the 17th, when he addressed them in the following words, which made a deep and lasting impression on the minds of all. "The day now approaches and is before the door, for which I have frequently and vehemently thirsted, when I shall be released from my great labours and innumerable sorrows, and shall be with Christ. And now, God is my witness, whom I have served in spirit, in the gospel of his Son, that I have taught nothing but the true and solid doctrine of the gospel of the Son of God, and have had it for my only object to instruct the ignorant, to confirm the faithful, to comfort the weak, the fearful, and the distressed, by the promises of grace, and to fight against the proud and rebellious, by the divine threatenings. I know that many have frequently and loudly complained, and do yet complain, of my too great severity; but God knows that my mind was always void of hatred to the persons of those against whom I thundered the severest judgments. I cannot deny but that I felt the greatest abhorrence at the sins in which they indulged, but I still kept this one thing in view, that if possible I might gain them to the Lord. What influenced me to utter whatever the Lord put into my mouth so boldly, without respect of persons, was a reverential fear of my God, who called, and of his grace appointed me to be a steward of divine mysteries, and a belief that he will demand an account of my discharge of the trust committed unto me, when I shall stand before his tribunal. I profess, therefore, before God, and before his holy angels, that I never made merchandise of the sacred word of God, never studied to please men, never indulged my own private passions or those of others, but faithfully distributed the talent intrusted to me, for the edification of the church over which I watched. Whatever obloquy wicked men may cast on me respecting this point, I rejoice in the testimony of a good conscience. In the mean time, my dearest brethren, do you persevere in the eternal truth of the gospel; wait diligently on the flock over which the Lord hath set you, and which he redeemed with the blood of his only begotten Son. And thou my brother, Lawson, fight the good fight, and do the work of the Lord joyfully and resolutely. The Lord from on high bless you, and the whole church of Edinburgh, against whom, as long as they persevere in the word of truth which they have heard of me, the gates of hell shall not prevail." Having warned them against countenancing those who disowned the king's authority, and made some observations on a complaint which Maitland had lodged against him before the session, he was so exhausted that he was obliged to desist from speaking. Those who were present were filled with both joy and grief by this affecting address. After reminding him of the warfare which he had endured, and the triumph which awaited him, and joining in prayer, they took their leave of him in tears.

When they were going out, he desired his colleague and Lindsay to remain behind, to whom he said: "There is one thing that greatly grieves me. You have been witnesses of the former courage and constancy of Grange in the cause of God; but now, alas! into what a gulph has he precipitated himself? I intreat you not to refuse to go, and tell him from me, That John Knox remains the same man now, when he is going to die, that ever he knew him when able in body, and wills him to consider what he was, and the estate in which he now stands, which is a great part of his trouble. Neither the craggy rock in which he miserably confides, nor the carnal prudence of that man (Maitland) whom he esteems a demi-god, nor the assistance of strangers, shall preserve him; but he shall be disgracefully dragged from his nest to punishment, and hung on a gallows before the face of the sun, unless he speedily amend his life, and flee to the mercy of God. That man's soul is dear to me, and I would not have it perish, if I could save it." The ministers undertook to execute this commission, and going up to the castle, obtained an interview with the governor, and delivered their message. He at first exhibited some symptoms of relenting, but having consulted with Maitland, he returned and gave them a very unpleasant answer. This being reported to Knox, he was much grieved, and said, that he had been very earnest in prayer for that man, and he still trusted that his soul would be saved, although his body should come to a miserable end.

After his interview with the session, he was much worse: his difficulty of breathing increased, and he could not speak without obvious and great pain. Yet he continued still to receive persons of every rank, who came, in great numbers, to visit him, and he suffered none to go away without exhortations, which he uttered with such variety and suitableness as astonished those who waited upon him. Lord Boyd came in and said, "I know, Sir, that I have offended you in many things, and am now come to crave your pardon." His answer was not heard, as the attendants retired and left them alone. But his lordship returned next day, in company with the Earl of Morton and the laird of Drumlanrig. His conversation with Morton was very particular, as related by the earl himself before his death. He asked him, if he was previously acquainted with the design to murder the late king. Morton having answered in the negative, he said, "Well, God has beautified you with many benefits which he has not given to every man; as he has given you riches, wisdom, and friends, and now is to prefer you to the government

His charge to Morton

of the realm. And therefore, in the name of God, I charge you to use all these benefits aright, and better in time to come than ye have done in times bypast; first to God's glory, to the furtherance of the evangel, the maintenance of the church of God, and his ministry; next for the weal of the king, and his realm, and true subjects. If so ye shall do, God shall bless you, and honour you; but if ye do it not, God shall spoil you of these benefits, and your end shall be ignominy and shame."

On Thursday the 20th, Lord Lindsay, the bishop of Caithness, and several gentlemen visited him. He exhorted them to continue in the truth which they had heard, for there was no other word of salvation, and besought them to have nothing to do with those in the castle. The earl of Glencairn (who had often visited him) came in, with lord Ruthven. The latter, who called only once, said, " If there be any thing, Sir, that I am able to do for you, I pray you charge me." His reply was, " I care not for all the pleasure and friendship of the world."

A religious lady of his acquaintance desired him to praise God for what good he had done, and was beginning to speak in his commendation, when he interrupted her. " Tongue, tongue, lady, flesh of itself is overproud, and needs no means to esteem itself." He put her in mind of what had been said to her long ago, " Lady, lady, the black one has never trampit on your fute," and exhorted her to lay aside pride, and be clothed with humility. He then protested as to himself, as he had often done before, that he relied wholly on the free mercy of God, manifested to mankind through his dear Son Jesus Christ, whom alone he embraced for wisdom, and righteousness, and sanctification, and redemption. The rest of the company having taken their leave of him, he said to the laird of Braid, " Every one bids me good night, but when will you do it? I have been greatly indebted unto you, for which I shall never be able to recompense you; but I commit you to one that is able to do it, to the eternal God."

Upon Friday the 21st, he desired Richard Bannatyne to order his coffin to be made. During that day he was much engaged in meditation and prayer. These words were often in his mouth; "Come, Lord Jesus. Sweet Jesus, into thy hands I commend my spirit. Be merciful, Lord, to thy church which thou hast redeemed. Give peace to this afflicted commonwealth. Raise up faithful pastors who will take the charge of thy church. Grant us, Lord, the perfect hatred of sin, both by the evidences of thy wrath and mercy." In the midst of his meditations, he would often address those who stood by, in such sentences as these: " O serve the Lord in fear, and death shall not be terrible to you. Nay, blessed shall death be to those who have felt the power of the death of the only begotten Son of God."

PERIOD VIII. 1570–1572 A. D.

On Sabbath 23d (which was the first day of the national fast), during the afternoon-sermon, he, after lying a considerable time quiet, suddenly exclaimed, " If any be present, let them come and see the work of God." Richard Bannatyne thinking that his death was at hand, sent to the church for Johnston of Elphingston. When they came to his bed-side, he burst out in these rapturous expressions: " I have been these two last nights in meditation on the troubled state of the church of God, the spouse of Jesus Christ, despised of the world, but precious in the sight of God. I have called to God for her, and have committed her to her head, Jesus Christ. I have fought against spiritual wickedness in heavenly things, and have prevailed. I have been in heaven, and have possession. I have tasted of the heavenly joys, where presently I am." He then repeated the Lord's prayer and creed, interjecting some devout aspiration at the end of every petition, and article.

After sermon many came in to visit him. Perceiving that he breathed with great difficulty, some of them asked, if he felt much pain. He answered that he was willing to lie there for years, if God so pleased, and if he continued to shine upon his soul, through Jesus Christ.

His breathing difficult.

When they thought him asleep, he was employed in meditation, and at intervals exhorted and prayed. "Live in Christ. Live in Christ, and then flesh need not fear death. Lord, grant true pastors to thy church, that purity of doctrine may be retained. Restore peace again to this commonwealth, with godly rulers and magistrates. Once, Lord, make an end of my trouble." Stretching his hands toward heaven, he said, "Lord, I commend my spirit, soul, and body, and all, into thy hands. Thou knowest, O Lord, my troubles: I do not murmur against thee." His pious ejaculations were so numerous, that those who waited on him could recollect only a part of them, for seldom was he silent, when they were not employed in reading or in prayer.—During the course of that night his trouble greatly increased.

Monday, the 24th of November, was the last day that he spent on earth. That morning he would not be persuaded to lie in bed, but, though unable to stand alone, rose between nine and ten o'clock, and put on his stockings and doublet. Being conducted to a chair, he sat about half an hour, and then went to bed again. In the progress of the day it appeared evident that his end drew near. Besides his wife and Richard Bannatyne, Campbell of Kinyeancleugh, Johnston of Elphingston, and Dr. Preston, three of his most intimate acquaintances, waited by his bed-side. Mr. Campbell asked him, if he had any pain. "It is no painful pain, but such a pain as shall, I trust, put end to the battle. I must leave the care of my wife and children to you," continued he, "to whom you must be a husband in my room." About three o'clock in the afternoon, one of his eyes failed, and his speech was considerably affected. He desired his wife to read the 15th chapter of 1st Corinthians. "Is not that a comfortable chapter?" said he, when it was finished. "O what sweet and salutary consolation the Lord hath afforded me from that chapter!" A little after, he said, "Now, for the last time, I commend my soul, spirit, and body," touching three of his fingers, "in-

to thy hand, O Lord." About five o'clock he said to his
wife, "Go read where I cast my first anchor;" upon
which she read the 17th chapter of John's gospel, and
afterwards a part of Calvin's sermons on the Ephesians.

After this he appeared to fall into a slumber, during
which he uttered heavy groans. The attendants looked
every moment for his dissolution. At length he awaked
as if from sleep, and being asked the cause of his sighing
so deeply, replied, "I have formerly, during my frail
life, sustained many contests, and many assaults of Satan; but at present that roaring lion hath assailed me
most furiously, and put forth all his strength to devour,
and make an end of me at once. Often before has he
placed my sins before my eyes, often tempted me to despair, often endeavoured to ensnare me by the allure-
ments of the world; but with these weapons, broken by
the sword of the spirit, the word of God, he could not
prevail. Now he has attacked me in another way;
the cunning serpent has laboured to persuade me that
I have merited heaven and eternal blessedness, by the
faithful discharge of my ministry. But blessed be God
who has enabled me to beat down and quench this
fiery dart, by suggesting to me such passages of Scripture as these: What hast thou that thou hast not
received? By the grace of God I am what I am:
Not I, but the grace of God in me. Being thus vanquished, he left me. Wherefore I give thanks to my
God through Jesus Christ, who was pleased to give me
the victory; and I am persuaded that the tempter shall
not again attack me, but, within a short time, I shall,
without any great bodily pain, or anguish of mind, exchange this mortal and miserable life for a blessed immortality through Jesus Christ."

He then lay quiet for some hours, except that now
and then he desired them to wet his mouth with a little
weak ale. At ten o'clock, they read the evening prayer,
which they had delayed beyond their usual hour,
from an apprehension that he was asleep. After they

concluded, Dr. Preston asked him, if he had heard the prayers. "Would to God," said he, "that you and all men had heard them as I have heard them: I praise God for that heavenly sound." The doctor rose up, and Mr. Campbell sat down before the bed. About eleven o'clock, he gave a deep sigh, and said, Now it is come. Richard Bannatyne immediately drew near, and desired him to think upon those comfortable promises of our Saviour Jesus Christ, which he had so often declared to others; and, perceiving that he was speechless, requested him to give them a sign that he heard them, and died in peace.

November 24th.

Upon this he lifted up one of his hands, and sighing twice, expired without a struggle.

He died in the sixty-seventh year of his age, not so much oppressed with years, as worn out and exhausted by his extraordinary labours of body and anxieties of mind. Few men ever were exposed to more dangers, or underwent such hardships. From the time that he embraced the reformed religion, till he breathed his last, seldom did he enjoy a respite from these, and he emerged from one scene of difficulties, only to be involved in another, and a more distressing one. Obliged to flee from St. Andrews to escape the fury of Cardinal Beatoun, he found a retreat in East Lothian, from which he was hunted by archbishop Hamilton. He lived for several years as an outlaw, in daily apprehension of falling a prey to those who eagerly sought his life. The few months during which he enjoyed protection in the castle of St. Andrews were succeeded by a long and rigorous captivity. After enjoying some repose in England, he was again driven into banishment, and for five years wandered as an exile on the continent. When he returned to his native country, it was to engage in a struggle of the most perilous and arduous kind. After the reformation was established, and he was settled in the capital, he was involved in a continual contest with the court. When he had retired from warfare, and thought only of ending his days in peace, he was again called into the field ; and, although scarcely able to walk, was obliged to remove from his flock, and to avoid the hatred of his enemies, by submitting to a new banishment. Often had his life been threatened ; a price was publicly set upon his head; and persons were not wanting who were disposed to attempt his destruction. No wonder that he was weary of the world, and anxious to depart. With great propriety might it be said, at his decease, that he rested from his labours.

On Wednesday the 26th of November, he was interred in the church yard of St. Giles. His funeral was attended by the newly elected regent, Morton, the nobility who were in the city, and a great concourse of people. When his body was laid in the grave, the regent pronounced his eulogium, in the well-known words, " There lies he, who never feared the face of man."

The character of this extraordinary man has been drawn with very opposite colours, by different writers, and at different times. The changes which have taken place in the public opinion about him, with the causes which have produced them, form a subject not uncurious nor unworthy of attention.

The interest excited by the ecclesiastical and political revolutions of Scotland, in which he acted so conspicuous a part, caused his name to be known throughout Europe, more extensively than those of most of the reformers. When we reflect that the Roman Catholics looked upon him as the principal instrument of the overthrow of their religious establishment in this country, we are prepared to expect that the writers of that persuasion would represent his character in an unfavourable light; and that, in addition to the common charges of heresy and apostasy, they would describe him as a man of a restless, turbulent spirit, and of rebellious principles. We will not even be greatly surprised though we find them charging him with whoredom, because, being a priest, he entered into wedlock, once and a second time; or imputing his change of religion to a desire of throwing off the bonds of chastity by which the Popish clergy were so strictly tied. But all this is nothing to the portraits which they have drawn of him, in which he is unblushingly represented, to the violation of all credibility, as a man, or rather a monster, of the most profligate character, who gloried in depravity, avowedly indulged in the most vicious practices, and to crown the description, upon whom providence fixed an evident mark of reprobation at his death, which was accompanied with circumstances which excited the utmost horror in the beholders. This might astonish us, did we not know, from undoubted documents, that there were a number of writers, at that time, who, by inventing or retailing such malignant calumnies, attempted to blast the fairest and most unblemished characters among those who appeared in opposition to the church of Rome, and that, ridiculous and outraged as the accusations were, they were greedily swallowed by the slaves of prejudice and credulity. The memory of none was loaded with a greater share of this obloquy than our Reformer's. But these accounts have long ago lost every degree of credit; and they now remain only as a proof of the spirit of lies, or of strong delusion, by which these writers were actuated, and of the deep and deadly hatred which was conceived against the accused, on account of his strenuous and successful efforts to overthrow the fabric of papal superstition and despotism.

Knox was known and esteemed by the principal persons among the reformed in France, Switzerland, and Germany. We have had occasion repeatedly to mention **Theodore de Beza.** his friendship with the Reformer of Geneva. Beza, the successor of Calvin, was personally acquainted with him; in the correspondence which was kept up between them by letters, he expressed the warmest regard, and highest esteem for him: and he afterwards raised an

affectionate tribute to his memory, in his *Images of* ADDEND
Illustrious Men. This was done, at a subsequent period,
by the German biographer, Melchior Adam, the Dutch
Verheiden, and the French La Roque. The late historian of the literature of Geneva, (whose religious sentiments are very different from those of his countrymen
in the days of Calvin), although he is displeased with
the philippics which Knox sometimes pronounced from
the pulpit, says, that he "immortalised himself by his
courage against Popery, and his firmness against the
tyranny of Mary," and that though a violent, he was
always an open and honourable enemy to the Catholics.

The affectionate veneration in which his memory was
held in Scotland, after his death, evinces that the influence which he possessed among his countrymen during
his life was not constrained, but founded on the opinion
which they entertained of his virtues and talents. Bannatyne has drawn his character in the most glowing
colours; and, although allowances must be made for the
enthusiasm with which a favourite servant wrote of a
beloved and revered master, yet, as he lived long in his
family, and was himself a man of respectability and
learning, his testimony is by no means to be disregarded.
"In this manner," says he, "departed this man of God : Richard
the light of Scotland, the comfort of the church within Banna-
the same, the mirror of godliness, and pattern and tyne's t
example to all true ministers, in purity of life, soundness timony.
in doctrine, and boldness in reproving of wickedness ;
one that cared not the favour of men, how great soever
they were. What dexterity in teaching, boldness in reproving, and hatred of wickedness was in him, my
ignorant dulness is not able to declare, which if I should
preis to set out, it were as one who would light a candle
to let men see the sun ; seeing all his virtues are better
known and notified to the world a thousand fold than I
am able to express."

Principal Smeton's character of him, while it is less
liable to the suspicion of partiality, is equally honour-

able and flattering. " I know not," says he, " if ever so much piety and genius were lodged in such a frail and weak body. Certain I am, that it will be difficult to find one in whom the gifts of the Holy Spirit shone so bright to the comfort of the church of Scotland. None spared himself less in enduring fatigues of body and mind ; none was more intent on discharging the duties of the province assigned to him." And again, addressing Hamilton, he says, " This illustrious, I say *illustrious*, servant of God, John Knox, I will clear from your feigned accusations and slanders, rather by the testimony of a venerable assembly than by my own denial. This pious duty, this reward of a well-spent life, all of them most cheerfully discharge to their excellent instructor in Christ Jesus. This testimony of gratitude they all owe to him, who, they know, ceased not to deserve well of all, till he ceased to breathe. Released from a body exhausted in Christian warfare, and translated to a blessed rest, where he has obtained the sweet reward or his labours, he now triumphs with Christ. But beware, sycophant, of insulting him when dead ; for he has left behind him as many defenders of his reputation as there are persons who were drawn, by his faithful preaching, from the gulph of ignorance to the knowledge of the gospel."

Principal Smeton's estimate of him.

The divines of the church of England who were contemporary with our Reformer, or who survived him, entertained a great respect for his character. I have already produced the mark of esteem which Bishop Bale conferred on him. Aylmer, in a work written to confute one of his opinions, bears a voluntary testimony to his learning and integrity. Bishop Ridley, who stickled more for the ceremonies of the church than any of his brethren at that period, and was displeased with the opposition which he made to the introduction of the English liturgy at Frankfort, expressed his high opinion of him, as " a man of wit, much good learning, and earnest zeal." Whatever dissatisfaction they felt at his pointed repre-

Bishop Ridley's opinion.

hensions of several parts of their ecclesiastical establishment, the English dignitaries rejoiced at the success of his exertions, and without scruple expressed their approbation of many of his measures which were afterwards severely censured by their successors. I need scarcely add, that his memory was held in veneration by the English Puritans. Some of the chief men among them were personally acquainted with him during his residence in England, and on the continent; others corresponded with him by letters. They greatly esteemed his writings, procured his manuscripts from Scotland, and published several of them.

But towards the close of the sixteenth century, there arose another race of prelates, of very different principles from the English reformers, who began to maintain the divine right of diocesan episcopacy, with the intrinsic excellency of a ceremonious worship, and to adopt a new language respecting other reformed churches. Dr. Bancroft, afterwards archbishop of Canterbury, was the first writer among them who spake disrepectfully of Knox, after whom it became a fashionable practice among the hierarchical party. This was resented by the ministers of Scotland, who warmly vindicated the character of their Reformer. King James, who began to long for his accession to the throne of England, and carried on a private correspondence with Bancroft for introducing episcopacy into Scotland, took great offence at this, and said that Knox, Buchanan, and the regent Murray, "could Opinion of not be defended, but by traitors and seditious theo- James VI. logues." Andrew Melville told him that they were the men who set the crown on his head, and deserved better than to be so traduced. James complained that Knox had spoken disrespectfully of his mother; to which Patrick Galloway, one of the ministers of Edinburgh, replied, "If a king or a queen be a murderer, why should they not be called so?" Walter Balcanquhal, another Balcanquhal, 1590 minister of the city, having, in a sermon preached October 29, 1590, rebuked those who disparaged the Reform- A.D.

ADDENDA.

er, the king sent for him, and in a passion protested, that "either he should lose his crown, or Mr. Walter should recant his words." Balcanquhal "prayed God to preserve his crown, but said, that if he had his right wits, the king should have his head, before he recanted any thing he spake." Long after the government of the church of Scotland was conformed to the English model, the Scots prelates professed to look back to their national Reformer with gratitude and veneration; and as late as 1639, archbishop Spottiswood described him as "a man endued with rare gifts, and a chief instrument that God used for the work of those times."

Arch-
bishop
Spottis-
wood,
1639 A.D.

Our Reformer was never a favourite with the friends of absolute monarchy. The prejudices which they entertained against him were taken up in all their force, subsequent to the revolution, by the adherents of the Stuart family, whose religious notions approximating very nearly to the popish, joined with their slavish principle respecting non-resistance of kings, led them to disapprove of almost every measure adopted at the time of the reformation, and to condemn the whole as a series of disorder, sedition, and rebellion against lawful authority. The spirit by which the Jacobitish faction was actuated, did not become extinct with the family which was so long the object of their devotion: it has only changed its object. The alarm produced by that revolution which of late has shaken the thrones of so many of the princes of Europe, has greatly increased this party; and with the view of preserving the present constitution of Britain, principles have been widely disseminated, which, if they had been generally received in the sixteenth century, would have perpetuated the reign of popery and arbitrary power in Scotland. From persons of such principles, nothing favourable to our Reformer can be expected. But the greatest torrent of abuse, poured upon his character, has proceeded from those literary champions who have come forward to avenge the wrongs, and vindicate the innocence of the peerless, and immaculate

The Jaco-
bite fac-
tion.

Mary, queen of Scots. Having conjured up in their im- agination the image of an ideal goddess, they have sacrificed, to the object of their adoration, all the characters which, in that age, were most estimable for learning, patriotism, integrity, and religion. As if the quarrel which they had espoused exempted them from the ordinary laws of controversial warfare, and conferred on them the absolute and undefeasible privilege of calumniating and defaming at pleasure, they have pronounced every person who spake, wrote, or acted against that queen, to be a hypocrite or a villain. In the raving style of these writers, Knox was " a fanatical incendiary, a holy savage, the son of violence and barbarism, the religious Sachem of religious Mohawks."

The increase of infidelity, and of indifference to religion in modern times, especially among the learned, has contributed, in no small degree, to swell the tide of prejudice against our Reformer. Whatever satisfaction such persons may express, or feel, at the reformation from Popery, as the means of emancipating the world from superstition and priestcraft, they must necessarily despise, or dislike men who were inspired with the love of religion, and who sought the acquisition of civil liberty, and the advancement of literature, in subordination to the propagation of the doctrines and institutions of Jesus Christ. Nor can it escape observation, that even among the friends of the reformed doctrine, in the pre- sent day, prejudices against the characters and proceedings of our reformers are far more general than they were formerly. Impressed with the idea of the high illumination of the present age, and having formed a correspondingly low estimate of the attainments of those which preceded it; imperfectly acquainted with the enormity and extent of the corrupt system of religion which existed in this country at the æra of the Reformation; inattentive to the spirit and principles of the adversaries with which our reformers were obliged to contend, and to the dangers and difficulties with which

ADDENDA. they struggled,—they have too easily received the calumnies which have been circulated to their prejudice, and hastily condemned measures which may be found, upon examination, to have been necessary to secure, and to transmit the invaluable blessings which they now enjoy.

Having given this account of the opinions entertained respecting our Reformer, I shall endeavour to sketch, with as much truth as I can, the leading features of his character.

Outline of Knox's character.

That he possessed strong natural talents is unquestionable. Inquisitive, ardent, acute; vigorous and bold in his conceptions; he entered into all the subtleties of the scholastic science then in vogue, yet, disgusted with its barren results, sought out a new course of study, which gradually led to a complete revolution in his sentiments. In his early years he had not access to that finished education which many of his contemporaries obtained in the foreign universities, and he was afterwards prevented, by his unsettled and active mode of life, from prosecuting his studies with leisure; but his abilities and application enabled him in a great measure to surmount these disadvantages, and he remained a stranger to none of the branches of learning cultivated in that age by persons of his profession. He united the love of study with a disposition to active employment, two qualities which are seldom found in the same person. The truths which he discovered he felt an irresistible impulse to impart unto others, for which he was qualified by a bold and fervid eloquence, singularly adapted to arrest the attention, and govern the minds of a fierce and unpolished people.

From the time that he embraced the reformed doctrines, the desire of propagating them, and of delivering his countrymen from the delusions and corruptions of Popery, became his ruling passion, to which he was always ready to sacrifice his ease, his interest, his reputation, and his life. An ardent attachment to civil liberty held the next place in his breast, to love of the reformed religion. That the zeal with which he laboured to advance these was of the most disinterested kind, no candid person who has paid attention to his life can doubt for a moment, whatever opinion he may entertain of some of the means which he employed for that purpose. "In fact, he thought only of advancing the glory of God, and promoting the welfare of his country." Intrepidity, a mind elevated above sordid views, indefatigable activity, and constancy which no disappointments could shake, eminently qualified him for the hazardous and difficult post which he occupied. His integrity was above the suspicion of corruption; his firmness proof equally against the solicitations of friends, and the threats of enemies. Though his impetuosity and courage led him frequently to expose himself to danger, we never find him neglecting to take prudent precautions for his safety. The opinion which his countrymen entertained of his sagacity, as well as honesty, is evident from the confidence which they reposed in him. The measures taken for advancing the reformation were either adopted at his suggestion, or submitted to his advice; and we must pronounce them to have been as wisely planned as they were boldly executed.

His ministerial functions were discharged with the greatest assiduity, fidelity, and fervour. No avocation or infirmity prevented him from appearing in the pulpit. Preaching was an employment in which he delighted, and for which he was qualified, by an extensive acquaintance with the Scriptures, and the happy art of applying them, in the most striking manner, to the existing circumstances of the church, and of his hearers. His powers of alarming the conscience, and arousing the passions, have been frequently mentioned; but he excelled also in opening up the consolations of the gospel, and calming the breasts of those who were agitated with a sense of their sins. When he discoursed of the griefs and joys, the conflicts and triumphs of genuine Chris-

His knowledge of the Scriptures

tians, he declared what he himself had known and felt. The letters which he wrote to his familiar acquaintances breathe the most ardent piety. The religious meditations in which he spent his last sickness were not confined to that period of his life; they had been his habitual employment from the time that he was brought to the knowledge of the truth, and his solace amidst all the hardships and perils through which he passed.

With his brethren in the ministry he lived in the utmost cordiality. We never read of the slightest variance between him and any of his colleagues. While he was dreaded and hated by the licentious and profane, whose vices he never spared, the religious and sober part of his congregation and countrymen felt a veneration for

him, which was founded on his unblemished reputation, as well as his popular talents as a preacher. In private life, he was both beloved and revered by his friends and domestics. He was subject to the occasional illapses of melancholy, and depression of spirits, arising partly from natural constitution, and partly from the maladies which had long preyed upon his health; which made him (to use his own expression) *churlish*, and less capable of pleasing and gratifying his friends than he was otherwise disposed to be. This he confessed, and requested them to excuse; but his friendship was sincere, affectionate, and steady. When free from this morose affection, he relished the pleasures of society, and among his acquaintances, was accustomed to unbend his mind from severer cares, by indulging in innocent recreation, and the sallies of wit and humour, to which he had a strong propensity, notwithstanding the grave tone of his general character.

Most of his faults may be traced to his natural temperament, and the character of the age and country in which he lived. His passions were strong; he felt with the utmost keenness on every subject which interested him; and as he felt he expressed himself, without disguise or affectation. The warmth of his zeal was apt to

betray him into intemperate language; his inflexible ADDENDA.
adherence to his opinions inclined to obstinacy; and his
independence of mind occasionally assumed the appearance of haughtiness and disdain. A stranger to compli-
mentary or smooth language, little concerned about the
manner in which his reproofs were received, provided
they were merited, too much impressed with the evil of
the offence, to think of the rank or character of the of-
fender, he often " uttered his admonitions with an acri-
mony and vehemence more apt to irritate than to reclaim." But he protested at a time when persons are
least in danger of deception, and in a manner which
should banish suspicions of the purity of his motives,
that, in his sharpest rebukes, he was influenced by hatred of the vices, not the persons of the vicious, and that
his aim was always to discharge his own duty, and, if
possible, to reclaim the guilty.

Those who have charged him with insensibility and
inhumanity, have fallen into a mistake very common
with superficial thinkers, who, in judging of the characters of persons who lived in a state of society very different from their own, have pronounced upon their moral qualities from the mere aspect of their exterior manners. He was stern, not savage; austere, not unfeeling;
vehement, not vindictive. There is not an instance of
his employing his influence to revenge any personal injury which he had received. Rigid as his maxims as to
the execution of justice were, there are more instances on
record of his interceding for the pardon of criminals, than
perhaps of any man of his time; and unless when crimes
were atrocious, or the safety of the state was at stake, he
never exhorted the executive authority to the exercise
of severity. The boldness and ardour of his mind, called His opin-
forth by the peculiar circumstances of the time, led him ion unto push his sentiments on some subjects to an extreme, changeable.
and no consideration could induce him to retract an opinion of which he continued to be persuaded; but his behaviour after his publication against female government.

proves that he was not disposed to improve them to the disturbance of the public peace. His conduct at Frankfort evinced his moderation in religious differences among brethren of the same faith, and that he was disposed to make all reasonable allowances for those who could not go the same length with him in reformation, provided they abstained from imposing upon the consciences of others. The liberties which he took in censuring from the pulpit the actions of individuals, of the highest rank and station, appear the more strange and intolerable to us, when contrasted with the silence of modern times; but we should recollect that they were then common, and that they were not without their utility, in an age when the licentiousness and oppression of the great and powerful often set at defiance the ordinary restraints of law.

In contemplating such a character as that of Knox, it is not the man, so much as the reformer, that ought to engage our attention. The admirable wisdom of providence in raising up persons endued with qualities suited to the work allotted them to perform for the benefit of mankind, demands our particular consideration. The Matt. iii. austere and rough reformer, whose voice once " cried in the wilderness" of Judea, who was " clothed with camel's hair, and girt about the loins with a leathern girdle," who " came neither eating nor drinking," who, " laying the axe to the root of every tree, warned a generation of vipers to flee from the wrath to come," saying even to Matt. xiv. the tyrant upon the throne, " It is not lawful for thee;" he, I say, was fitted for " serving the will of God in his generation;" and " wisdom was justified" in him, according to his rank and place, as well as in his Divine Master, whose advent he announced, who " did not strive, nor cry, nor cause his voice to be heard in the streets; nor Matt. xii. break the bruised reed, nor quench the smoking flax." To those who complain, that they are disappointed at not finding, in our national Reformer, a mild demeanour, courteous manners and a winning address, we may say

in the language of our Lord to the Jews concerning the
Baptist; "What went ye out into the wilderness for to
see? A reed shaken with the wind? What went ye out
for to see? A man clothed in soft raiment? Behold, they
which are gorgeously apparelled, and live delicately, are
in king's courts. But what went ye out for to see? A
prophet? Yea, I say unto you, and more than a prophet."
Those talents which fit a person for acting with propri- Matt. xi. 7.
ety and usefulness in one age and situation, would alto- Luke vii.
gether unfit him for another. Before the reformation, 24.
superstition shielded by ignorance, and armed with power, governed with gigantic sway. Men of mild spirits,
and gentle manners, would have been as unfit for taking
the field against this enemy, as a dwarf or a child for
encountering a giant. "What did Erasmus in the days
of Luther? What would Lowth have done in the days
of Wicliffe, or Blair in those of Knox?" It has been
justly observed concerning our Reformer, that "those
very qualities which now render his character less amiable, fitted him to be the instrument of providence for
advancing the reformation among a fierce people, and
enabled him to face danger, and surmount opposition,
from which a person of a more gentle spirit would have
been apt to shrink back." Viewing his character in this
light, if we cannot regard him as an amiable man, we may,
without hesitation, pronounce him a Great Reformer.

There are perhaps few who have attended to the active and laborious exertions of Knox, who have not been His stat-
led insensibly to form the opinion that he was of a ro ure.
bust constitution. This is however a mistake. He was
of small stature, and of a weakly habit of body; a circumstance which serves to give a higher idea of the vigour of his mind. His portrait seems to have been taken
more than once during his life, and has been frequently
engraved. It continues still to frown in the bed-cham-
ber of queen Mary, to whom he was often an ungracious
visitor. We discern in it the traits of his characteristic
intrepidity, austerity, and keen penetration. Nor can

we overlook his beard, which, according to the custom of the times, he wore long, and reaching to his middle; a circumstance which I mention the rather, because some writers have assured us, that it was the chief thing which procured him reverence among his countrymen. A popish author has informed us, that he was gratified with having his picture drawn, and expresses much horror at this, after he had caused all the images of the saints to be broken.

There is one charge against him which I have not yet noticed. He has been accused of setting up for a prophet, of presuming to intrude into the secret counsel of God, and of enthusiastically confounding the suggestions of his own imagination, and the effusions of his own spirit, with the dictates of inspiration, and immediate communications from heaven. Let us examine the grounds of this accusation a little. It is proper to hear his own statement of the grounds upon which he proceeded in many of those warnings which have been denominated predictions. Having in one of his treatises, denounced the judgments to which the inhabitants of England exposed themselves, by renouncing the gospel and returning to idolatry, he gives the following explication of the warrant which he had for his threatenings.

Knox on his prophetic warnings.

"Ye wald knaw the groundis of my certitude. God grant that, hering thame, ye may understand, and stedfastlie believe the same. My assurances ar not the mervalles of Merlin, nor yit the dark sentences of prophane prophesies; but the plane treuth of Godis word, the invincibill justice of the everlasting God, and the ordinarie cours of his punismentis and plagis frome the beginning ar my assurance and groundis. Godis word threatneth destructioun to all inobedient; his immutabill justice man requyre the same; the ordinar punishments and plaguis schawis exempillis. What man then can ceis to prophesie?" We find him expressing himself in a similar way in his defences of the threatenings which he uttered against those who had been guilty of the

murder of king Henry, and the regent Murray. He re- ADDENDA.
fused that he had spoken "as one that entered into the
secret counsel of God," and insisted that he had merely
declared the judgment which was pronounced in the divine law. In so far then his threatenings, or predictions
(for so he repeatedly calls them) do not stand in need
of an apology.

There are, however, several of his sayings which cannot be vindicated upon these principles, and which he
himself rested upon different grounds. Of this kind
were, the assurance which he expressed, from the beginning of the Scottish troubles, that the cause of the Congregation would ultimately prevail; his confident hope
of again preaching in his native country, and at St. Andrews, avowed by him during his imprisonment on board
the French galleys, and frequently repeated during
his exile ; with the intimations which he gave respecting the death of Thomas Maitland, and Kircaldy of
Grange. It cannot be denied that his contemporaries
considered these as proceeding from a prophetic spirit,
and have attested that they received an exact accomplishment. The most easy way of getting rid of this His pre-
delicate question is, by dismissing it at once, and sum- dictions
marily pronouncing that all pretensions to extraordi- held to be
nary premonitions, since the completing of the canon visionary.
of inspiration, are unwarranted, that they ought, without examination, to be discarded and treated as fanciful
and visionary. Nor would this fix any peculiar imputation on the character or talents of our Reformer, when
it is considered that the most learned persons of that age
were under the influence of a still greater weakness, and
strongly addicted to the belief of judicial astrology.
But I doubt much if this method of determining the
question would be consistent with doing justice to the
subject. I cannot propose to enter into it in this place,
and must confine myself to a few general observations.
Est periculum, aut neglectis his, impia fraude, aut suscep-
tis anili superstitione, obliyemur. On the one hand, the

ADDENDA. disposition which mankind discover to pry into the secrets of futurity, has been always accompanied with much credulity, and superstition; and it cannot be denied, that the age in which our Reformer lived was prone to credit the marvellous, especially as to the infliction of divine judgments upon individuals. On the other hand, there is great danger of running into scepticism, and of laying down general principles which may lead us obstinately to contest the truth of the best authenticated facts, and even to limit the Spirit of God, and the operation of providence. This is an extreme to which the present age inclines. That there have been instances of persons having presentiments and premonitions as to events that happened to themselves and others, there is, I think, the best reason to believe. The *esprits forts*, who laugh at vulgar credulity, and exert their ingenuity in accounting for such phenomena upon ordinary principles, have been exceedingly puzzled with these, a great deal more puzzled than they have confessed; and the solutions which they have given are, in some instances, as mysterious as any thing included in the intervention of superior spirits, or divine intimations. The canon of our faith is contained in the scriptures of the Old and New Testament; we must not look to impressions or new revelations as the rule of our duty; but that God may, on particular occasions, forewarn persons of some things which shall happen, to testify his approbation of them, to encourage them to confide in him in peculiar circumstances, or for other useful purposes, is not, I think, inconsistent with the principles of either natural or revealed religion. If this is enthusiasm, it is an enthusiasm into which some of the most enlightened and sober men, in modern as well as ancient times, have fallen. Some of the reformers were men of singular piety; they "walked with God;" they were "instant in prayer;" they were exposed to uncommon opposition, and had uncommon services to perform; they were endued with extraordinary gifts,

Presentiment and premonition.

and, I am inclined to believe, were occasionally favoured with extraordinary premonitions, with respect to
certain events which concerned themselves, other individuals, or the church in general. But whatever intimations of this kind they enjoyed, they did not rest the
authority of their mission upon them, nor appeal to
them as constituting any part of the evidence of those
doctrines which they preached to the world.

Our Reformer left behind him a widow, and five
children. His two sons, Nathanael and Eleazar, were
born to him by his first wife, Mrs Marjory Bowes. We
have already seen that, about the year 1566, they went to
England, where their mother's relations resided. They
received their education at St. John's College, in the
university of Cambridge, and after finishing it, died in
the prime of life. It appears that they died without
issue, and the family of the Reformer became extinct in
the male line. His other three children were daughters
by his second wife. Dame Margaret Stewart, his widow,
afterwards married Sir Andrew Ker of Fadounside, a
strenuous supporter of the Reformation. One of his
daughters was married to Mr. Robert Pont, minister of
St. Cuthberts ; another of them to Mr. James Fleming,
also a minister of the Church of Scotland ; Elizabeth,
the third daughter, was married to Mr. John Welch,
minister of Ayr.

Mrs. Welch seems to have inherited a considerable
portion of her father's spirit, and she had her share of
hardships similar to his. Her husband was one of those
who resisted the arbitrary measures pursued by James
VI. for overturning the government and liberties of the
presbyterian Church of Scotland. For attending a meeting of the General Assembly at Aberdeen, in July 1605,
when the king had sent directions for adjourning it,
sine die, (in pursuance of a scheme laid for abolishing
that court), he was imprisoned ; and for afterwards declining the Privy Council, as not the proper judges of
that cause, he, along with other five ministers, was

arraigned, and, by a packed and corrupted jury, found
guilty, and condemned to the death of traitors. Leaving
her children at Ayr, Mrs. Welch attended her husband in
prison, and was present at Linlithgow, with the wives of
the other pannels, on the day of trial. When informed
of the sentence, these heroines, instead of lamenting
their fate, praised God who had given their husbands
courage to stand to the cause of their Master, adding
that, like Him, they had been judged and condemned
under the covert of night.

The sentence having been commuted into banishment,
she accompanied her husband to France, where they
remained for sixteen years. Mr. Welch, having lost his
health, and the physicians informing him that the only
prospect which he had of recovering it was by returning
to his native country, ventured, about the year 1622, to
come to London. His wife, by means of some of her
mother's relations at court, obtained access to the king, to
petition for liberty to him to go to Scotland for the sake of
his health. The following conversation is said to have
taken place on that occasion. His majesty asked her,
who was her father. She replied, Mr. Knox. " Knox
and Welch!" exclaimed he, " the devil never made such
a match as that."—" Its right like, Sir," said she, " for
we never speired his advice." He asked her, how many
children her father had left, and if they were lads or
lasses. She said, three, and they were all lasses. " God
be thanked!" cried the king, lifting up both his hands;
" for an they had been three lads, I had never bruiked
my three kingdoms in peace." She urged her request,
that he would give her husband his native air. " Give
him the devil!" a morsel which James had often in his
mouth. " Give that to your hungry courtiers," said she,
offended at his profanity. He told her at last that, if
she would persuade her husband to submit to the
bishops, he would allow him to return to Scotland.
Mrs. Welch, lifting up her apron, and holding it to-

wards the king, replied, in the true spirit of her father, ADDENDA.
" Please your Majesty, I'd rather kep his head there."

The account of our Reformer's publications has been partly anticipated in the course of the preceding narrative. Though his writings were of great utility, it was not by them, but by his personal exertions, that he chiefly advanced the Reformation, and transmitted his name to posterity. He did not view this as the field in which he was called to labour. " That I did not in writing communicate my judgment upon the Scriptures," says he, " I have ever thought myself to have most just reason. For, considering myself rather called The writ-
of my God to instruct the ignorant, comfort the sorrow- ing of
ful, confirm the weak, and rebuke the proud, by tongue, books not
and lively voice, in these most corrupt days, than to Knox's
compose books for the age to come, (seeing that so much mission.
is written, and by men of most singular erudition, and yet so little well-observed); I decreed to contain myself within the bounds of that vocation, whereunto I found myself especially called." This resolution was most judiciously formed. His situation was very different from that of the early Protestant reformers. They found the whole world in ignorance of the doctrines of Christianity. Men were either destitute of books, or such as they possessed were calculated only to mislead. The oral instructions of a few individuals could extend but a small way; it was principally by means of their writings, which circulated with amazing rapidity, that they benefited mankind, and became not merely the instructors of the particular cities and countries where they resided and preached, but the Reformers of Europe. By the time that Knox appeared on the field, their judicious commentaries upon the different books of Scripture, and their able defences of its doctrines, were laid open to the English reader. What was more immediately required of him was to use the peculiar talent in which he excelled, and, " by tongue and lively voice," to imprint the doctrines of the Bible upon the hearts of

his countrymen. When he was deprived of an opportunity of doing this, during his exile, there could not be a more proper substitute than that which he adopted, by publishing familiar epistles, exhortations, and admonitions, in which he briefly recalled to their minds the truths which they had received, and excited them to adhere unto them. These were circulated and read with far more ease, and to a far greater extent, than large treatises could have been.

Of the many sermons preached by him during his ministry, he never published but one, which was extorted from him by peculiar circumstances; and that one affords a very favourable specimen of his talents. If he had applied himself to writing, he was qualified for excelling in that department. He had a ready command of language, expressed himself with perspicuity, and with great animation and force. Though he despised the tinsel of rhetoric, he was acquainted with the principles of that art, and when he had leisure and inclination to polish his style, wrote both with propriety and eloquence. Those who read his letter to the queen regent, his answer to Tyrie, his papers in the account of the dispute with Kennedy, or even his sermon, will be satisfied of this. During his residence in England, he acquired the habit of writing the language according to the manner of that country, and in all his publications which appeared during his life-time, the English and not the Scottish orthography, and mode of expression, are used. In this respect, there is a very evident difference between them and the vernacular writings of Buchanan.

How his literary reputation has been impaired. The freedoms which have been used with his writings, in the editions commonly read, have greatly injured them. They were translated into the language which was used in the middle of the seventeenth century, by which they were deprived of the antique costume which they formerly wore, and contracted an air of vulgarity which did not originally belong to them. Besides this, they have been reprinted with innumerable omissions.

interpolations, and alterations, which frequently affect the sense, and always enfeeble the language. Another circumstance which has impaired his literary reputation is, that the two works which have been most read, are the least accurate and polished, as to style, of all his writings. His tract against female government was hastily published by him, under great irritation of mind at the increasing cruelty of queen Mary of England. His History of the Reformation was undertaken during the confusions of the civil war, and was afterwards continued, at intervals snatched from numerous avocations. The collection of historical materials is a work of labour and time; but the digesting and arranging of them into a regular narrative require much leisure, and undivided attention. The want of these sufficiently accounts for the confusion that is often observable in that work. But notwithstanding of this, and of particular mistakes, it still continues to be the principal source of information as to ecclesiastical proceedings in that period, and, in all the leading facts, has been confirmed by the examination of other documents, although great keenness has been discovered in attacking its genuineness and accuracy.

The History of the Reformation a book of reference to the period.

His defence of *Predestination*, the only theological treatise of any size which was published by him, is rare, and has been seen by few. It is written with perspicuity, and discovers his controversial acuteness, with becoming caution, in handling that delicate question.

I have thus attempted to give an account of our national Reformer, of the principal events of his life, of his sentiments, his writings, and his exertions in the cause of religion and liberty. If what I have done shall contribute to set his character in a more just, or full light, than that in which it has been generally represented; if it shall be subservient to the illustration of the ecclesiastical history of that period, or excite others to pay more attention to the subject; above all, if it shall be the means of suggesting, or confirming proofs of the

ADDENDA. superintendence of a wise and merciful providence, in
the accomplishment of a revolution of all others the
most interesting and beneficial to this country, I shall
not think any labour which I have bestowed on the
subject to have been thrown away, or unrewarded.

GRAVE OF JOHN KNOX.
Parliament Square, Edinburgh.

INDEX.
